With the abolition of slavery in the American South, the largest slave population in the hemisphere gained independence from institutional powers that had absorbed its social being into masters' and mistresses' households. Ex-slaves seized emancipation as the occasion to reclaim their persons and their labor, precipitating a social movement that linked immediate relations, family, kinship, community, labor-sharing, and mutual aid to arenas of political action.

This book explores from the vantage of the South Carolina countryside the upheavals in daily life that underlay broad social transformations engendered by emancipation and the fashioning of wage relations. Going beyond current discussions about the meaning of freedom for former slaves, it offers a portrait of freedpeople's actual social life that sheds light on their new relations with yeomen Republican allies.

Ex-slaves' projects of "grass-roots reconstruction" were a dual struggle to blunt new coercions embedded in terms of postbellum employment, and to elude the personal domination of the old order. Freed men and women gradually mounted public and collective repudiations of the reasoning that had supported their owners' rights to command human property. At the same time, they challenged emergent claims that subjection to landowners' management and to the discipline of an abstract market constituted freedom.

The Work of Reconstruction

The Work of Reconstruction
From Slave to Wage Laborer in South Carolina, 1860–1870

JULIE SAVILLE

University of California, San Diego

CAMBRIDGE
UNIVERSITY PRESS

Published by the Press Syndicate of the University of Cambridge
The Pitt Building, Trumpington Street, Cambridge CB2 1RP
40 West 20th Street, New York, NY 10011-4211, USA
10 Stamford Road, Oakleigh, Melbourne 3166, Australia

First published 1994

Printed in the United States of America

Library of Congress Cataloging-in-Publication Data

Saville, Julie.
    The work of reconstruction : from slave to wage laborer in South
Carolina, 1860–1870 / Julie Saville.
      p.   cm.
    Includes bibliographical references (p.) and index.
    ISBN 0-521-36221-0
    1. Reconstruction – South Carolina.   2. Slave labor – South
Carolina.   3. Plantation workers – South Carolina – History – 19th
century.   4. South Carolina – History – Civil War, 1861–1865.
5. South Carolina – History – 1865– 6. Afro-Americans – South
Carolina – History – 19th century. I. Title.
F274.S38   1994   93–47430
331.6'3960730757'09034 – dc20   CIP

A catalog record for this book is available from the British Library.

ISBN 0-521-36221-0 hardback

For my parents
Betty Jase Saville and Alphonso F. Saville, Jr.

Contents

Contents

Acknowledgments

So many people have helped me with this project. To acknowledge their support is to reach the straightest portion of a long and winding course.

At the beginning, there were the words of my Louisiana-born grandmother, Mrs. Julia Jase. During my childhood, neither of us dreamed, while her stories unfolded about kin who had experienced slavery and emancipation in Rapides Parish, Louisiana, that she would be stimulating an adult's quest for understanding. During my graduate studies, words of scholarship and counsel from C. Vann Woodward brought new worlds into view, and in the process inspired a topic for dissertation research. My appreciation for John W. Blassingame's insights about life and labor as a historian deepens with the passage of time. David Montgomery, who supervised the writing of the dissertation on which this study is based, remained a source of invaluable criticism, and the substance and spirit of his advice continue to enrich the meaning of the historian's work.

One of life's good fortunes is to receive comments as thoughtful as the queries and suggestions that this manuscript has received at various stages. Harold D. Woodman considerately assessed three chapters with insight that proved crucial to my completion of the dissertation. Evaluations of the dissertation from David Brion Davis and Gerald D. Jaynes helped me see the subject with new eyes. Eugene D. Genovese's rich comments on an earlier version of the book manuscript improved this study and inspired another project. The anonymous reader for Cambridge University Press left me with much to ponder while suggesting how to bring this investigation to a close. I am grateful for the ending and the beginnings that these remarks have made possible.

Friends and family also lent assistance at critical moments. To Collette Willis Lashley, Deborah Anita Dobbs, and Gwendolyn Lipsey – wherever they are – I remain grateful for their ready hospitality during my first research trip to Columbia, South Carolina. George Heltai, Agnes Heltai, and Lucille S. Whipper offered their vast understandings of human affairs during my sojourn in Charleston, South Carolina. M. Nanalice Saville read the manuscript with a poet's eye and a sister's heart. My brother, Alphonso F. Saville, III, and my sister-in-law, Patricia Heard Saville, taught me the secrets of the grain of mustard seed. My nephews Marshall Patrick and Alphonso, IV, paid me the great compliment of renewing their commitment to their own studies. Willda Shaw Jackson and Frank Seales, Jr., read early drafts of the dissertation, cheerfully admonishing me to earn the interest of those who have not formally scrutinized the mysteries of the past.

I have also drawn upon unparalleled combinations of judgment and friendship. Joye L. Bowman, Kandioura Dramé, and Karen E. Fields patiently offered comments on early drafts of several dissertation chapters. Lawrence N. Powell, Clarence L. Mohr, and C. Peter Ripley offered encouragement as the work progressed (and even when it did not). The work never could have proceeded without the unstinting gifts of counsel and exemplary scholarship from Barbara Jeanne Fields, Nan Elizabeth Woodruff, and John Higginson. At the Freedmen and Southern Society Project at the University of Maryland, I found wisdom and camaraderie without bounds in discussions with Ira Berlin, Steven F. Miller, Joseph P. Reidy, and Leslie S. Rowland. Theresa Singleton, Irene Silverblatt, and David Barry Gaspar generously spared time from their own research to help me think through problems that arose as the study neared completion.

Colleagues at the University of California, San Diego, made southern California a wonderful place to teach, write, and think. I am particularly indebted to Steven Hahn's astute comments on an earlier version of the manuscript, Michael E. Parrish's helpful editorial suggestions, and Stephanie McCurry's generous sharing of documents and formulations shaped by her own engagement with South Carolina. Rachel N. Klein's compassion and wisdom saw me through many a paragraph and many a day. Although they never commented directly on the manuscript, Michael Bernstein and Robert C. Ritchie, now director of research at the Huntington Library, always found time to offer an encouraging word.

Archivists offered patient guidance. The late Sara Dunlap Jackson, Walter Hill, and Michael Musick in particular smoothed my visits to the National Archives. The staff of the South Caroliniana Library, especially its director, Allen H. Stokes, Jr., and George D. Terry of the McKissick Museum at the University of South Carolina extended a wide range of assistance. I am also thankful for assistance from the staff of the South Carolina Department of Archives and History, the South Carolina Historical Society, the Southern Historical Collection at the University of North Carolina, and Perkins Library at Duke University. The aid of Susannah Galloway, bibliographer at Central University Library at the University of California, San Diego, and the university's Interlibrary Loan and Government Documents staff was indispensable.

Institutional support permitted me to overcome otherwise insurmountable obstacles to research and writing. A predoctoral fellowship at the Carter G. Woodson Institute of Afro-American and African Studies at the University of Virginia provided a combination of financial support, scholarly discussion, and working time without which I could not have completed the dissertation. I remain grateful to Armstead L. Robinson, William E. Jackson, and Mary F. Rose of the Woodson Institute. A postdoctoral fellowship from the National Research Council and resources of the University of California's Graduate Seminar in Southern History permitted me to revise the manuscript for publication. The book's fifth chapter began to take shape during a semester's visit at the Postemancipation Societies Project at the Center for African and African-American Studies at the University of Michigan, stimulated by thoughtful questions from Rebecca Scott, Frederick Cooper, Neil Foley, and students in the comparative emancipation seminar. Kristin Webb and Michael Gorman, graduate students in United States history at the University of California, San Diego, offered critical research assistance in the last stages of revision.

I had often read about Frank Smith's remarkable qualities as an editor before I benefited from them myself. His judgment and extraordinary patience were the salvation of the author and the manuscript. Janis Bolster generously guided me through the intricacies of turning a manuscript into a book. Cary Groner's skillful copyediting improved my prose.

To all mentioned here, and to others remembered but left unnamed because of constraints of space, my appreciation is everlasting. Because they believed in me and in this project with a dedication that only parents can summon, this work is dedicated to my mother and to the memory of my father.

Abbreviations Used in Notes

AFIC	American Freedmen's Inquiry Commission
AgH	*Agricultural History*
AHR	*American Historical Review*
AMA	American Missionary Association
CtY	Manuscripts and Archives, Yale University
DLC	Manuscripts Division, Library of Congress
GaHQ	*Georgia Historical Quarterly*
JAH	*Journal of American History*
JNH	*Journal of Negro History*
JSH	*Journal of Southern History*
JSocH	*Journal of Social History*
LH	*Labor History*
PR	Press
Pt	Part
r	reel number
RG	Record Group
SCDAH	South Carolina Department of Archives and History
SCHM	*South Carolina Historical Magazine*
SCHS	South Carolina Historical Society
SCL	South Caroliniana Library
UNC	Southern Historical Collection, University of North Carolina, Chapel Hill
Univ	University
WiM	Manuscripts Division, University of Wisconsin, Madison
WMQ	*William and Mary Quarterly*

Bracketed numbers refer to copies of documents consulted in files prepared by editors of the Freedmen and Southern Society Project at the University of Maryland.

A Note on Spellings

I have tried to let material cited in the notes retain as much of its original flavor as possible, and to this end have used *sic* only when spelling errors could be construed as my own rather than as those of my sources, or could lead to other confusion about meaning.

Given a wide variation in the rendering of regional place names, I have opted to standardize with a possessive apostrophe such names as St. John's River and St. Matthew's Parish.

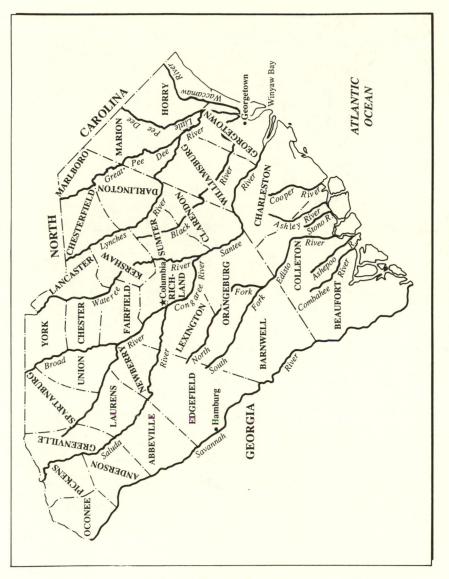

South Carolina in 1868

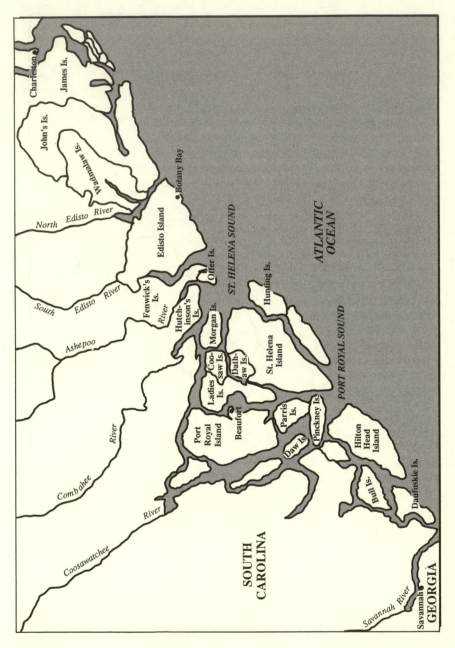

The Sea Islands of South Carolina

Introduction

Slaves of necessity made their ways by a separate path to the ranks of American labor. Their masters held claims to their persons rather than to their trades or working time. As chattel property, slaves were excluded not merely from the body politic but from civil society. A symbol of the most extreme form of human dependency, the status of slavery was consignment to what has been memorably termed "social death."[1]

No matter how separate their path, American slaves became equal participants in nineteenth-century struggles to establish workers' standing in the American Republic. The emancipation of four million slaves, the political harvest of Southern slaveowners' bid to shatter an emerging national state, also formed a national counterpoint to global developments. With the abolition of slavery in the American South, the largest slave population in the hemisphere gained independence from institutional powers that had absorbed its social being into masters' and mistresses' households.

The narrative that follows is indebted to studies of the Civil War, emancipation, and Reconstruction in the United States for the extent to which they have examined national reunification in broad comparison with slavery and serfdom and the convulsions that their abolitions unleashed.[2] Indebted, but without the intent to declare that this installment closes out the account.

This examination of the fashioning of wage relations in the South Carolina countryside in the immediate aftermath of emancipation views historic transformations of the nineteenth century from the vantage of small places. Ex-slaves in South Carolina, like their rural counterparts else-

---

1. Patterson, *Slavery and Social Death.*
2. Principal obligations are to Woodward, "Price of Freedom"; Genovese; *Roll, Jordan, Roll;* Montgomery, *Beyond Equality;* Davis, *Slavery in the Age of Revolution;* Mintz, "Rural Proletariat"; Woodman, "Post–Civil War Southern Agriculture"; Powell, *New Masters;* Foner, *Nothing But Freedom;* Fields, *Slavery and Freedom;* Berlin et al., eds., *Freedom;* Hahn, "Class and State"; Fox-Genovese, *Within the Plantation Household;* Jones, *Peasantry in the French Revolution;* Scott, *Slave Emancipation in Cuba;* Cooper, *From Slaves to Squatters;* Kolchin, *Unfree Labor;* Higginson, *Working Class in the Making;* and Holt, *Problem of Freedom.*

where, assessed fundamental changes in their circumstances from concrete upheavals in daily life. From horizons opened by the rich investigations of others, I argue that emancipation entailed a dual struggle for ex-slaves. They gradually mounted public and collective repudiations of the personal sovereignty on which their masters' and mistresses' rights to command human property had rested. At the same time, they challenged emergent claims that subjection to landowners' management and to the discipline of an abstract market constituted freedom.

Emancipated workers themselves rarely elaborated the larger convictions that undergirded their specific acts. However, an embarrassingly rich documentary record has captured more fragments of their stated principles and episodic behaviors than a single researcher – or this one, at any rate – can digest alone. I hope that the narrative that follows captures both the specificity of ex-slaves' circumstances and the fullness of their judgments and passions; for acts that were of the moment resonated into broader historical changes as they evolved in specifically regional contexts.

Underlying the course of Reconstruction was a simultaneous transformation of petty commodity production in the Old North, and of slave society in the Old South. By 1850, centralized factory production, outwork, and longer payment schedules of falling piece rates had drained meaning from the artisan organization of tailoring and shoemaking in the North. In part, these crafts felt the effects of plantation slavery's geographical expansion. Growing Southern markets for cheap but serviceable shoes, "Negro brogans," ready-made apparel, and "Negro cottons" helped spawn terms of wage labor in textile and shoe production that organizing tailors and shoemakers denounced as "wage slavery." The whips that cracked in the westward march of the plantation regime probably echoed in the early metamorphoses of these crafts into the North's "sweated trades."[3] The material base of Northern free labor ideology was being eroded even as military victory opened opportunity to establish a free labor society in Dixie.

Notwithstanding the erosion of the productive relations of the small workshop by factory organization and outwork, entrepreneurial justifications of wage labor generally spoke in muted tones on the eve of the Civil War.[4] In the 1850s, free labor critics of slavery most uniformly pro-

---

3. Wilentz, *Chants Democratic*, pp. 31, 120, 125, 223, 316, 380; Dawley, *Class and Community*; Laurie, *Working People of Philadelphia*.
4. However, the deaths of at least two tailors at the hands of New York City police during an intensive wave of strikes in 1850 did mark "the first time" that "urban American workers had been slain by the forces of order in a trade dispute." Wilentz, *Chants Democratic*, p. 380.

claimed the virtues of a republican social order – of small producers who owned land and tools and traded in a local market – when they condemned the aristocratic pretensions, economic stagnation, and moral backwardness of Southern slave society.[5] Blind to the expansion of wage employment, they deemed ownership of property a cornerstone of civic virtue and insisted that wage labor was but a temporary feature of Northern working life.

Republican president Abraham Lincoln clearly articulated this free labor vision in his annual message to Congress in December 1861. Rejecting outright the assumption that "nobody labors unless somebody else, owning capital, somehow by the use of it induces him to labor," Lincoln depicted a social order that accorded neither continuous wage labor nor unrestrained capital accumulation a significant role in the historical development of the United States. Although he conceded, "A few men own capital, and that few avoid labor themselves, and, with their capital, hire or buy another few to labor for them," Lincoln argued that "there is not, of necessity, any such thing as the free hired laborer being fixed to that condition for life":

> The prudent, penniless beginner in the world labors for wages awhile, saves a surplus with which to buy tools or land for himself, then labors on his own account another while, and at length hires another new beginner to help him. This is the just and generous and prosperous system which opens the way to all – gives hope to all, and consequent energy and progress and improvement of condition to all.[6]

Curiously, celebrating the toiler's rise to property-owning status and self-employment became free labor's conventional manner of expressing praise for working people.[7]

Demands of Northern labor organizations exposed fissures in the cornerstone of free labor ideology. Hence, free labor marched southward to battle against slavery to the strain of discordant notes. The judgment of Northern labor radicals echoed in an editorial by a wartime journalist in Port Royal who pronounced that "labor for wages, as the only means of subsistence, is but a modified servitude."[8] A more strongly insistent entrepreneurial view of free labor resonated in the authoritative declaration of an army commander, stationed in the South Carolina capital of Columbia, who at war's end advised that "the liberty given [the freedpeople]

5. Foner, *Free Soil.*
6. *Official Records of the Union and Confederate Armies,* ser. 3, vol. 6, pp. 709–21, quotation at p. 720 (hereafter cited as *OR*).
7. The observation derives from Montgomery's seminal study of Northern labor during Reconstruction, *Beyond Equality,* especially pp. 30–32.
8. Beaufort, SC *Free South,* 17 Jan. 1863, p. 1, cols. 1–2.

simply means liberty to work, *work* or *starve.*"[9] These divergent views reflect the fragmentation of free labor ideology, as conceptions of freedom rooted in the ownership of productive property and self-employment collided with evolving entrepreneurial justifications of wage labor.

Ownership of one's person and the right to sell one's labor were insistently proffered to former slaves as the measure of freedom.[10] A consideration of slaves' responses to this conception of freedom in the new order that began to evolve in South Carolina in the aftermath of Union occupation and Northern military victory should help us more precisely to describe the character of social relationships that came generally to be called free.[11] Challenges to the evolving character of wage labor issued not only from an urban Northern labor movement but also from former slaves little inclined to accept such terms of wage employment as the fulfillment of emancipation.

Struggles over the immediate terms of human labor proved to be inseparable from conflict over envisioned human possibilities. What led some people to stake human life on decisions to take a morning meal or to drive grazing cattle from a swampy patch of ground? Why did people, few of whom could read or write, claim authority to interpret written law? How did recently emancipated men and women try to blunt new uncertainties embedded in the terms of their liberation without falling back on slavery's real, if costly, guarantees? Making no distinctions between political and economic struggles, South Carolina's agricultural laborers understood the planting of a new social order to be the work of Reconstruction.

9. Ralph Ely to J. A. Clark, 25 Jan. 1866, Letters and Reports Received Relating to Freedmen and Civil Affairs, ser. 4112, 2d Military District, RG 393 Pt 1 [C-1412]. See also Foner, "Abolitionism and the Labor Movement," in Foner, *Politics and Ideology,* pp. 57–76; Glickstein, "'Poverty Is Not Slavery'"; and the masterful exploration of the relationship between attacks on slavery and defense of forms of coercion of an emerging industrial capitalism offered by Davis, *Slavery in the Age of Revolution.*
10. Fields, *Slavery and Freedom,* early delineated the terms of the conflict.
11. Cooper, *From Slaves to Squatters,* pp. 25–33, urged a more specific analysis of postemancipation social orders.

1

Freedom Versus Freedom: Competing Visions of Emancipation

Slaves brought to emancipation ethical standards of human relations. Values that were a landmark of the world that they had known as slaves shaped their earliest efforts to define the terms of emancipation. Freed adults who lived outside the state's two principal cities, district seats, and market villages shared an expectation about emancipation so widespread it is tempting to regard it as elemental: Slavery had not died intestate but rather had bequeathed to them intact whatever improvements of condition their struggles as slaves had garnered. The origins of what freedpeople insisted was slavery's legacy lay in struggles that had shaped the work routines of slave laborers on antebellum plantations and farms.

Antebellum Field Slaves' Labor: Regional Overviews

Nineteenth-century slaves produced and enjoyed independent management of an agricultural surplus, composed most often of food crops but occasionally of the plantation's commercial staple.[1] They also made and traded articles of local use, such as baskets, horse collars, furniture, or

1. Suggestive explorations of slaves' attempts to establish household economies are offered in McDonald, "'Goods and Chattels'"; see also Berlin, "Time, Space"; Fields, "Nineteenth-Century American South," especially p. 9; and Genovese, *Roll, Jordan, Roll*, pp. 535–40. Clifton, "Jehossee Island," ignores the issue, whereas Armstrong, "From Task Labor to Free Labor," Morgan, "Work and Culture," and idem, "Ownership of Property," offer an optimistic assessment of the antebellum operation and postbellum fate of these customary productive and marketing arrangements. Thoughtful investigations of slaves' quasi-independent productive and economic activities in regions of the Caribbean and the American South in Berlin and Morgan, eds., *Culture and Cultivation*, caution against some of the more sanguine inferences that have at times been drawn, in the North American context, from slaves' possession of or access to productive property. For ownership or long-term use of horses and mules by slaves in Beaufort district, see claims of Edward Brown, Robert Bryant, Caesar Dias, William Drayton, Anne Goethe, David Harvey, John Morree, Henry Newton, Benjamin Platts, Philip Reid, Andrew Riley, Pompey Smith, Benjamin Stafford, Benjamin Tyson, Eliza Washington, Moses M. Washington, Mack Duff Williams, and Nero Williams, all in Beaufort County SC case files, Approved Claims, Southern Claims Commission, 3d Auditor, RG 217. Quoted description of slaves' horses appears in [endorsement], Summary

5

Group of slaves at Drayton's plantation, Hilton Head, Photography by Henry P. Moore, spring 1862. Courtesy of New Hampshire Historical Society, F3809.

pottery; many slaves also raised barnyard fowl and swine that their owners did not appropriate outright. Under exceptional circumstances, older slave men managed to acquire draft animals, although in coastal Beaufort district purchases during the Civil War itself were the predominant means by which some slave artisans and foremen acquired "a pretty cheap horse – such as slaves usually owned." Most slaves on large and small places probably cultivated garden patches whose produce was marked for household consumption. Cleared lands reserved for more general use by the plantation community had probably been attached only to large plantations, especially those of the low-country rice region. Such provision grounds were most regularly cultivated by adult field workers able to complete their daily quotas or "tasks" of work on the plantation staple in less time than the nine hours of daytime labor that the majority of slaves normally required.[2] Slaves able to meet this test of endurance thereby gained a portion of each day, especially between late May and early September, when intense field cultivation was intermittent, to raise crops of corn, potatoes, peas, and "upland" rice.

Work in provision grounds was not by nature free from supervision. Where slaves produced the bulk of their subsistence, as in the coastal rice region, quotas of daily labor at times also structured work on fairly extensive provision grounds, thereby obligating slaves to raise a fixed portion of the plantation community's food supply.[3]

Report, Claim of Moses M. Washington, 4 Dec. 1876, ibid. See also Testimony of Sam'l B. Smith, Esq. before the American Freedmen's Inquiry Commission, 19 Nov. 1863, Letters Received, ser. 12, RG 94 [K-90].

2. Excerpt from "Rules on the Rice Estate of P. C. Weston," reprinted in U. B. Phillips, ed., *Plantation and Frontier*, vol. 1, p. 117. Morgan, "Work and Culture," too readily associates work on gardens and provision grounds with "leisure," minimizes the interdependence of task and gang labor even in the rice area under slavery, and ignores the changed conditions of postwar task work. The latter problem is considered more closely in Chapter 4. Under no circumstances should antebellum task labor be likened to the task-oriented labor of a free peasantry described in Thompson, "Time." McDonald, "'Goods and Chattels,'" Joyner, *Down by the Riverside*, and Berlin and Morgan, "Labor and the Shaping of Slave Life in the Americas," in Berlin and Morgan, eds., *Cultivation and Culture*, 1–45, avoid making the equation. Leslie S. Rowland analyzes customary arrangements associated with task labor in a forthcoming study of nineteenth-century rice production. A summary of Rowland's findings appears in Hahn, "Hunting, Fishing, and Foraging," p. 61n.

3. See a copy of the tasks adopted on Henry Middleton's Weehaw plantation printed in Johnson, *Social History of the Sea Island*, p. 84; see also "Memorandum of Tasks," *Southern Agriculturist*, 7 (June 1834): 298. A similar range of practices regulating the cultivation of provision grounds is discussed in David Barry Gaspar, "Sugar Cultivation and Slave Life in Antigua before 1800," p. 115; Woodville K. Marshall, "Provision Ground and Plantation Labor in Four Windward Islands: Competition for Resources during Slavery," p. 206; Dale Tomich, "*Une Petite Guinée*: Provision Ground and Plantation in Martinique, 1830–1848," p. 244; all in Berlin and Morgan, eds., *Cultivation and Culture*.

On cotton farms and plantations in the interior, slaves who gave roughly ten hours daily to field labor produced supplements to allowances largely by nighttime work, Sunday labor, and toil on recognized holidays. Although the task organization of field labor seems to have been rare in interior cotton districts, work in gangs did not bar slaves from producing a marketable surplus. Slaveowners generally designated a few days throughout the growing season on which slaves were permitted to tend crops exempted from their masters' direct claims. Yeoman slaveowner David Golightly Harris of Spartanburg district, who adopted tasks in cotton work only in May 1860, nevertheless noted, "Every year I give time to make themselves a crop – though I am not prepair to say I think it a good plan."[4] In most regions, labor in subsistence production was augmented when slaveowners set aside certain week days or portions of Saturdays for all people to cultivate food crops.[5]

Nineteenth-century slaveowners thus encouraged the production of a local food supply that complemented their aim to render their properties self-sufficient. It was with a degree of satisfaction that Thomas B. Chaplin, a small cotton planter on St. Helena Island, gave his slaves part of a Thursday in October 1851 to "break in" their corn. "Some of them have excellent corn, better than any of mine," he recorded in his journal. "I like to see this & will always encourage it."[6] At times, such customs seemed so deeply entrenched that they provided a standard by which both masters and slaves judged the fairness of plantation routine. Charles Manigault, for example, heir to rice plantations on South Carolina's Cooper River and owner of Gowrie rice plantation on Argyle Island in the Savannah River, thought it rather hard that the latter place had no high ground where his slaves could raise provisions. Manigault therefore prohibited his overseer's keeping poultry "because this is the only thing my people can raise for themselves (they having no spot to plant) except the trifle near their houses & near my dwelling." He could see value in an arrangement that "enable[s] them to procure some little extra Comforts for themselves" and "tends to attach them to their homes."[7]

4. David Golightly Harris Farm Journals, 2 June 1860, UNC; Thomas B. Chaplin Journal, 9 Oct. 1851, SCHS.
5. Faust, *James Henry Hammond*, p. 100, notes the practice on Hammond's Barnwell district plantations. See also Joseph P. Reidy, "Obligation and Right: Patterns of Labor, Subsistence, and Exchange in the Cotton Belt of Georgia, 1790–1860," pp. 138–54; Steven F. Miller, "Plantation Labor Organization and Slave Life on the Cotton Frontier: The Alabama–Mississippi Black Belt, 1815–1840," pp. 155–69; John Campbell, "As 'A Kind of Freeman?': Slaves' Market-Related Activities in the South Carolina Up Country, 1800–1860," pp. 243–75; all in Berlin and Morgan, eds., *Cultivation and Culture*.
6. Thomas B. Chaplin Journal, 9 Oct. 1851, SCHS.
7. Charles Manigault to James Haynes, 1 March 1847, in Clifton, ed., *Argyle Island*,

At the same time, however, masters looked askance at connotations of entitlement that slaves attached to these arrangements. Edward Barnwell Heyward, whose grandfather Nathaniel Heyward's ownership of some seventeen rice plantations and nearly twenty-five hundred slaves had made him one of the largest slaveowners in the antebellum South, illustrates both the extent and the limits of masters' tolerance. In December 1861, young Heyward was superintending the relocation of his wife's slaves by railroad from Savannah to a Wateree River cotton plantation near Columbia that he had purchased several years earlier. In good humor, Heyward likened slaves' painstaking accumulation to roguery, even as he hired six drays from an Irish carter in order "to transport the peoples 'plunder'" to the depot. He was rather amused when one woman "asked to bring *her poultry*."[8] Property claiming property!

At emancipation, therefore, many slaves claimed ownership of a largely perishable property that had originated in a fragile network of customary practices. From guarantees of minimum subsistence and habits of long-term use, slaves fashioned claims of entitlement that had somewhat contained their masters' claims to absolute dominion. They attached great significance to the poultry, hogs, and food crops over which they enjoyed an independence of management that approached proprietorship. These products of overwork and strained exertion supplemented and lent variety to the meager weekly rations. Customary arrangements by which slaves transferred and inherited the fruits of their nonplantation labors fulfilled obligations of community and reinforced ties of kinship whose networks were not bounded by the limits of their owners' properties.[9]

Assertions of customary rights penetrated the very organization of plantation labor. A localized struggle shaping work routines underlay the nonstandardized, often idiosyncratic character of antebellum plantation labor. Plantation work routines were not identical, even when the plantations were – as in the following instance – adjacent properties of a single owner. In November 1864, overseer S. H. Boineau anticipated trouble when the wives of drivers from two different Heyward plantations on the Combahee River were brought to work on the same Heyward place in an attempt to speed up the rice harvest and hasten evacuation of the estates.

p. 49. See also Easterby, ed., *R. F. W. Allston*, pp. 24, 257–60. Overseers were typically excluded from plantation subsistence production.

8. "Barney" [Edward Barnwell Heyward] to "Tattie" [Catherine Clinch Heyward], 30, 31, [Dec. 1861?], Edward Barnwell Heyward Papers, SCL. See also Thomas Wentworth Higginson, Extracts of Testimony, Department of the South, Report of the American Freedmen's Inquiry Commission, Letters Received by the Adjutant General's Office, 1861–70, M 619, r 200 (hereafter cited as AFIC Testimony).

9. Gutman, *Black Family*, explores the importance of slaves' kinship networks in the transmission of cultural values; see also the studies cited in notes 1, 2, 3 and 5 in this chapter.

Boineau observed what seems to have become a fairly general practice on many low-country plantations of compensating drivers and other workers whose full-time engagements in plantation business denied them time to work in gardens and provision grounds. On the Heyward properties one form of this restitution was periodically to release drivers' wives from work on the crop. Nevertheless, Boineau had never "allowed [driver Mathias's] wife but the half of every Saturday." The wife of the driver March, on the other hand, was by the custom on her place allowed "half of every day," a practice Boineau regarded as "a great nuisance." "[D]o instruct me," Boineau wrote his employer Charles Heyward, "whether Mathias wife is to be allowed the same liberty that March will claim for his wife or if March's wife shall be brought to the standard that Mathias wife now hold."[10] Such particularized work arrangements on two different Heyward plantations suggest the extent to which low-country slaves could blunt the intrusion of their masters' proprietorship in some details of plantation life.

At the same time, there were pronounced limits to the independent management that low-country slaves achieved over work routines.[11] Slaves' individual accountability for the performance of their tasks compromised their ability to lend a friend or mate a helping hand. The range of tasks to which slaves might devote their daytime labor fell short of task-oriented allocations of working time that a more independent peasantry might enjoy. Taking time for a morning meal before beginning the chores of the day was virtually unknown, and family meals were most often confined to the more general sociability that prevailed on Sunday.[12] Even the

10. [S. H.] Boineau to Ch[arles] Heyward, 16 November 1864, Heyward Family Papers, SCL.

11. Mintz, "Slavery and the Rise of Peasantries," reprinted in *Historical Reflections/Reflexions Historiques*, 6, no. 1 (Summer 1979): 226, notes that Tadeusz Lepkowski used the term "peasant-breach" to describe the extensive role that Haitian slaves played in the production and distribution of that island's food supply. See Tadeusz Lepkowski, *Haiti*, 2 vols., (Havana, Cuba, 1968, 1969) vol. 1, pp. 59–60. For differing assessments of the usefulness of the concept, see Cardoso, "Peasant Breach" and Tomich, "*Une Petite Guinée,*" in Berlin and Morgan, eds., *Cultivation and Culture*. In addition to the essays cited in notes 3 and 5 above, see also Higman, *Slave Populations*, pp. 180–88. I am aware of no instance in which antebellum slaves produced the dominant portion of a local food supply. The significance of slaves' individualized accountability for labor services is explored in Kolchin, *Unfree Labor*, pp. 58–64, 79–87, 91–95. Suggestive analysis of struggles unleashed by Antiguan slaves' determination to defeat statutory repeal of their deeply rooted roles in local production and marketing appears in Gaspar, "Slavery, Amelioration, and Sunday Markets." A persuasive argument that rejects suggestions that a peasantry emerged in postemancipation Guyana – where ex-slaves, though petty landholders, nevertheless remained dependent on occasional wage labor on estates in order to sustain a family living – is offered in Rodney, "Plantation Society in Guyana."

12. Laura Towne, AFIC Testimony; Henry McMillan, AFIC Testimony; both in M 619, r 200.

weekly punctuations of plantation labor brought by the religious calendar yielded at harvest to the pressures of a ripening crop. During the harvest, or when the crop was "in the grass," Sunday field labor was not
unknown. Able low-country field hands probably managed by overexertion to gain a greater portion of daylight for nonplantation pursuits than
their counterparts in short-staple cotton districts. Nevertheless, the press
of the harvest or an urgent need for intensive cultivation dissolved divisions between "slaves' time" and time that belonged to masters' work.[13]

At bottom, slaves' proprietary claims to animals and crops were no sol-
vent of their own status as human property. In March 1849, St. Helena
Island's small planter Thomas Chaplin rendered the slave Peter fullest acknowledgment of Peter's title in a hog. Chaplin hurriedly approached a
relative to borrow cash so that he might immediately pay Peter for a hog
that Peter had traded some time earlier. Chaplin made haste because the
fullest exaction of the slaves' status as property had fallen on Peter – he
was being sold from the neighborhood.[14]

In the low country, then, no regional customs of labor effectively isolated slaves from power relations fundamental to slavery. Like their counterparts elsewhere, low-country slaves had every reason to understand
why the Savannah, Georgia, Baptist minister Garrison Frazier, who had
bought himself and his wife in the early 1850s, pronounced masters' personal dominion over labor the essence of slavery. Asked to define slavery,
when Secretary of War Edwin P. Stanton and Union army commander
William T. Sherman conferred with twenty-one black ministers in Savannah shortly after Union troops had occupied the city late in December
1864, the sixty-seven year old Frazier replied, "Slavery is receiving by ir-
resistible power the work of another man, and not by his consent."[15] At
certain seasons, for certain slaves, task labor modified but did not over-
turn masters' claims of ownership.

Twilight of Slavery, Dawn of Freedom

By the spring of 1865, the old order was again under siege in South Carolina. Federal military and naval occupation, which had jolted coastal
plantation districts in November 1861 with the invasion of Port Royal,

13. Students of slavery and emancipation remain indebted to Rose, *Rehearsal for Recon-
     struction,* where harvest stretch-outs are noted on pp. 126–27. See also Black Oak
     Agricultural Society, Minutes, 24 Aug. 1847, pp. 61–62 (typescript), SCHS.
14. Thomas B. Chaplin Journal, 3 March 1849, SCHS. See also Rosengarten, *Tombee,* p.
     150.
15. "Minutes of an interview between the colored ministers and church officers at Savan-
     nah with the Secretary of War and Major General Sherman," 12 Jan. 1865, in *OR,*
     ser. 1, vol. 47, part 2, quotation at p. 39; *Liberator,* 24 Feb. 1865; Quarles, *Negro in
     the Civil War,* pp. 322–24; McPherson, ed., *Negro's Civil War,* p. 299.

renewed with Sherman's march in the winter of 1864–65.[16] In all likelihood, a larger slave population was at work in Confederate Carolina in
January 1865 than had been present at the time of secession, its numbers
swollen by relatively successful evacuations of slaves from islands north
of St. Helena Sound in the winter of 1861–62 and by refugee slaveowners from the Mississippi Valley, Alabama, and Georgia, who reversed the
routes of westward expansion after 1863 to seek a Carolina refuge for
slavery. The different paths by which these slaves would attempt breaks
with the old order were shaped by underlying differences in the social organization of slave society in the state's distinctive crop regions, and by
the fortunes of war.

Initially, the course of federal invasion reinforced regional differences
in South Carolina's slave communities. Slaves tended to gain greater
wartime independence from the supervision of a resident Confederate
population in coastal districts, where planters' seasonal absenteeism, the
wide use of slave drivers to supervise field labor, and a dense concentration of large plantation-slave majorities had supported the relative success with which antebellum slaves had gained intermittently independent
management of their working time and community life. Like their counterparts in Port Royal, slaves on the mainland seized the visible dismantling of slavery, occasioned by planters' hurried flight on the eve of
Sherman's march, to order their lives in accordance with their views of
freedom and their expectations about Northern liberators.

Along the Combahee and Savannah rivers, many planters had evacuated rice plantations on the heels of the fall of Port Royal, only to return
some of their slaves to cultivate lands again in 1863 and 1864 under the
oversight of strategically positioned Confederate troops. Many of these
diminished rice-plantation communities did not gain effective freedom
from Confederate supervision until Sherman's armies reached the coast in
the winter of 1864–65. During a six-month interval between the masters'
panicked flight and the occupation of the coastal mainland by Northern
troops in the summer of 1865, plantation slaves and nonslaveowning
residents of the pinelands confiscated and redistributed whatever rations,
stock, and household property the rice barons and marching Confederate troops had left behind.[17] Clear testimony to slaveowners' weakened

16. The early and successful Northern occupation of Port Royal, coupled with the virtual
    absence of Southern whites, brought slaves in the occupied islands into almost imme-
    diate acquaintance with Northern terms of freedom, even before emancipation be-
    came a Union war measure in 1863. The character of this singular wartime encounter
    is considered in Chapter 2.
17. S. H. Boineau to Charles Heyward, 21 April, 28 Dec. 1863, 6 Oct., 7, 19 Dec. 1864,
    Heyward Family Papers, SCL; Clifton, ed., *Argyle Island*, p. 344. The 1865 confisca-
    tions in the unoccupied coastal zones are treated separately in Chapter 3.

power, such seizures at times exposed plantation residents to new vulnerabilities. In mid-May of 1865, overseer S. H. Boineau left his home in the pinelands to survey the state of affairs on his former employer's Combahee River plantations. The slaves, whom Boineau had in January reported "odorly and respectful more so than one could expect under the circumstances" of impending Union advance, had later moved furniture from the "Big House" to their quarters. By the time of Boineau's May visit, however, the furniture had "all been taken away from them by the backwoods people" and "bands of robbers [were] prowl[ing] about Combahee for the purpose of picking up any article and robbing the poor blacks of what their masters left for them."[18] The demise of a slaveowning patriarch thus sometimes spawned competing claims to his patrimony.

Where slaves' numbers seemed to suggest strength, a condition more often realized in the spring of 1865 along the coastal rivers north of Charleston – emptied of former owners, unoccupied by Union or Confederate armies, and unvisited by roaming Rebel bands – the expulsion of overseers was an early matter of business. Overseer W. C. Munnerlyn was a remnant of the old order left on Keithfield rice plantation on Georgetown's Black River until 10 March when, he later complained, he was "driven off by the negroes of the plantation assisted by the [ex-slave] crew of a Government Transport."[19]

The imminent march of Sherman's armies through South Carolina in the winter of 1864–65 was the stimulus for slaves in the interior to make those claims and assertions – often recorded in owners' plaints of impudence and negligence – whose very openness cast off the indirection and coded ambiguities that had suffused antebellum slaves' cultural expressions.[20] Masters (who were mostly mistresses as Confederate conscription absorbed the menfolk) spotted the changes and read in the new gestures slaves' conviction that the days of the old order could be counted. "It seems that people are getting afraid of negroes," confided the wife of a Spartanburg farmer in the journal of her absent husband early in 1865.[21]

As the prospects of Confederate victory receded, slaves found that new opportunity and unprecedented peril seldom traveled far apart. In plantation areas along the interior rivers, which were not effectively occupied

---

18. S. H. Boineau to Ch[arles] Heyward, 6 Jan. 1865, [S. H.] Boineau to [Edward Barnwell] Heyward, 15 May 1865, Heyward Family Papers, SCL.
19. W. C. Munnerlyn, 17 Jan. 1866, M 869, r 21, 0370; Charles Manigault to Louis Manigault, 30 April 1865, in Clifton, ed., *Argyle Island*, p. 353. See also Pringle, *Chronicles of Chicora Wood*, pp. 264–65.
20. See Genovese, *Roll, Jordan, Roll*, pp. 97–112, 594; Roark, *Masters Without Slaves;* Litwack, *Been in the Storm So Long;* Levine, *Black Culture and Black Consciousness,* pp. 3–54; and Robinson, *Bitter Fruits of Bondage.*
21. David Golightly Harris Farm Journals, 3 Jan. 1865, UNC.

by Northern troops until the summer of 1865, some of the last officially Confederate assignments of Rebel troops issued from headquarters established on large plantations. Confederate soldiers diligently lent the weight of armed strength to overseer's duties on large plantations of the Santee in the spring of 1865. Their military oversight provoked slaves to a rash of arson and threats when troops relinquished rice field duties for engagements on the fields of battle. In alarm, planters took refuge in the nearby village of Pineville.[22]

In the last months of war, broken remnants of Confederate regiments turned their attention to "repressing rebellion amongst the negroes," while slaves offered Yankee invaders valuable news of troop movements, hideouts, and local geography. It was almost as though the guerilla warfare that some Union officers had expected to erupt in South Carolina in the wake of Sherman's march came to be directed not against armed Union troops but against unarmed slaves. In the closing days of the Confederacy, James White, overseer for Mrs. Amelia Parker for more than five years, treated a serious, though fairly common, violation of plantation discipline as an act of war. In early April 1865, six men, who were among the hundred slaves that Parker had removed from her plantation in St. Andrew's Parish near Charleston to one on the Black River in Clarendon district the year before, took to the woods rather than suffer the overseer's customary punishment of flogging people who were not in the fields by sunrise. White and some neighbors tracked the men down with bloodhounds, shot one of them, and had the five survivors locked up in a Manning jail. One month later, White and twenty neighbors took the men back to the plantation and hanged them, attempting to establish on the plantation what defeat on the battlefront had denied.[23]

In keeping with the qualities of the season, the springtime of emancipation brought at best unsteady and reversible trends toward liberation. Harry, a driver on a plantation in the interior parish of St. John's Berkeley, misjudged the times. Union troops had already visited plantations in his neighborhood early in March. Some people had walked off, cursed but unharmed by their owners, when a few soldiers approached Harry and asked him to show them where a party of Confederate soldiers was hiding out in the swamp. Harry led them to a hiding place that he had discovered. The soldiers then revealed themselves to be Confederate scouts

22. *OR*, ser. 1, vol. 47, part 3, pp. 1042–43. See also *Official Records of the Union and Confederate Navies in the War of the Rebellion* (hereafter cited as *ORN*), ser. 1, vol. 12, p. 298; *OR*, ser. 1, vol. 14, pp. 292, 298–306, 541.

23. Quincy A. Gilmore to Carl Schurz, 27 July 1865, Generals' Papers and Books, ser. 159, RG 94 [V-120]; "Certificate of Freedmen relative to outrages committed," 3 Aug. 1865, M 869, r 20, 0436; Jervey and Ravenel, *Two Diaries*, p. 13; *Nation*, 21 Dec. 1865, p. 780.

only "pretending to be Yankees" and, so a diarist recorded, they summarily "hung the traitor" Harry.[24]

In short, in the wake of Sherman's march, it required a fine eye to distinguish the twilight of slavery from the dawn of freedom. Although as many as ten thousand slaves from the interior and upper districts may have followed Sherman's armies, most stayed behind.[25] It was not simply deference to a master's authority that inclined most slaves to wait until their former owners personally announced news of Confederate defeat and confirmed reports of their emancipation.[26] The strongest defense of their expected legacy from slavery – for those men and women in interior and upper districts who had not been uprooted by wartime hiring, work on Confederate fortifications, Union military service, or evacuation – was to stay at home. But they went to plant that spring while a fragile, threatened freedom was blowing in the wind, hopeful that, although they sowed as slaves, they stood to reap on other terms.

Along the coastal rivers that spring, most slaves slowed without the surveillance of their former owners. Unlike their counterparts further inland, few low-country planters saw the new order ushered in from the vantage point of their coastal plantations. Rice planter Gabriel Manigault contemptuously dismissed reports from his Cooper River plantation that "the Negroes are working after their own fashion" as he busied himself that April searching for "a white woman to do the drudgery" in his Charleston residence after his former house slaves walked off.[27] Refugee low-country planters let coastal properties go unattended in 1865 and relied on the cultivation of interior plantations to which they had removed during the war. Not until the winter of 1866–67 did Edward Barnwell Heyward visit Combahee plantations that he had inherited in 1865. He did release the "family negroes" to return there after they harvested the 1865 crop on his Wateree place – "to stay there *alone*, like a naughty child in a closet, to remain there till they were in a good humour," Heyward planned – confident that they would become "pretty sick of it and 'long for the fall and Mass Barnwell.'"[28] Indeed, some low-country cotton planters who applied for the restoration of their properties in the fall of 1865 insisted that they had not abandoned their properties at all. Maintaining residences in Charleston, "the capital of the plantations," they proposed that seasonal

24. Jervey and Ravenel, *Two Diaries*, p. 17.
25. Williamson, *After Slavery*, p. 35; Berlin et al., eds., *Freedom*: ser. 1, vol. 1: *Destruction of Slavery*, doc. 39, pp. 154–55.
26. Cf. Litwack, *Been in the Storm So Long*, pp. 185–86.
27. Charles Manigault to Louis Manigault, 30 April 1865, in Clifton, ed., *Argyle Island*, pp. 353–54.
28. Edward Barnwell Heyward to Allen [Cadwaller Izard], 16 July 1866, Heyward Family Papers, USC.

custom rather than Union occupation had dictated their absences. Merchant and bank clerk Francis G. Cart explained that "he never lived on the plantation but only visited it from time to time" and that "his people remained on the plantation under the control of the headman who was his agent" until agents of the Freedmen's Bureau relocated them. In a similarly optimistic vein, an Ashley River cotton planter, who for thirty years had been in the habit of "spending about one half of the year at the plantation, & the other half at Charleston," left his plantation the day before Charleston surrendered, having "engaged a white man to stay on the place & take charge of things" and "urged upon his then servants to remain & plant as usual."²⁹

Such admonitions went unheeded. During the prolonged absences of their onetime owners, freedpeople in the low country introduced fundamental changes when they set out to construct from the wrecked remains of slavery a life and labor worthy of free people.

By June 1865, there had emerged rough, though by no means fixed, contrasts in the conditions under which South Carolina's rural freedpeople would begin to assert their views of freedom. In the low country, ex-slaves pursued autonomy within the framework of larger communal structures by occupying and collectively working land under the wartime guarantee of a field order issued by Union general William T. Sherman or the de facto warranty of slaveowner flight. In much of the rest of the state, early struggles for autonomy in the face of a resident planting and refugee Confederate population more often required individualized assertions of will, freedom of movement, and attempts to establish some portion of time that an employer could not claim.

During their short, uncontested occupation of coastal plantations, ex-slaves in the rice region north of Charleston introduced patterns of land use and production that were rooted in a conception of freedom older than the historically peculiar form held out to them by Northern emancipators. Precise description of the organization of work in these short-lived farming communities is difficult. Most often, they entered the written record only as "disorderly," "barbaric" obstacles to the ideals of bourgeois agrarian society. Nevertheless, sketchy accounts suggest that ex-slaves proceeded to subdivide and fence in provision lands and the old slave gardens, with an eye toward household cultivation of particular tracts.³⁰

29. Applications for restoration of property, Francis G. Cart, 4 Oct. 1865, J. Pinckney Clement, 25 Sept. 1865, Ex-parte William Davidson, 5 Oct. 1865, all in M 869, r 26, 0004–07, 0085–90, 0359–63. The apt description of Charleston appears in Easterby, ed., *R. F. W. Allston*, p. 23.
30. [Affidavit], Cassius Middleton, 25 Jan. 1866, enclosed in Capt. Woodbury C. Smith to Lieut. Henry Krebbs, 2 Feb. 1866, Letters Received, Returns of Prisoners, and Reports of Arrests, ser. 482, Georgetown, SC, Military Installations, RG 393 Pt 4. Ex-

These practices emerged most clearly on Santee and lower Waccamaw River rice plantations that had been abandoned by their owners early in 1865. A community of more than seventy freedpeople formerly owned by Georgetown's rice-planting physician Alexius M. Forster rejected the antebellum order of work on their Waccamaw River place during Forster's absence. In an attempt to surmount the inequality of land in Friendfield plantation's provision grounds, freedpeople allocated noncontinuous strips in different fields among plantation households. An army officer who reported that on Friendfield in 1865 "in nearly every case the small amount of land tilled by each hand was divided into 3 or 4 patches situated in as manny [*sic*] fields" was certain that because the next year's contract would require them to "work together," that "the labor [would be] more advantageously employed." Their "separate division of each subdivision of the plantation" fostered an "unwillingness to do anything except cultivate their own little lots."[31] That "evil," reported Ammiel J. Willard (who before enlistment was a New York lawyer, and who would later enjoy a lengthy tenure on the bench of the South Carolina state court), must yield to the right to direct their labor, which in his view, ownership of the plantation had vested in the planter. Willard despaired at his efforts in 1865 to reconcile the household-oriented cultivation of freedpeople on Friendfield with the property rights of landowner Forster. "Such a system cannot be maintained for any length of time," he lamented, "as it is contrary to the Laws of Nature and Civilization as I understand them."[32] By midcentury, Willard was not alone in his suspi-

---

slaves on the same Waccamaw River plantation attempted to employ the overlapping property relations of the antebellum plantation in order to justify their use of wood from a summer house to fence in their gardens. A slave foreman explained that the people "got the boards and made fences around their gardens" rather than see slaves from another plantation make use of wood from their plantation's summer house. See [affidavit], Benj. King, 27 Jan. 1866, ibid.

31. Harry Seton to B. F. Smith, 21 Jan. 1866; Woodbury C. Smith to B. F. Smith, 20 April 1866; [contract], Dr. A. M. Foster [*sic*], Jan. 1866, enclosed in S. Willard Saxton to [B. F.] Smith, 10 Feb. 1866; all in M 869, r 11; A. J. Willard to George W. Hooker, 7 Nov. 1865, M 869, r 8; J. H. Sheckelfod and others to O. O. Howard, 17 Jan. 1866, enclosed in wrapper labeled J. H. Shackleford and others, 17 Jan. 1866, M 752, r 24, 0513–15; Easterby, ed., *R. F. W. Allston*, pp. 155–56.

32. A. J. Willard to George W. Hooker, 7 Nov. 1865, M 869, r 11; Williamson, *After Slavery*, pp. 330, 364, 413; U. S. Army, *Official Register*, part 8, p. 206, a useful reference kindly brought to my attention by Leslie Rowland. It is important not to equate the agricultural reorganization that freedpeople undertook with the antebellum task system. The freedpeople on rice plantations between February and June 1865 constructed an agricultural community that enjoyed the task orientation of free peasants, with households assuming continuous responsibility for the same plots of land. It is doubtful that the time spent in cultivation was as prolonged as field cultivation under slave tasks had required. The judgment that ex-slaves in the low country "were tenaciously striving to retain and even extend the fundamentals of their former system" offered in Morgan, "Work and Culture," p. 584, is misleading.

cion that the emergence of absolute rights of property in land was extending the dominion of the landowner, but not all parties to that discovery dated the "laws of nature and civilization" from this transformation. Those who did excised self-employment as a necessary condition for economic independence in rural life.

Freedpeople wanted land. Contemporary testimony to the primacy of that desire was virtually unanimous; a later generation came to characterize their expectation as a claim for "forty acres and a mule."[33] Broad agreement on this question may actually have obscured the varying meanings of land to most plantation slaves. In occupying the very land that, as sites of tillage, hunting, gathering, and ceremonial burials, had established its kinship to their generations of kin past, present, and to be born, some ex-slaves in the low country briefly knew a kind of freedom as common to former slaves' wants as it was rare to their experiences. For, more than any other category of property, land was not separate from the ex-slaves' sense of community. Like kinship, it made identity objective.[34] Attempts to maintain a link with particular land led some freedpeople to plant a patch on the old "home place" after they took up residence elsewhere; others made the reverse arrangement.[35] Their dilemma reminds us that they reckoned severance costly, even when part of freedom's price.

Decisions to purchase and move to land other than "home" land did not automatically transform the values that freedpeople attached to land. In January 1867, thirty-eight men and women moved their families from Edisto Island rather than sign contracts to work on plantations recently restored to absent landowners. They had arranged to purchase in two or three yearly installments thirty-acre tracts on Bulow plantation in St. Andrew's Parish on the mainland. When they learned that the seller's right to the plantation was in dispute, the "People of Bulow Plantation" wrote to request Governor Robert K. Scott's "information advicement:"[36]

33. James C. Beecher to T. D. Hodges, 2 Dec. 1865, Letters and Reports Received Relating to Freedmen and Civil Affairs, ser. 4112, 2d Military District, RG 393 Pt 1; Preliminary Report of American Freedmen's Inquiry Commission; Laura Towne, AFIC Testimony, both in M 619, r 200; Fleming, "'Forty Acres and a Mule,'" 46 tersely judges, "For several years after the close of the Civil War, the negroes of the South believed that the estates of the whites were to be confiscated by the Washington Government, and that each negro head of a family would obtain from the property thus confiscated 'forty acres and a mule.'"

34. Fields, "Introduction," in Fields with Fields, *Lemon Swamp and Other Places,* p. xvii; and Joyner, *Down By the Riverside,* p. 42.

35. Rose, *Rehearsal for Reconstruction,* pp. 282–83, 289; Pearson, ed., *Letters from Port Royal,* p. 234.

36. Hector Robinson et al. to Robert K. Scott, 26 Nov. 1867, Governors' Papers, SCDAH; Endorsement of George A. Williams, 10 July 1867, on [affidavit], [Henry] Knight, 10 Aug. 1867, M 869, r 14.

[O]ut of all thing we wont the land   we wants to finish pay for the
30 a[cres] to make ourselves a Home stead   we do not matter who
the plantation belonce to   if he will request of us to commence to
pay him again . . . still we are willing to do so for what we can or may
obtain the 30 a[cres] for a home stead sir.

Their expressed willingness to "pay again" previously paid installments
was not market-oriented calculation. Ownership of land remained an
end in itself, even after those who could turned to purchase to lay a claim
to some.

Not only does the "forty acre" slogan obscure values that are foreign
to the idea of land as a commodity, but, by drawing attention to a fixed
measure of land, it tends to distort the character of the farming that
ex-slaves undertook. Sherman's Field Order 15, issued in January 1865,
set forty acres as the maximum amount of land that freed heads of
households might claim in a territory stretching along the coast south
of Charleston to the St. John's River in northern Florida and embrac-
ing the sea islands and mainland for thirty miles inland.[37] Nevertheless, freed families in the low country seldom attempted to cultivate
land in lots as large or as regularly defined as forty acres. When Francis
Singleton, formerly worked as a driver by his owner Philip Givens,
joined with other slaves to purchase Givens's Port Royal plantation
sold under the Direct Tax Act in 1863, they immediately divided it into
twenty-two–acre tracts, Singleton and another freedman holding the
title in trust for the joint proprietor–cultivators.[38] Such uniform divisions seem fairly common where ex-slaves acquired plantations lands
by collective purchases.[39] Nevertheless, the larger portion of land
claimed under Sherman's field order showed "a strange looseness in regard to the assignment of the forty acre tracts" that James Chaplin
Beecher, youngest son of Lyman Beecher and officer of the North
Carolina-raised Thirty-fifth United States Colored Infantry, attributed to
the laxity of local bureau agents. The "so called 40 acre tract[s],"
Beecher impatiently noted, "vary in size from eight acres to (450) four

---

37. OR, ser. 1, vol. 47, part 2, pp. 60–62. The significance of Sherman's wartime order is
discussed in Chapter 3.
38. H. G. Judd to Rufus Saxton, 13 Oct. [1865], Correspondence Relating to the Restoration of Property, ser. 3108, Beaufort, Subordinate Field Office Records, RG 105.
39. In addition to the document cited in note 38, see Hector Robinson et al. to Robert K.
Scott, 26 Nov. 1867, Governors' Papers, SCDAH. Direct evidence about how freedpeople arranged these collective purchases is still wanting. Because ex-slaves respected
mutuality and reciprocity more than market equality, there seems little reason to assume that all households contributed the same amount of cash toward the purchase,
or that given disparities in the sizes of the land-buying households, all household members worked exclusively on a single subdivided tract.

hundred and fifty."⁴⁰ Had Beecher's assessment considered the subsistence needs of family workers, relying on open range grazing of stock and cooperative household labor, organized in extended family settlements, where perhaps the construction of meeting houses and schools was envisioned, he might have discovered beneath the variability of the acreage a constancy of purpose.

The expectation that land would accompany emancipation was not restricted to ex-slaves on the coast. An army officer commanding in Sumter district in the late summer of 1865 thought that fully two-thirds of the freedpeople in his district expected to receive land, many of them assuming it would be the land that they were then working. His energetic efforts to disabuse them of the notion were to no avail. "I have been about the District," he explained, "and done all that is in my power to do away with the expectation, but I no sooner get back than there is another story started."⁴¹ No less than their low-country counterparts, ex-slaves in interior plantation districts shared an expectation common to the mass of servile workers in the age of emancipation, who almost invariably interpreted news that land was not to accompany their emancipation as an unfaithful characterization of the freedom offered them.⁴²

Outside the low country, the path from slavery did not favor the direct social and agricultural changes that ex-slaves on the seaboard briefly undertook. Instead, the disintegration of slavery in interior and upper districts in 1865 was marked by outbreaks of violence that had their origins in wartime stresses of plantation slavery, planters' attempts to salvage legal recognition of the institution from the wreck of military defeat, and the impact of freedpeople's wartime struggles.

40. In the same report Beecher complained, "Of all the 40 acre tracts held upon Johns and Wadmalaw Islands, only five have ever been measured or properly surveyed. The custom has been for any colored man to announce that he has staked out 40 acres upon a certain plantation upon which announcement his blank is filled out." James C. Beecher to M. N. Rice, 7 Feb. 1866, enclosed in wrapper labeled Headquarters, Military District of Charleston, 16 Feb. 1866, Letters and Reports Received Relating to Freedmen and Civil Affairs, ser. 4112, 2d Military District, RG 393 Pt 1.

41. F. H. Whitt[en?] to O. D. Kinsman, 1 Oct. 1865, M 869, r 20, 0481; C. H. Howard to R. Saxton, 29 Nov. 1865, M 869, r 20, 0183–93; E. A. Kozlay to H. W. Smith, 28 Nov. 1865, M 869, r 20, 0291; Ralph Ely to J. Clark, 26 Dec. 1865, Miscellaneous Reports Received, ser. 3157, Columbia, Subordinate Field Office Records, RG 105; F. H. Whitt[en?] to C. Fillebrown, 4 Nov. 1865, Letters and Reports Received Relating to Freedmen and Civil Affairs, ser. 4112, 2d Military District, RG 393 Pt 1.

42. In British Guiana, ex-slaves were certain that planters and local justices, who informed them that emancipation granted them neither the huts they had lived in nor their former provision grounds, were betraying the queen's intent. A special magistrate sent to British Guiana later recalled the former slaves on one estate who insisted "that it was all nonsense that the Queen made them free without giving them a free house and land; and they called upon me to carry out that proposition. . . . I attempted to explain the system of tenancy, but I could not make them comprehend it in the least; they had no idea of paying anything at all." Quoted in Hall, "Flight from the Estates," p. 18.

Observers were struck by the amount of corn and other food crops under cultivation in the old short-staple region in the summer of 1865.[43] Whether the increased acreage in grain reported in many districts was a product of wartime agricultural shifts or of springtime replanting in areas that had suffered heavy losses of stock, tools, and other farming properties, the cereals did not require work forces as large or as intensively employed as the antebellum staple.[44] In upper districts, even the largest cotton planters had resisted the use of task work in cultivation, insisting that it led to overexertion and tended to promote slaves' independent management of their time.[45] Reduced labor requirements of the corn crops now threatened to give plantation slaves greater free time in the wake of the march of an army that had proclaimed them free for all time. In a move to hinder both developments after military surrender, planters welcomed the services of Confederate scouts and armed bands in maintaining plantation discipline and restricting movement from the plantation. Some conceded military defeat but, so a Boston newspaper correspondent concluded during a summer tour, "made a strenuous effort to keep their former slaves on their plantations for the avowed object of having them still in their possession when, after the complete restoration of civil government, the emancipation proclamation would be declared unconstitutional and the negroes reduced to their former condition." The revived patrols, pass systems, and armed scouts that Union troops found in place in many upper districts in the summer of 1865 make the reporter's account credible.[46]

The need to force slaves to remain on the place took on added urgency before July 1865 for the area's small farmers as well. The attempts of would-be free people to establish a larger social identity could not be fully

43. Boston *Daily Advertiser*, 5 Aug. 1865, p. 2, col. 3; F. H. Whitt[en?] to [C.] Fillebrown, 28 July 1865, Letters and Reports Received Relating to Freedmen and Civil Affairs, ser. 4112, 2d Military District, RG 393 Pt 1.
44. Analysis of agricultural and social conditions behind Confederate lines in South Carolina is still needed, although earlier studies strongly suggest that calls to reduce cotton acreage scarcely enjoyed the full support of the planter class. A rich study of the social struggles that erupted on the Confederate homefront in the Mississippi Valley is offered in Robinson, *Bitter Fruits of Bondage*, where the author concludes that because corn could be cultivated with one-third the labor required for cotton, slaves used the reduced labor requirements of such provision crops to reduce their work loads during the war. See also Robinson, "Worser Than Jeff Davis: The Coming of Free Labor during the Civil War, 1861–1865," in Glymph and Kushma, eds., *Postbellum Southern Economy*, pp. 11–43; Gates, *Agriculture and the Civil War* pp. 13–21, 74; Thomas, *Confederate Nation*, p. 200; and Ramsdell, *Behind the Lines*.
45. Faust, *Design for Mastery*, pp. 74–75, 100; idem, "Culture, Conflict, and Community."
46. Boston *Daily Advertiser*, 5 Aug. 1865, p. 2, col. 3; Charles C. Soule to O. O. Howard, 12 June 1865, Miscellaneous Reports Received, ser. 3157, Columbia, Subordinate Field Office Records, RG 105; James C. Beecher to Stewart M. Taylor, 29 Sept. 1865,

satisfied on an owner's farm. On smaller plantations and farms in the interior, the workplace and the networks of slave community life did not
converge as readily as on large plantations. Assertions of claims to land
seem to have been less common on smaller places, where ex-slaves could
often begin to organize their work on the basis of household labor only
by first trying to gather in one place families dispersed over neighboring
farms.[47]

Small slaveowners often recalled the direct manner in which their onetime slaves asserted their autonomy from the insistent claims of an equally
direct sense of ownership. Newberry farmer John Hair spotted the change
in his tanner and field worker William right away:

> [S]o soon as he found out he was free he was not like the same man.
> he gave me more impudence that I ever thought I could take from any
> man white or black. he never asked my permission to leave one sin-
> gle time, although he did not stay at home on an average one night
> in the week. . . . In addition to all that he ruined three good hides for
> me which I am convinced he did intentionally or carelessly and did
> not care. as he never has done so until he found out he was free.

Although the ex-slave tanner returned to pass the Christmas holidays in
the quarters, he had quit Hair's place after the 1865 harvest. In February,
he returned to collect a ten-dollar payment that Hair regarded as a reward
to which only "each hand was entitled to that stayed at home and did
his duty."[48]

Like the tanner William, former slave John Watt pressed no claim for
land but did mark his emancipation by reclaiming variable portions of
his time and by directly rebuffing whatever behavior by his owners-
turned-employers he found disrespectful of his new condition. Exasper-
ated by the "impudence" that he regarded as both personal affront and
as violation of their contract, Watt's employer J. G. McKim explained
why he threw Watt off the place after the crops were laid by in August
1866:[49]

r 20, 0029; Chas. H. McCreery to C. H. Howard, 10 Nov. 1865, r 20, 0339; C. C.
Bowen to C. H. Howard, 23 Oct. 1865, r 7; all in M 869. Cf. E. A. Kozlay to C. H.
Howard, 27 Oct. 1865, r 20, 0268, M 869.

47.   Gutman, *Black Family*, especially pp. 102–84, suggests that the existence of extended
       family networks among slaves belonging to different owners was not solely a function
       of the size of the slaveowning unit, since marriage without coresidence and multiple
       ownership of extended slave families were features of larger slaveholdings in the up-
       per South and the southwest cotton kingdom as well. Family reorganization in inte-
       rior districts of South Carolina is more fully considered in Chapter 4.

48.   John Hair to nn, 9 Feb. 1866, Letters Received, ser. 3156, Subordinate Field Office
       Records, Columbia, RG 105.

49.   J. G. McKim to Gen. Runkle, 6 Aug. 1866, Letters Received, ser. 3156, Subordinate
       Field Office Records, Columbia, RG 105.

He paid no regard to the contract; and told me repeatedly that he did not care a *damn* for it; would not work, was insolent; would leave his work and visit the adjoining plantation during work hours, would frequently come home one hour by Sun in the morning, and have his breakfast to cook and get to work 2 hours by sun when he was required by the Contract to go to work by Sun rise. And tell me that he was free now and would go when he pleased and return when he pleased, would leave the plantation his task half finished without permission and stay away two days at a time. . . . Would swear in the presence of my family and . . . give my wife impudince in my absense. . . . I would not keep him on my plantation if he would work for nothing

For McKim, Hair, and other small slaveowners, mastery had most often manifested itself as the right continuously to command work that had often claimed their slaves' labor no less than their own. Charges of "impudence" attest to the persistent, personalized challenges to such authority in the intimacy of daily contact.

Familiarity born of work in common with their slaves at a number of different chores did not erode the personal power that small slaveowners could exercise over their slave property. Such work did seem to leave them ill suited to itemize and parcel out work routines that were shaped more by fitful seasonal demands than by a division of labor among slave workers or between master and slave. Many small slaveowners thus failed in early contracts to describe the work that they would require of their now employees in terms of specific chores, claiming instead "there entier servis," requiring them "when not engaged in working or gathering the crop to do whatever she [the farmowner] may desire," or stipulating that a former slave "do bind herself to obey me as before."[50]

Perhaps in part because Union troops had skirted his district in their wartime marches, it was a small planter in Anderson district who most fully defended the view that employers' rights to workers' time was unrestricted. After the crops had been laid by in July 1865, William Tunro proposed to his former slaves that they "sign a contract for their lifetime." Robert Perry, his wife, and two other men refused, and Tunro drove them away. Heading for Columbia, the former slaves were about fifteen miles from Tunro's place when Tunro's neighbors overtook them. The search party took the men into the woods and shot them.[51]

50. William Agnew, Jan. 1867, Sarah H. Barmore and Blindford [1867?], Labor Contracts, ser. 3037, Abbeville, Subordinate Field Office Records, RG 105; Lovie Ewbanks and Jean [1865?], Labor Contracts, ser. 3090, Barnwell, Subordinate Field Office Records, RG 105.
51. The woman's fate is unrecorded. The slaveowner's name is variantly reported as Tunro, Turno, and Turns in G. Pillsbury to O. D. Kinsman, 30 Dec. 1865, r 11; G.

Widely if not invariably horrified by reports of murder and assault that reached them in the upper districts, Freedmen's Bureau agents and army officers compiled accounts of "outrages," the category literally pronouncing them acts beyond the bounds of society.[52] The violence that preceded the close of the 1865 agricultural season in upper districts in part reflected a struggle for power specific to the disintegration of the social relations of the small slaveholding. The farm, where work of master and slave had often overlapped and where chores were seldom defined as quotas whose completion might temporarily mark the end of the slave's daily obligation, was most often the source of claims by former slaveowners to the full time of their now-free workers. Yet it was also on the farm that freedpeople's longing for reunion with kin might lure them to other places. In the snubs, oathes, and rejoinders that challenged the etiquette of dependency in the close quarters of the farm, in the insistence that freedom allowed movement and even change of residence, and in a determination to reclaim portions of their time, freedpeople on smaller farms asserted views of freedom that challenged most directly the notion of right that had informed small slaveowners' views of authority.

It was chiefly in the low country and on large plantations in the interior that brief, undisturbed occupation of abandoned plantation lands and joint long-term residence of extended family households first combined to permit former slaves to act on their conviction that free people worked for themselves, and through the possession of land, controlled the product of their labor for the support of their families and community settlements. So abstract a formulation of the ex-slaves' view of freedom may not adequately distinguish them from the majority of nineteenth-century American working people, for whom the possession of land still symbolized an alternative to wage labor and only a small portion of whom by midcentury had begun to frame collective assertions of right as wage-earning employees. Nevertheless, such goals set freedpeople on a collision course with Northern emancipators and former slaveowners alike.

Pillsbury to H. W. Smith, 30 Dec. 1865, r 20, 0377; O. S. B. Wall to O. D. Kinsman, 6 Nov. 1865, r 20, 0505; all in M 869. That same fall, five ex-slave men in Edgefield district wrote to report the murder of a black Methodist minister, "one of our most respectable friends," and concluded that "there is no safety of our lives here. . . . we hear of many men being found dead in different places." See David Harris et al. to nn, 30 Nov. 1865, M 869, r 20, 0181.

52. Endorsement of A. Ames, 8 Nov. 1865, on Ralph Ely to Chas. A. Carleton, 7 Nov. 1865, Letters and Reports Received Relating to Freedmen and Civil Affairs, ser. 4112, 2d Military District, RG 393 Pt 1; Charles H. McCreery to C. H. Howard, 10 Nov. 1865, M 869, r 20, 0339; R. M. Fulton to Ralph Ely, 13 Feb. 1866, Registers of Letters Received, ser. 3155, Columbia, Subordinate Field Office Records, RG 105. Cf. Charles C. Soule to O. O. Howard, 12 June 1865, Miscellaneous Reports Received, ser. 3157, Columbia, Subordinate Field Office Records, RG 105.

Rebels and "Rebels in Disguise"

No surviving record has yet indicated that the tidings of any Northern bearer of the "good news" of emancipation departed from two tenets common to artisan, evangelical, and free labor antislavery.[53] All could agree that abolition transferred to former slaves ownership of their persons and guaranteed them freedom from arbitrary corporal punishment. Two soldiers laid out the groundwork of the new order in the summer of 1865. "You are now free," one explained, "but you must know that the only difference you can feel yet, between slavery and freedom, is that nei-ther you nor your children can be bought or sold." Defining the limits of acceptable coercion, a second soldier announced, "Shooting and whipping are done with."[54] However, not even this minimalist program would survive the first year of emancipation intact.

In not a few instances, the occupying army's intention to prohibit corporal punishment merely substituted for the slaveowners' lash the standard form of military discipline – physical restraint, or "tying up" – occasionally with dire results.[55] Soldiers detailed to service as Freedmen's Bureau agents often put down with force of arms freedpeople's widespread refusals to sign midsummer contracts.[56] Captain F. M. Montell introduced freedom of contract on the Cooper River at the end of a musket. Montell's desire to "get a place on Cooper river" was probably aroused in July when he was making contracts on the river's eastern branch. From his bargain with Cooper River rice planters Ball, Read, Huger, and Hazelton for 10 percent of any share he collected on their behalf, Montell stood to acquire ready cash to support his prospective planting venture. His personal stake in the outcome of the 1865 contracts whetted the zeal with which the officer encouraged ex-slaves in the region to sign contracts to work for their former owners. The former slave Tober described Montell's "mode of persuasion": "Mr. Montell had him [Tober] cornered up against

---

53. Foner, "Abolitionism and the Labor Movement," in Foner, *Politics and Ideology;* Glickstein, "Poverty Is Not Slavery"; Rose, *Rehearsal for Reconstruction,* especially pp. 63–85, 209, 298–313, compares the tenets of free labor and evangelical antislavery in Port Royal; Powell, *New Masters,* pp. 97–122, closely considers the conflict between the free labor tenets of Northern planters and the economic views of the freedpeople.
54. [Speech], "To the Freed People of Orangeburg District," enclosed in Charles C. Soule to O. O. Howard, 12 June 1865, M 752, r 17, 0053–61; "Certificate of Freedmen relative to outrages committed," 3 Aug. 1865, M 869, r 20, 0436.
55. W. F. Redding to H. W. Smith, 3 Nov. 1865, r 20, 0390; H. G. Judd to [Rufus] Saxton, 23 Sept. 1865, r 20, 0214–33; Reuben Tomlinson to O. D. Kinsman, 27 Sept. 1865, r 20, 0441; all in M 869; Powell, *New Masters,* p. 118.
56. Geo[rge] H. Nye to C. [R?] Fillebrown, 9 Aug. 1865, Letters and Reports Received Relating to Freedmen and Civil Affairs, ser. 4112, 2d Military District, RG 393 Pt 1.

a brick chimney with the muzzle of a musket against his breast & ordered him to sign the contract."[57] By the end of the year, physical coercion had played no small role in imposing contracts meant to demonstrate to freed-people that self-employment was not a condition of their emancipation.

Perhaps because Andrew Johnson's advisors ensured that at war's end the articulation and enforcement of bureau policy increasingly fell to commissioned officers, Northern antislavery often spoke to the newly free in its most conservative tones.[58] Upon the establishment of garrisons and special military commissions to supervise contracts outside the Sherman reserve during the summer of 1865, officers optimistically put down swords and took up pens to draft addresses that would "disabuse the ne-groes of [their] false and exaggerated ideas of freedom."[59] They were nev-ertheless slated to join the swelling ranks of the century's reformers whose optimistic faith that they were messengers carrying the age's universal proclamations of freedom to all men would splinter on collision with views of freedom different from their own.[60]

Would-be instructors to former slaves of their "true position and prospects" often found their audiences patient and courteous, but "not disposed to place any large amount of confidence in the judgment of those whose duty it is to look after their interests."[61] The lessons bitterly disap-pointed both students and teachers. Charles C. Soule, a captain in the black Fifty-fifth Massachusetts Volunteer Infantry, energetically launched a speaking tour around Orangeburg district shortly after his

57. W. F. Reading to Rufus Saxton, 20 Nov. 1865, M 869, r 8; Easterby, ed., *R. F. W. Allston*, p. 214, where the bureau officer is mistakenly identified as Montate.
58. McFeely, *Yankee Stepfather*, pp. 65–83; Wagstaff, "Call Your Old Master."
59. Charles C. Soule to O. O. Howard, 12 June 1865, Miscellaneous Reports Received, ser. 3157, Columbia, Subordinate Field Office Records, RG 105. See also E. A. Kozlay to T. D. Hodges, 5 Dec. 1865, Letters and Reports Received Relating to Freed-men and Civil Affairs, ser. 4112, 2d Military District, RG 393 Pt 1; [circular letter], Headquarters Acting Assistant Commissioner [Ralph Ely], 22 Nov. 1865, Letters Re-ceived, ser. 3156, Columbia, Subordinate Field Office Records, RG 105; James C. Beecher to H. W. Smith, 26 Dec. 1865, M 869, r 7; F. H. Whitt[en?], to C. [R?] Fille-brown, 4 Nov. 1865, Letters and Reports Received Relating to Freedmen and Civil Affairs, ser. 4112, 2d Military District, RG 393 Pt 1.
60. The disintegration of systems of bound labor in Europe and portions of the Americas as a global consequence of the slow ascendance of industrial capitalism is deftly treated in Hobsbawm, *Age of Revolution, 1789–1848*, especially pp. 180–201, and idem, *Age of Capital*, especially pp. 173–92. Indispensable to an appreciation of the historical specificity of the failures of emancipation and Reconstruction in the south-ern United States is Woodward, "Price of Freedom," in Sansing, ed., *What Was Free-dom's Price?*, pp. 93–113. Montgomery, *Beyond Equality*; Sproat, *The Best Men*; and Foner, *Reconstruction*, pp. 488–511, explore the evolution of American liberalism's antidemocratic face.
61. Charles C. Soule to O. O. Howard, 12 June 1865, Miscellaneous Reports Received, ser. 3157, Columbia, Subordinate Field Office Records, RG 105; A. J. Willard to George W. Hooker, 7 Nov. 1865, M 869, r 8, 0633–40.

company arrived in early June. Two weeks later, he and his fellow officers had addressed nearly two thousand whites and ten thousand freedpeople. To ex-masters, Soule stressed "the necessity of making equitable contracts with their workmen, of discontinuing corporal punishment, and of referring all cases of disorder and idleness to the military authorities." To ex-slaves, he explained "in plain and simple terms their new position as freedmen, their prospects, their duties, and their continued liability to punishment for faults and crimes." Looking backward, Soule identified many hard-won rights under slavery – customary possession of fowl, stock, and farm tools, as well as access to small gardens or provision grounds and the time in which to work them – as the first casualties of free labor. Slaves' guaranteed minimal subsistence and shelter now became in-kind payments to be "earned" by free workers. Surveying present conditions in Orangeburg district, Soule prohibited many of the very steps that freedpeople had undertaken to order their work and family life more harmoniously. Looking ahead, he justified and prescribed a subordination of the social, domestic, and working lives of wage earners that a postwar Northern organized labor movement would vigorously challenge. So sweeping an effort should be shared in full measure:[62]

> You have heard many stories about your condition as freemen. You do not know what to believe: you are talking too much; waiting too much; asking for too much. . . . Listen, then, and try to understand just how you are situated. . . . You may have a harder time this year than you have ever had before; it will be the price you pay for your freedom. You will have to work hard, and get very little to eat, and very few clothes to wear. . . . Do not expect to save up anything or to have much corn or provisions ahead at the end of the year. . . . You do not own a cents worth except yourselves. The plantation you live on is not yours, not the houses, nor the cattle, mules and horses; the seed you planted with was not yours, and the ploughs and hoes do not belong to you. . . . [F]ree people everywhere else work Saturday, and you have no more right to the day than they have. . . . Every man must work under orders . . . and on a plantation the head man who gives all the orders is the owner of the place. Whatever he tells you to do you must do at once, and cheerfully. . . . Some people must be rich, to pay the others, and they have the right to do no work except to look out after their property. . . . Remember that all your working time belongs to the man who hires you. . . . [W]hen a husband and wife live on different places . . . this year, they have their crops

62. Charles C. Soule to O. O. Howard, 12 June 1865, Miscellaneous Reports Received, ser. 3157, Columbia, Subordinate Field Office Records, RG 105; [speech], "To the Freed People of Orangeburg District," enclosed in Charles C. Soule to O. O. Howard, 12 June 1865, M 752, r 17, 0053–61.

planted on their own places and they must stay to work them. At the
end of the year they can live together. Until then they must see each
other only once in a while. . . . Remember that even if you are badly
off, no one can buy or sell you.

Soule was quickly made to know that freed audiences pronounced the
officers bearing such tidings "rebels in disguise." The epithet, variations
of which rang widely in the state, suggests how ex-slaves rated their liberators' understanding of freedom.[63]

The origins of freedpeople's disillusion may be found in part in the conditions that surrounded the introduction of the military-supervised
contract system on the mainland in 1865. At the same time that army officers assumed a prominent role in proclaiming a landless emancipation,
military-supervised contract boards were parceling out and assigning
exclusive shares to a harvest that had been sown and cultivated according to slavery's overlapping and less-than-absolute rights of property.
These first divisions of what had long been indivisible brought to the fore
competing claims of right and justice.

The proportion of planters who sought military approval of contracts
in 1865 is not clear, but at least two circumstances inclined both resident
and refugee planters to tolerate if not to favor the system. Where contracts
were introduced before crops were laid by in late July, resident planters
seized upon contracts as an opportunity to keep their labor force undi-
minished during what they quickly informed arriving soldiers was "the
most critical stage" of cultivation, when workers were needed in larger
numbers than they would again be needed until the harvest. District commanders accepted the urgency of the planters' appeal and, whenever possible, required freedpeople to sign contracts with their former owners,[64]
even if, as Soule explained, the contracts temporarily confirmed antebellum patterns of residence that would permit families to "see each other
only once in a while." On abandoned places, nonresident planters hastened in the summer to secure contracts guaranteeing them shares of a
crop from whose division there are some indications that laborers might
have either excluded them altogether or turned over a smaller share than
the contracts awarded. To an outside observer, it might well seem that the

63. Charles C. Soule to O. O. Howard, 12 June 1865, Miscellaneous Reports Received,
    ser. 3157, Columbia, Subordinate Field Office Records, RG 105; Endorsement of E.
    W. Everson, 4 April 1866, on nn to "General Skott," 22 March 1866, M 869, r 21,
    0009; Myers, ed., *Children of Pride*, p. 1292.
64. Charles C. Soule to O. O. Howard, 12 June 1865, Miscellaneous Reports Received,
    ser. 3157, Columbia, Subordinate Field Office Records, RG 105; [circular letter],
    Headquarters Acting Assistant Commissioner [Ralph Ely], 22 Nov. 1865, Letters Re-
    ceived, ser. 3156, Columbia, Subordinate Field Office Records, RG 105; A. J. Willard
    to Geo[rge] W. Hooker, 20 Oct. 1865, M 869, r 8, 0650–54.

thirty-eight workers on the Santee River rice plantation north of Charleston managed by Thomas Doar fared well in 1865. Their June contract secured them two-thirds of all crops except fodder at a time when the shares promised to ex-slaves in other contracts throughout the state more commonly ranged from one-tenth to one-half. In September, however, three ex-slave men, acting on behalf of the people of Springfield plantation, disputed Doar's right to even a third of the crop. Measuring their share against the contract's requirement that they quit the place after the harvest, leaving behind all agricultural implements, they found the seemingly generous share wanting.[65]

On abandoned places where no threat of eviction was imminent, ex-slaves were more willing to divide their surplus – that is, the portion of their crops in excess of what they could live on until the following July, when their gardens would bear again. Two ex-mistresses who returned to St. Helena Island in August and "went from house to house among their fathers [sic] slaves, pleading their poverty" received liberal donations of grits, potatoes, plates, spoons, and some cash. But freedpeople in the settlements that had emerged during wartime occupation of St. Helena limited their donations, "made partly from pity, and partly to let their former owners see how well they can take care of themselves." As ex-slaves made clear to a New Englander then living on St. Helena, it was with the greatest unease that they presented gifts to those who made no reciprocal offerings and whose very return threatened the wartime land tenures on which these gift exchanges rested: "Although to the first who came back the people gave liberally they are becoming more cautious, for they say that two come for every one they send relieved, and that is a new way 'maussa' has of making them work for him."[66] Charity honored reciprocal obligations that had originated in master's antebellum household within new bounds.

Dean of South Carolina letters William Gilmore Simms encountered a similarly constrained charity in August when he sought assistance from the military contract board to secure a quarter share of the crops raised during his absence from Woodlands, his Barnwell district plantation. Simms and family had left Woodlands, sending off a year's provisions, shortly before Union soldiers reached the neighborhood in February. The troops' levies stripped the plantation of tools, work animals, and remaining food supplies. The forty-seven freedpeople who re-

---

65. "Copy of Usual Contract," T. W. Doar [c. June 1865]; R. Tomlinson to Thomas Dorr [sic], 29 Sept. 1865; both in Letters and Reports Received Relating to Freedmen and Civil Affairs, ser. 4112, 2d Military District, RG 393 Pt 1; Cha[rle]s Devens to W. L. M. Burger, 23 Oct. 1865 [C-1361].
66. W. E. Towne to Rufus Saxton, 17 Aug. 1865, M 869, r 8.

mained at Woodlands had gone to work, improvising some rude hoes
from saw blades and railroad iron and rehabilitating several condemned
army mules, to plant about seventy-five acres of corn along with some
rice and potatoes. Simms's former slave Billy Curry, whom the bureau
had appointed foreman during Simms's absence and awarded a quarter
of the crops grown on the place, countered Simms's claim for a fourth of
the crops. Curry announced his willingness to share half of his fourth
with Simms, "'cos Ise willin to help Massa Gilmore troo de hard
times.'" But Curry "objected to taking the food from the other hands,
inasmuch as they had scarcely sufficient to feed them until July
next."[67] Curry would have restricted the share that Simms could justly
claim by first guaranteeing a year's subsistence for the other freed families on the place.

After the crops were laid by, many planters in the upper districts
showed their faith that a new order had indeed been inaugurated. In late
July, a grudging acknowledgment that "[t]he negroes . . . are now so 'de-
moralized' that they can no more be made good reliable slaves" accompanied the first wave of evictions from interior plantations, as the
disabled, the elderly, and women with large numbers of nonworking children were among the first to be pared from the plantation community's
work force.[68] At the same time, reports came from other places that
planters had stopped issuing rations once garden crops had been harvested, freeing themselves of the obligation to feed now-free workers during the preharvest lull.[69]

Struggles during the lay-by season anticipated a pattern that would intensify after the first crops of freedom were harvested. On large and small
places freedpeople declined to perform the farm chores of the lay-by and
postharvest seasons – fencing, cutting wood, gathering fodder, clearing
new ground, and ditching – without compensation in addition to that
promised in their contracts. Others turned to the promise of land in the
Sherman reserve; an estimated four hundred freedpeople in Orangeburg

67. "Report," James C. Beecher, 23 June 1865; Beecher to Stewart M. Taylor, 23 Sept.,
    6 Oct. 1865; all in M 869, r 7; Oliphant, Odell, and Eaves, eds., *Simms Letters*, vol.
    4, pp. 478–80, 482, 499, 502.
68. Boston *Daily Advertiser*, 5 Aug. 1865, p. 2, col. 3; James C. Beecher to Stewart M.
    Taylor, 29 Sept. 1865, r 20, 0029; J. E. Bryant to S. Willard Saxton, 4 Aug. 1865, r
    7; all in M 869.
69. G. P. McDougall to Mrs. Mary Tilmon, 16 Aug. 1866, idem to Mrs. Martha Lowery,
    17 Aug. 1866, idem to O. H. Moore, 20 Aug. 1866, all in Letters and Endorsements
    Sent, ser. 3051, Anderson, Subordinate Field Office Records RG 105; C. R. Becker to
    J. Devereux, 1 Aug. 1866, Miscellaneous Records Relating to Complaints, ser. 3035,
    Abbeville, Subordinate Field Office Records, RG 105; H. G. Judd to [S. W.] Saxton,
    16 Sept. 1865, M 869, r 20, 0214.

district alone sold their shares of 1865 crops and hired cars for the coast.[70] A portent of things to come, such conflicts were an opening round in the disputed settlements and contested work practices of the postwar South. In them we can read former slaves' critiques of Southern slavery and of Northern freedom.

70. Charles Devens to W. L. M. Burger, 31 Jan. 1866, enclosed in wrapper labeled Daniel E. Sickles, Semi-monthly report, 13 Jan. 1866, Letters and Reports Received Relating to Freedmen and Civil Affairs, ser. 4112, 2d Military District, RG 393 Pt 1; Ralph Ely to C. H. Howard, 14 Dec. 1865, M 869, r 9.

2

A Measure of Freedom: Plantation Workers and the Wartime Introduction of Wage Labor in Port Royal

Eluding the Confederacy's Grasp

The federal invasion of the Carolina coast that began with the occupation of lower Beaufort district in November 1861 reclaimed for the Union a region comprising one of the antebellum South's largest plantation-slave populations. The sheer number of black people living in this first area of large slaveholdings to fall to federal invasion astounded many a Northern newcomer. The Boston schoolteacher Elizabeth Hyde Botume recorded her impressions when her boat docked in Beaufort in the fall of 1864:

> Negroes, negroes, negroes. They hovered around like bees in a swarm. Sitting, standing, or lying at full-length, with their faces turned to the sky. Every doorstep, box, or barrel was covered with them, for the arrival of the boat was a time of great excitement. . . . The town of Beaufort was filled to overflowing with ex-slaves.[1]

By the time of the Civil War, of course, slaves had formed a majority of the population along the Carolina coast for more than a century.[2] During the war, however, an almost continuous incursion of fugitive slaves increased the density of the black population in the area occupied by Union troops. Where federal control was staked out in small planting and farming regions, fugitive slaves penetrated Union lines singly and seldom in groups of more than ten people. However, during the four-year occupation of the Carolina coast, they came by scores and at times by the hundreds.[3]

1. Botume, *First Days*, pp. 31–33.
2. Wood, *Black Majority*; Littlefield, *Rice and Slaves*.
3. Arrivals in small groups seem most common among fugitives who sailed small (and often rickety) dugouts toward ships in the federal coastal blockade. Analysis of the timing and significance of wartime escapes is offered in Berlin et al., eds., *Destruction of Slavery*; Gutman, *Black Family*, pp. 227, 320–21, 367–75; Mohr, "Before Sherman"; and Robinson, "Day of Jubilo," pp. 224–78. Leslie S. Rowland shared preliminary findings from her manuscript "Self-Emancipation: The Destruction of Slavery in Ken-

Planting sweet potatoes on James Hopkinson's plantation on Edisto Island, SC, photograph by Henry P. Moore, spring 1862. Courtesy of The New-York Historical Society, New York, NY.

Early in February 1862, Edward L. Pierce, a Boston attorney appointed as a special agent to investigate and report to the Treasury Department on conditions in newly occupied Beaufort district, distinguished the sources of the slave population behind Union lines in his first report to Secretary of the Treasury Salmon P. Chase. Secured federal territory then embraced, Pierce guessed, between ten and twelve thousand slaves. Some eight thousand of them were on plantations "within our lines . . . by the invitation of no one; but they were on the soil when our army began its occupation." Another two thousand slaves were refugees who had come in to the army camp on Hilton Head Island and to Beaufort Village on Port Royal Island from outlying areas before Union control became secure. Nearly half of these early slave refugees were from somewhere other than Port Royal and Hilton Head islands, and fugitives from the main-

tucky, 1861–1865." See also Williamson, *After Slavery,* pp. 4–8; Litwack, *Been in the Storm So Long,* pp. 51–59; Ripley, *Slaves and Freedmen,* pp. 25–40; Wiley, *Southern Negroes,* pp. 8–12; and Quarles, *Negro in the Civil War,* pp. 57–77. Accounts of fugitives sailing to coastal blockades appear in ORN, ser. 1, vol. 12, part 2, pp. 457, 460–61, 509, 546, 678–80, and in ser. 1, vol. 13, p. 447.

land were among them. While Pierce was preparing his report, he learned that forty-eight people had successfully escaped from a single plantation near Grahamville on the mainland. Reportedly led by the driver, they required four days to travel the fifteen or so miles to Port Royal, making their way in small boats past Confederate pickets at night and keeping hidden during the day.[4]

The majority of the slave refugees on Hilton Head and Port Royal had fled rebel snipers and nighttime raiding parties who, for six weeks after the federal invasion, tried to reverse the failure to evacuate slaves from those islands.[5] As United States naval forces made their first expedition to Beaufort on 9 November, they encountered a crew of slave boatmen headed there "to make some arrangements." The boatmen told a naval officer that "many of them had been shot by their masters" and expressed their belief that "all of the blacks would come in [to Beaufort] to avoid being murdered." Later that day, when Union naval forces entered Beaufort, slaves were there to greet them. An officer reported the slaves "rejoiced to see me, crowding around in large numbers and cheering the flag." They told him that "their masters had been firing at them and driving them back into the woods to prevent their communicating with United States forces."[6]

The overt violence that erupted on Port Royal plantations during Confederate evacuation unleashed the fury of the slaves' attack on Beaufort, which was in abated progress when Union troops arrived. Few of Beaufort's elegant residential comforts found their way back to the quarters on outlying plantations. Instead, smeared with excrement, smashed, shredded, and otherwise dismantled beyond use, the wrecked remains of planters' personal property spoke of a contemptuous effacement and destruction. Vengeful rage as much as mass seizure and redistribution of forbidden goods seems to have fueled the slaves' assault. Small wonder that the one white resident of Beaufort that Union troops could find – a storekeeper and "poor fellow" of Northern birth – had become crazed by some combination of fear and whiskey during the slaves' "perfectly wild" rampage. The naval commander whose troops spent two days stopping the rioting judged the rioters ready to "commit any act of retaliation that opportunity offered."[7]

Federal occupation of lower Beaufort had been reasonably swift; Confederate armed forces in the area were relatively weak. The slaves who lived south of St. Helena Sound had been largely successful in resisting

4. Edward L. Pierce to Salmon P. Chase, 3 Feb. 1862, in Moore, ed., *Rebellion Record*, vol. 1, supplement, pp. 303, 306, quotation at p. 304.
5. S. F. Du Pont to Gideon Welles, 25 Nov. 1861, 13 Dec. 1861, in ORN, ser. 1, vol. 12, part 2, pp. 320–21, 398.
6. Dan Ammen to S. F. Du Pont, 9 Nov. 1862, J. Glendy Sprotson to D. Ammen [9 Nov. 1861], ibid., pp. 336–37, 337–38.
7. Concerning the articles that slaves had taken from plantation houses back to the quarters, Pierce observed that "it is not true that they have, except as to very simple articles,

removal, and within three months federal control of the islands south of St. Helena Sound had been secured. Within those three months, slaves who lived on the two hundred island plantations and in island camps had most often won their struggles to hide from, escape, or destroy slavery's unusually weak defenses in a relatively calm theater of war.[8]

North of the sound, Confederate evacuation proved more vigorous when it began in earnest after the invasion of lower Beaufort. As planters hauled slave women and children off to the mainland, Confederate troops and attachments to evacuated kin kept slave men away from the Yankees and at work getting in the cotton crop. From an army camp in Virginia, Edisto planter Micah Jenkins wished his brother John luck in moving their slaves up-country:

> I fully approve your determination to enforce obedience among our
> negroes at any alternative. I would shoot the first who refused to
> move; but I would manage to have force enough so as to insure [sic]
> their going.[9]

John Jenkins had force enough. The morning that Northern troops landed on Edisto, most of Jenkins's slaves ran to them and he feared that "we had lost all our People." But the invasion pitted slave against master before Union military strength was committed to the abolition of the right to own slaves. As a result, the Yankees did not carry Jenkins's slaves off, but did use some of the men to help load "a lot of Potatoes" on board a federal steamer. Jenkins returned to his plantation that night, burned out the slave quarters, the crops of cotton and corn, and "gott in all the Negros." Aided by federal indifference to slaves who sought Northern protection – as well as by his access to family lands removed from the zone of conflict, state armed transport, and a bit of ready cash from the sale of plantation stock – Jenkins quit Edisto Island for the interior "satisfied that the Yankees took off none" of his slaves.[10]

The force employed to maintain subordination during evacuation departed starkly from the antebellum ideal of measured force.[11] During

as soap or dishes, generally availed themselves of [abandoned] property." See Edward L. Pierce to Salmon P. Chase, 3 Feb. 1862, in Moore, ed., *Rebellion Record,* vol. 1 supplement, p. 308; S. W. Saxton Diary, 12 March 1862, Saxton Papers, CtY; Botume, *First Days,* pp. 27–28; J. Glendy Sprotson to D. Ammen [9 Nov. 1861], *ORN,* vol. 12, part 2, pp. 337–38 and enclosed reports on pp. 338–39; Dan Ammen to S. F. Du Pont, 9 Nov. 1861, ibid., pp. 336–37. The attack on Beaufort is analyzed in Rose, *Rehearsal for Reconstruction,* pp. 106–07.

8.   The estimated number of plantations in the occupied district is offered in Edward L. Pierce to Salmon P. Chase, 3 Feb. 1862, in Moore, *Rebellion Record,* vol. 1 supplement, p. 303.
9.   Micah Jenkins to John Jenkins, 21 Nov. 1861, Jenkins Family Papers, SCL.
10. John Jenkins to Marcelline R. Jenkins, 4 Dec. 1861, Jenkins Family Papers, SCL.
11. Post-Enlightenment legitimations of physical coercion in the master–slave relationship are considered in Genovese, *Roll, Jordan, Roll,* pp. 27–28, 37–38, 50–51, 65; and in Kolchin, *Unfree Labor,* pp. 128–30.

evacuation, violent and lethal force was deployed against the entire slave community, not against refractory individual slaves. To drive slaves away, Confederate troops, on occasion led by Master himself, burned the slaves' quarters, destroyed provisions, and shot at slaves not to caution but to kill. Starkly, evacuation revealed the master's power to protect as his power also to destroy. Exposure to that spectacle lay behind the terror, confusion, and alarm widely reported among slave refugees who eluded the Confederacy's grasp.

Early in December, a Union naval expedition landing on Hutchinson's Island, which lies near Edisto on the northern border of St. Helena Sound, visited a plantation that had been the site of such an evacuation. The cabins, the overseer's house, and the picked cotton had all been burned a few days earlier.

> The scene was one of complete desolation; the smoking ruins and cowering figures which surrounded them, of those negroes who still instinctively clung to their hearthstones, although there was no longer any shelter for them, presented a most melancholy sight, the impression of which was made even stronger by the piteous wailing of the poor creatures, a large portion of whom consisted of the old and decrepit.

Some slaves fled Hutchinson's and other islands north of St. Helena Sound after their cabins were burned. December naval expeditions found them lined along the beaches of the lower coastal rivers, "with their household effects piled up about them." During a single reconnaissance up the North Edisto River in mid-December, nearly 150 slaves came aboard federal vessels "all in a great state of alarm."[12] Their eyes had seen glory and horror in the coming of freedom.

More losers than winners figured among the slaves who lived on the small islands bordering St. Helena Sound to the north and on Edisto Island. Probably two-thirds of Edisto's slave population was moved behind Confederate lines between November 1861 and January 1862.[13]

Inducing Wage Labor behind Federal Lines

While Union troops fought to gain full possession of Edisto in January 1862, successful slave refugees came behind Union lines at rates without precedent, even in Yankee Port Royal. The slave population on the Union-

---

12. P[ercival] Drayton to S. F. Du Pont, 9 Dec. 1861, in *ORN,* ser. 1, vol. 12, part 2, pp. 388–90; S. F. Du Pont to Gideon Welles, 12 Dec. 1861, ibid., p. 388; P[ercival] Drayton to S. F. Du Pont, 21 Dec. 1861, ibid., pp. 405–06; John Jenkins to Marcelline R. Jenkins, 4 Dec. 1861, Jenkins Family Papers, SCL.

13. A tentative estimate based on an approximate 1860 slave population of six thousand on Edisto Island.

controlled eastern end of Edisto Island increased from 1,000 to 2,300 people "within a few days" in late January.[14]

The early wartime experiences of refugees to the north of the sound is less well known than that of slaves who lived in the portion of Beaufort district held by Union troops for the duration of the war. In the summer of 1862, about four thousand slave refugees, roughly one-third of the South Carolina slaves who had claimed federal protection by that date, were living in what came to be only temporary settlements, scattered almost the length of the Carolina coast from North Island at the entrance to Georgetown's Winyah Bay, to the Botany Bay settlement on the North Edisto River, to Otter and Hutchinson's islands bordering St. Helena Sound.[15] During the summer of 1862, refugees in the temporary camps were transported to Yankee Port Royal, as Northern military forces were withdrawn or reduced in the waters and forts near the settlements.

During the first nine months of Northern occupation, refugees in these temporary camps, like those at the more continuously settled camps on Port Royal and Hilton Head, supplied a disproportionate number of the men and women who worked for wages in the occupied area. They worked as laborers in the Quartermaster's Department, provided the "acclimated persons" needed on board ships in the blockading squadron "in such duties as involve much exposure to sun and heat" after the "hot season" commenced, and did cooking and laundry for soldiers in camp. It seems likely that male refugees were also the earliest large source of soldiers in the slave regiments organized in the Department of the South beginning in 1863.[16] Uprooted from their home plantations, these early refugees began a path from slavery bereft of the support that undisturbed

14. Edward L. Pierce to Salmon P. Chase, 3 Feb. 1862, in Moore, *Rebellion Record,* vol. 1, supplement, p. 303.

15. This tentative estimate is based on scattered reports of the number of slaves evacuated from Union settlements during the summer of 1862. Twenty-three hundred people seem to have been removed from North Island, 1,500 people were transported from Edisto, and eventually 245 people left Hutchinson's Island. See W. T. Truxton to S. F. Du Pont, 13 June 1862, Geo B. Balch to S. F. Du Pont, 25 July 1862, in *ORN,* ser. 1, vol. 13, pp. 96–98, 212–13; [R.] Saxton to E. M. Stanton, 17 July, 16 Aug. 1862, Saxton Papers, CtY; Edward L. Pierce to Salmon P. Chase, 2 June 1862, in Moore, ed., *Rebellion Record,* vol. 1 supplement, p. 316.

16. Precise figures have been located only for the number of laborers in the quartermaster's department on Hilton Head Island. Of the 472 people at the Hilton Head camp, only 77 were from Hilton Head Island. The number of slaves on the Hilton Head quartermaster's payroll ranged from 63, on 1 December 1861, to 137 on 1 February 1862. Williamson, *After Slavery,* pp. 13, 25, also carefully notes the early preponderance of refugees among the department's laborers and soldiers, though his judgment that as a result of this employment they were introduced into a "money economy" is less insightful. See also Edward L. Pierce to Salmon P. Chase, 3 Feb. 1862, in Moore, ed., *Rebellion Record,* vol. 1 supplement, p. 313; S. F. Du Pont, General Order No. 11, 15 May 1862, in *ORN,* ser. 1, vol. 13, p. 5.

occupation of the old homesite promised to communities left in possession of the plantations after their owners fled. People on the old home
places structured priorities differently than the refugee wage employees.

When Northern soldiers first encountered slaves living on their home
plantations, they found them "perfectly convinced that we have come to
free them, and in consequence most friendly." In late November the commander of an expedition around St. Helena Sound and up the Ashepoo
River was gratified that "whenever we call on them for assistance [they]
work like Turks," reporting "I overheard one of them say that they ought
to work for us, as we were doing so for them." However, as the occupying forces and Treasury agents became sufficiently organized to establish
"order" in the department – seizing provisions, cattle, horses, and carts
on the separate plantations and transporting them to central military
stores, drafting workers to pick and bale cotton at a time when only half
the provision crops had been gathered – complaints about the unreliabil-
ity of slave workers commenced.[17]

It came as no small surprise to John H. Filler of the Fifty-fifth Pennsylvania Volunteers, whose regiment established its headquarters on Hilton
Head Island in December 1861, that a desire to work to earn money was
not an innate human aspiration. "It is with the greatest difficulty that they
can be induced to do any work for pay which is freely offered them,"
Filler observed in disgust. "All they want is their corn-meal, hominy,
sweet potatoes, and oysters. As long as they have these they won't
work."[18] Conditions in the refugee camps help explain why slave refugees
rather than slaves living on their plantation supplied the bulk of the earliest wage workers.

Removed from their own plantations, slaves living in the refugee camps
nevertheless had to depend on abandoned plantations as sources of food
and shelter. Those who reached the camps enjoyed the protection of federal arms from nearby forts or patrol boats, and occasionally they were
issued military rations. They were made to know, however, that they were
expected to procure their own food. Trailing behind armed gun boats,
crews of slave boatmen rowed small boats and canoes up the coastal
rivers to bring back supplies from abandoned plantations. On a single
such expedition in mid-December 1861, twenty male "contrabands"
rowed up the Ashepoo River to Fenwick's Island under armed escort and
collected potatoes, corn, lumber, a corn mill, two horses, a cart, and other
supplies for the use of refugees in the camp where they were living. Not

17.   P[ercival] Drayton to "My Dear Wise," 30 Nov. 1861, idem to S. F. Du Pont, 28 Nov.
      1861, in *ORN,* ser. 1, vol. 12, part 2, pp. 272–74, 321–23.
18.   Jno. H. Filler to Edward McPherson, 30 Dec. 1861, Edward McPherson Manuscripts, DLC.

all rebel property was up for grabs, however. A naval officer who regularly led slaves assembled at Botany Bay on forays to collect food complained, "If I go anywhere to enable them to collect corn or potatoes, they begin to plunder the houses of furniture and other articles entirely useless to them."[19]

Confederate troops visited isolated islands in search of supplies or slaves, adding to the number of refugees. Ripening summer food crops drew raids from Confederate troops pressed for food in their own camps. About fifty Confederate "rangers" raided a settlement on Hutchinson's Island early in July 1862 and took off a large number of chickens and a few hogs. They told the people that they would "continue to come down and carry off crops as fast as they ripened." To the close margins of existence on Hutchinson's had been added the threat of armed attack. In June 1862, the Marsh plantation on Hutchinson's Island was attacked by Confederate soldiers. A majority of the slaves on Hutchinson's had earlier declined to move to Edisto or St. Helena, because Hutchinson's "was their home." After the June raid, however, seventy people then decided to go to Hilton Head. Where circumstances permitted, they abandoned homes and left the refugee settlements as they had come in – in the extended families that composed segments of a plantation. Two slave men approached a naval officer at Botany Bay, explained that they were "anxious to obtain work," and asked for transportation for themselves and their families. The group of fifty people secured passage to Port Royal.[20]

In the occupied area around Port Royal, the number of people who lived someplace other than their home plantation increased throughout the war. Port Royal and Hilton Head islands probably received the largest numbers of such refugees. But in February 1862, when Edward Pierce prepared his first report to Secretary Chase, the majority of slaves behind Union lines, and particularly on St. Helena and Ladies islands, were probably still living on their home plantations. It seemed to Pierce that there, except for occasionally bagging and baling cotton at the direction of Treasury agents, they "have had nothing to do."[21]

19. Danl. Ammen to S. F. Du Pont, 21 Jan. 1862, J. W. A. Nicholson to Saml F. Du Pont, 13 Dec. 1861, A. C. Rhind to S. F. Du Pont, 7 Feb. 1862, in *ORN*, ser. 1, vol. 12, part 2, pp. 516–17, 392–93, 520–21. See also Danl. Ammen to Saml. F. Du Pont, 29 Dec. 1861, 8 Jan. 1862, and Thomas A. Budd to S. F. Du Pont, 14 Jan. 1862, ibid., pp. 431–32, 464–65, 463.

20. I. B. Baxter to Capt. Balch, 24 July 1862, in *ORN*, ser. 1, vol. 13, pp. 202–03; W. T. Truxton to S. F. Du Pont, 13 June 1862, 13 July 1862, ibid., pp. 96–98, 185; Danl. Ammen to S. F. Du Pont, 21 Jan. 1862, *ORN*, ser. 1, vol. 12, part 2, pp. 516–17.

21. Edward L. Pierce to Salmon P. Chase, 3 Feb. 1862, in Moore, ed., *Rebellion Record*, vol. 1 supplement, p. 307.

Discussions of what the plantation slaves should do became entangled in an increasing controversy over the disposition of plantation lands forfeited under the Direct Tax Act of 1862. In brief, the conflict in Port Royal (which has received memorable treatment elsewhere) pitted advocates of an emancipated, "self-employed" landowning yeomanry against proponents (usually would-be employers or prospective investors) of emancipated wage workers on cotton plantations. At issue – argued the utopian communalist, anti–land monopolist, Garrisonian abolitionist father of Port Royal's military governor, Rufus Saxton – were the "proper uses of the negro in the social economy." But differences over the character of that society and economy were at the heart of the dispute.[22]

Proposals to employ island residents to tend vast acres of abandoned cotton lands sprouted within months of Union occupation, on the eve of the 1862 planting season. A group of Vermont entrepreneurs wrote Secretary Chase in February, promoting their scheme to employ laborers to plant twenty thousand acres on Edisto.[23] Nevertheless, private employers did not gain a foothold in Port Royal until the spring of 1863, when about fifty of an estimated two hundred plantations in the military department were sold by auction under the aegis of the Direct Tax Commission.[24]

The agency's auctions, it is worth noting, struck slaves in the islands as somewhat peculiar. With the help of a Northern amanuensis who meant to reproduce the sound of his speech, "Uncle Smart," a church elder and former slave from Port Royal Island, asked a Northern teacher on the sea islands who was returning to Philadelphia in 1864 to "tell Linkum dat we wants land – dis bery land dat is rich wid de sweat ob we face and de blood ob we back. We born here; we parents' graves here; we donne oder country; dis yere our home." There crept into his missive a muted criticism of the strangeness of "Northern" ways: "De Nort folks hab home, antee? What a pity dat dey don't love der home like we love we home, for den dey would never come here for buy all way from we."[25] Claims to land rooted in nonmarket notions of economy were peculiar to the terms in which ex-slaves claimed a share of the freed soil in occupied Port Royal.

22. J[onathan] A. Saxton to J. J. Childs, 15 March 1864; Louise Saxton Clapp, "Samuel Willard Saxton: A Memorial by his Daughter," both in Saxton Papers, CtY. On land controversies in the Union-occupied sea islands, see Rose, *Rehearsal for Reconstruction*, pp. 173–78, 200–16, 272–96; and Berlin et al., eds., *Wartime Genesis*, especially pp. 16–18, 36–37, 48–49, 59, 87–344.

23. Ellis, Britton, and Eaton to Hon. S. P. Chase, 3 Feb. 1862, vol. 19, item 46, Port Royal Correspondence, 5th Agency, RG 366 [Q-20]; [William H. Reynolds] to Hon. S. P. Chase, 1 Feb. 1862, vol. 19, item 45, Port Royal Correspondence, 5th Agency, RG 366 [Q-5].

24. Edward Philbrick to AFIC, 17 Aug. 1863, AFIC Testimony M 619, r 200, 0416–27.

25. McPherson, ed., *Negro's Civil War*, p. 298.

Among the civil and military officials headquartered in the Department of the South at Port Royal, evangelical antislavery traditions formed the principal channel by which slave residents' claims to land received a wider hearing. At the center of official attempts to secure such claims were the department's military governor, Rufus Saxton, the Methodist minister Mansfield French, and Abram D. Smith, one of three commissioners appointed to administer the Direct Tax Act in South Carolina.[26] In a move to halt the further alienation of landholdings from freedpeople after auctions in the spring of 1863, Saxton finally obtained, in December, President Lincoln's approval of revised instructions to the tax commissioners. The new instructions did not restrict preemption to the largely unimproved tracts reserved for ex-slaves as part of the "charitable" purposes of the Direct Tax measures.[27] Early in 1864, some freed families staked out and started to plant preempted tracts, on Saxton's assurance that the government intended to guarantee their right to purchase at $1.25 per acre at least twenty acres of any forfeited lands they might claim. However, only a minority of freed families were prepared to take advantage of the terms of the December 1863 preemption measure. Not more than five hundred families on Port Royal and St. Helena islands deposited with Saxton's aide A. P. Ketchum a total of $5,000 to purchase improved plantation lands.[28]

More than freedpeople's lack of the minimum cash deposit, their want of money to purchase seed, tools, and farm animals, or the refusal by a majority of the tax commissioners to accept payments tendered under the December instructions, impeded preemption. Freedpeople themselves looked askance at the plan to secure them preferred purchase options as

26. Rose, *Rehearsal for Reconstruction*, pp. 278–79; A. D. Smith, AFIC Testimony, M 619, r 200. Abram D. Smith should not be confused with Austin D. Smith, a New York attorney appointed a special agent of the Treasury Department in 1864 to investigate the freedpeople's complaints enclosed in a petition to Abraham Lincoln. The circumstances surrounding the petition are discussed later in this chapter.

27. Abraham Lincoln to Tax Commissioners for the District of South Carolina, 16 Sept. 1863, in Basler, ed., *Collected Works of Abraham Lincoln*, vol. 6, pp. 453–49; "Additional Instructions to the Direct Tax Commissioners for the District of South Carolina," 16 Dec. 1863, enclosed in R. Saxton to E. M. Stanton, 7 Feb. 1864, in *OR*, ser. 3, vol. 4, pp. 118–20; *Statutes At-Large of the United States*, vol. 12, pp. 640–41; Wm. Henry Brisbane to Hon. Joseph J. Lewis, 12 Dec. 1863, General Correspondence, ser. 99, South Carolina, Records Relating to Direct Tax Commissions in the Southern States, RG 58 [Z-2]; Rose, *Rehearsal for Reconstruction*, pp. 202–03, 285–96.

28. [R.] Saxton to Charles Sumner, 6 Dec. 1863, Saxton Papers, CtY; William F. Allen Diary, typescript, 28 Nov. 1863, WiM, reports that "upwards of $4000" was paid in within eight days. Five hundred is a very rough upper limit of the number of families, and is offered in the absence of more direct evidence. It assumes that the $5,000 represented only 40 percent of the purchase price of the minimal twenty-acre tracts, or ten dollars per family. Estimates of the number of freed families on Port Royal and St. Helena islands have been surprisingly hard to come by.

would-be smallholders. Sentimentalism coated the announcement of pre-emption at a St. Helena church meeting in January 1864, where one of the speakers explained the Latin derivation of the term preemption and the social significance of the measure as tears brimmed his eyes.[29] Never-theless, the emotional, almost revivalistic coating did not help all former slaves swallow the plan's kernel of absolute property rights.

Advocates of preemption for the most part proposed conceptions of land use foreign to most freedpeople. For, to select twenty or forty acres of arable plantation land was generally to lose access to other plantation lands – most notably marsh and woodland – of critical importance for fuel, fertilizer, pasturage, herbs, and game. Ex-slaves who in 1864 were living on home places that had been sold the previous year, viewed pre-emption with special misgiving. They often understood preemption not as an opportunity to buy land but as an obligation to leave home. After the people on St. Helena's Big House plantation (which had been pur-chased by Boston engineer Edward Philbrick in 1863) reflected that "they were going to be required to buy land away from their old homes," they told a young teacher on the place that they "thought it was as bad [as] to be sold" themselves. Indeed, preemption seemed to them to introduce a new form of inequality. They thought it "rather hard," the teacher wrote, "that they don't have the same chance to buy land on their own planta-tions that others do."[30] People who did preempt land on new places did not necessarily approve the terms. Glasgow, a spiritual leader among slaves on St. Simon's Island, off the Georgia coast, went ahead and staked out forty acres on a St. Helena plantation where a large number of slave refugees from St. Simon's had been settled. Nevertheless, Glasgow made it clear that his preference was "to go back to St. Simons, where the land is much better."[31]

The invitation to pursue personal advantage while continuing to show consideration for the welfare of others seemed to some freedpeople an outright contradiction. Gabriel caught the entrepreneurial spirit when he announced that he was "going to take twenty acres in the creek, and charge for the right to fish." But Robin recalled that a speaker who an-nounced preemption arrangements on St. Helena had also admonished

29. Accounts of the St. Helena preemption meeting appear in Rose, *Rehearsal for Recon-struction*, pp. 285–87; William F. Allen Diary, typescript, 17 Jan. 1864, pp. 98–100, WiM; Williamson, *After Slavery*, pp. 55–58; Pearson, ed., *Letters from Port Royal*, pp. 243–45.

30. Pearson, ed., *Letters from Port Royal*, p. 230; William F. Allen Diary, typescript, 10 Nov. 1863, p. 15, 25 Nov. 1863, p. 32, 17 Jan. 1864, p. 101, WiM. Rose, *Rehearsal for Reconstruction*, p. 289, observes that "generally in areas where the freedmen could preempt their own home plantations, there was little trouble."

31. William F. Allen Diary, typescript, 26 May 1864, p. 198, 25 March 1864, p. 160, WiM.

the people "not to wear horns and have sharp elbows." From the ensuing quarrels and the contentious putting down and pulling up of stakes, Robin had begun to fear that "dis one hab horns and dat one hab sharp elbows."[32]

It was primarily among themselves that ex-slaves tried to reconcile their conception of land with less familiar terms of land use implicit in preemption. Their strong attachments to particular lands, which they attempted to farm in extended family networks where private and community property overlapped, differed from the system of exclusive property rights in privately owned land subdivided into unfamiliar, spatially uniform units as proposed in the preemption measure. Community pressures for enforcing the old ways were strong. Robin was fairly certain that if he left Big House to stake out a claim on Hope Place or on the Pope plantation, "the people would knock him with a pole." In the end, it seems that more people tried to claim land on preemption's ethically unfamiliar terms than were able to make the reconciliation. Although all the men on Big House went to stake out claims, so the teacher William Allen recalled, only three men succeeded in staking out tracts – and their stakes were pulled up by others. The most common outcome, Allen noted, was, "Everyone says he is 'all confus 'bout dis land.'"[33]

On one of the St. Helena plantations that he had purchased in 1863, Boston businessman Edward Philbrick found the people "in a state of confusion" about buying land: "They had got the impression at church, from the earnest way in which they were urged to buy, that they *must* buy land, *nolens volens*." As head of a consortium that was the largest land purchaser and employer in the Port Royal region, Philbrick was buoyed by reports that people working on his plantations "all say they had rather stay where they are and work for me."[34] Events would demonstrate that the freedpeople preferred to stay because of reservations about preemption, not because they endorsed Philbrick's schemes of plantation management. Perhaps because in 1864 preemption died in Washington, its ambivalent reception in the slaves' quarters has been overlooked.

Secretary of the Treasury Chase endorsed the South Carolina tax commissioners' refusal to accept ex-slaves' proffered payments of the 40 percent of the purchase price that the December 1863 instructions required.

32. William F. Allen Diary, typescript, 17 Jan. 1864, pp. 101–02, WiM. Magdol, *Right to the Land*, pp. 174–86, notes that kinship seems to have structured residence patterns when freedpeople in Port Royal selected plots for preemption. See the diagrams of subdivided plantation lands submitted for preemption claims in Magdol, *Right to the Land*, pp. 178–79.
33. William F. Allen Diary, typescript, 17 Jan. 1864, pp. 101, 105, WiM.
34. Pearson, ed., *Letters from Port Royal*, pp. 246–47; Rose, *Rehearsal for Reconstruction*, p. 306n.

Saxton's insistent urging of ex-slaves' prior claim to lands in the department proved no match for the government's claim to revenue from confiscated rebel estates. After a member of the Direct Tax Commission for South Carolina advised Chase of legal weaknesses and contradictions in the new instructions, Chase suspended them, and the land auctions went forward in the spring of 1864 without preemption. That same spring witnessed the sale by auction of all movable property – farming tools, horses, draft animals, carts, and wagons – on the plantations.

At the land sales, few freedpeople managed to outbid the Northern purchasers and lessees, lured in "hungry swarms," so Saxton's father thought, by "reports of the fabulous wealth to be dug out of the cotton mines of the Sea Islands."[35] By 1864, a bare 3.8 percent of the estimated eighty thousand cultivable acres in the department had been bought by former slaves.[36] In sales of plantation stock, tools, and carts, northern landowners were less decisive victors. Perhaps in part because freedpeople more widely recognized personal ownership of these cheaper articles, sales of such plantation goods did not provoke as much "confusion" among them as did the sale of plantation lands. There is an occasional hint that, in bidding against each other, ex-slaves enjoyed winning even when they tried to give the impression that they were not pressing for maximum advantage. When Henry outbid Titus during the property auction on their place, he prefaced his higher bid with the joking apology, "Well Titus, I won't strain you."[37] A more collective spirit guided freedpeople on Fripp Point, another St. Helena plantation purchased by Edward Philbrick. They pooled their cash and outbid Philbrick's superintendent William Gannett for some of the plantation's mules, cows, and carts.

A relative of one of Port Royal's earliest free labor emissaries later reflected that, in gaining such purchases, ex-slaves manifested an "ungracious, not to say ungrateful spirit" toward the superintendents, "who had been using these things ever since they came into possession" of the plantations. The Fripp Point people and other former slaves occasionally acquired plantation utensils and stock through purchases at the auctions; they more generally lost plantation lands. Only the former outcome sparked a few disgruntled Yankee planters to question the justice of a process that did not more certainly link ownership with long-term use.[38]

35. J. A. Saxton to J. J. Childs, 15 March 1864, Saxton Papers, CtY.
36. William F. Allen Diary, typescript, 24 April 1864, p. 183, WiM, recounts a conversation with Reuben Tomlinson in which the latter judged that of the eighty thousand cultivable acres in the department, some three thousand had been purchased by ex-slaves at the 1863 and 1864 auctions.
37. William F. Allen Diary, typescript, 29 March 1864, p. 163, WiM.
38. Pearson, ed., *Letters from Port Royal,* p. 255; William F. Allen Diary, typescript, 8 March 1864, p. 146, WiM.

Legal title to plantation lands and movable property, as well as cash or ready credit to purchase farm tools and animals, launched wartime planters in the department; but these things did not guarantee the quick consolidation of wage labor on the plantations. Even though the number of privately owned plantations roughly doubled between 1863 and 1864,[39] alternatives to year-long wage work on the plantations were not eliminated. By various combinations of short-term wage labor in army and navy camps, cultivation of tracts of marginal plantations lands, housekeeping chores for plantation superintendents and teachers, and marketing, portions of the freed community shaped work to somewhat limit their dependence on the terms of labor that were evolving on the plantations. At the same time, plantation workers began after the land auctions to initiate strategies that would become lasting features of postwar attempts to contain the incursions of wage labor on low-country plantations. By the end of the war, few of the conditions and structures then associated with the Northern introduction of plantation wage labor had gone unchallenged by the roughly forty-five hundred agricultural workers in the department.[40]

Wartime Planting

Employing some five hundred workers on thirteen plantations on St. Helena, Ladies, and Morgan islands, the planting operations consolidated by Edward Philbrick shepherded the introduction of wage labor into long-staple cotton production on a scale perhaps never again attempted in the state after emancipation.[41] Philbrick was somewhat apologetic to the American Freedmen's Inquiry Commission about the scale of his wartime cotton planting. In August 1863, he advised the commission's members that only the uncertainty of military events warranted his large venture in cotton, "for under ordinary conditions of peace there is no reason why cotton should not be successfully raised by small proprietors with small capital."[42]

39. This rough estimate is based on Philbrick's judgment that around fifty plantations were sold to private owners in 1863 and on Allen's account that thirteen thousand acres were sold by auction that year, that only "a part" of the twenty-seven thousand acres slated for auction in 1864 was sold. See Edward Philbrick to AFIC, 17 Aug. 1863, Letters Received by the Adjutant General's Office, 1861–70, M 619, r 200, 0416–27, and William F. Allen Diary, typescript, 24 April 1864, p. 183, WiM.
40. J. A. Saxton to J. J. Childs, 15 March 1864, Saxton Papers, CtY, gives the number of agricultural laborers at that time as 4,448, comprising 1,199 men, 2,533 women, and 716 children.
41. The estimated number of Philbrick's employees is offered in Rose, *Rehearsal for Reconstruction,* p. 306n.
42. Edward Philbrick to AFIC, 17 Aug. 1863, Letters Received by the Adjutant General's Office, 1861–70, M 619, r 200, 0416–27.

Wartime endorsements of large agricultural ventures envisioned employment of freed laborers on a scale fanciful by prevailing Northern employment standards. Consider the unsolicited recommendations that a District of Columbia "water cure" physician offered to Freedmen's Bureau chief Oliver Otis Howard in June 1865. From the nation's capital, hydrotherapist George Bayne contemplated the establishment of government "township corporations" in which some two thousand freed men, women, and children would be employed on ten thousand acres of land. Each family was to enjoy its "own quarters" in a "general domicile" that would also house a "mess room in which each family would have its own table." Proceeds from the sale of crops would "reimburse the government," while weekly compensation at rates "a trifle less than current prices" would be paid to laborers in "scrip currency" that they could immediately claim in order to pay for "board and clothing" or redeem at six-month intervals for "stock of the corporation." In 1865, Bayne thought his plan an improvement on nearly three years of free labor experiments at Port Royal because his model did not leave freedpeople "scatter[ed] . . . over the countryside, each in his hovel, and each with his plough and hoe."[43]

The doctor may have exerted a more far-reaching influence on hydrotherapy than on economic reconstruction of the South. Nevertheless, by a somewhat different route, wartime planters in Port Royal came to endorse the spirit if not the letter of the doctor's prescription for the ills of slavery. Philbrick eventually placed greater faith in private rather than government landowning and justified rent for household cabins rather than Bayne's barracks-style dwellings.[44] Nevertheless, he and his superintendents expended much energy in search of arrangements by which a subsistence wage would tie laborers to cotton cultivation as surely as Bayne's scrip payments and town shares would have rendered them propertyless workers fixed in Southern "township corporations."

The trail of Philbrick's quest was charted over a peculiar ambivalence in free labor assessments of slave society. On the one hand, free labor critics of slavery were loath to deny the central role of overt physical force in coercing slave labor, as Northern defenders of slave society did. On the other hand, when faced with the discipline that force could achieve on large numbers of workers, they were respectful, if not frankly awed. Tracing the force and discipline to a single source – owning humans as property – they were confident that wage labor would eliminate the forceful

43. George Bayne to [O. O. Howard], 1 June 1865, M 752, r 13, 0671–74.
44. Philbrick charged in-kind rents for pasturage and corn lands, but assessment of rents for cabins remained by war's end a phantom of the fancy of a northern teacher who resided on one of his places. See the discussion later in this chapter.

component of the master–slave relationship without sacrificing discipline itself. Reinforced by a tendency in evangelical antislavery agitation to segregate slavery from other social relationships, free labor entrepreneurs ignored conflicting views of wage employment in the North and endorsed a competitive labor market as an effective agency for disciplining free workers.[45] The slaveowner was both the source of the physical coercion that they decried as immoral and the obstacle to other sources of labor discipline that they judged moral. A wartime plantation superintendent on St. Helena Island and his Harvard classmate succinctly posed for readers of the *North American Review* free labor's classic indictment of Southern slavery: "[I]n slavery, not only are natural rights denied, but what is quite as injurious, necessary wants are supplied."[46]

The last "injury" was addressed first. In 1863, when he first came into possession of thirteen sea-island plantations, Philbrick decided to discontinue all in-kind payments to his employees. He had rued their influence since 1862, when he had been hired as a superintendent in the region's federally sponsored cotton planting operations. At that time, Philbrick had taken special efforts to show plantation workers that they were receiving supplies or cash payments only after and in measure with their cotton work. Many had begun to ask to be "made sensible" what work the supplies and cash were for. It had seemed to Philbrick, however, that laborers too readily held the government's intermittent issues of cloth, corn, bacon, and molasses to the standard of the old slave allowances, to whose spare amounts all field hands had been evenly entitled. Workers had found that the government issues came at unpredictable times. The system compared unfavorably, some people made known, with "the time when they used to obtain shoes, dresses, coats, flannels, food, etc., from their masters."[47]

As a government superintendent on St. Helena in September 1862, Philbrick had issued a yard of cotton cloth for each "task," or quarter acre, of cotton that the people had hoed in July. In consequence, "Some people . . . got twenty-two yards, and many got only two or three." Though he reported that "all took it thankfully and seemed content that they got any," the woman Rosetta had disputed the ethics and the mathematics of his accounting. Rosetta had hoed four tasks in July and, by

45. The basis for considering the particular role of free labor antislavery within a larger antislavery tradition is explored in Davis, *Slavery in the Age of Revolution;* Foner, *Free Soil;* and in "Abolitionism and the Labor Movement in Antebellum America," in Foner, *Politics and Ideology,* pp. 57–76; see also Glickstein, "'Poverty is Not Slavery,'" pp. 195–218; and Cooper, *Slaves to Squatters,* pp. 25–33.
46. [Gannett and Hale], "Freedmen at Port Royal," p. 1.
47. Testimony of E. W. Hooper, Extracts of Testimony, Department of the South, Report of the AFIC, Letters Received by the Adjutant General's Office, 1861–70, M 619, r 200; Pearson, ed., *Letters from Port Royal,* p. 146.

Philbrick's calculation, had therefore earned four yards of cloth. Before "paying" her, Philbrick deducted a dress that Rosetta had been "given" in the spring from the four yards of cloth her July hoeings had earned. By that formula, "she got nothing now." Rosetta did not find four yards of cloth to be equivalent to a dress: "She didn't take it very kindly," Philbrick reported, "and growled about the dress being too small for her, so she couldn't wear it, whereupon I offered to take it back, but I haven't heard any more about it."[48] Whether Rosetta had children to clothe, or intended to sew herself a better-fitting garment, or simply desired to swap a bit of cloth for tobacco or some other article that had not been issued, is uncertain. We can only safely conclude that walking away empty-handed from a plantation distribution of cloth had been for her a novel and unjust outcome.

Nor was it only clothing and dietary staples that field workers especially expected to be made available to them in adequate shares. While still a government superintendent, Philbrick paid people cash in May 1862 for the cotton they planted. A female teacher watching the payments observed that "one woman, who had not done so much work, was disturbed at not getting as much money as the others and Mr. Philbrick could not make her understand." Plantation workers held even voluntary offerings not presented as compensation – gifts, as the Northern donors understood them – to the standard of evenness. Harriet Ware, a Philadelphia teacher on St. Helena Island, thought that the arrival in May 1862 of denim cloth earmarked for sale would permit her to "give away the made clothes with more freedom." However, laborers' strong insistence that all receive alike did not dissolve with the wartime debut of the plantation store:

> We thought we should enjoy the giving more things, now that the goods have come by the piece which they prefer to buy, but they are so jealous, and it is so hard to keep the run of so many families so as to distribute the garments equally, that it is hard work, and proves the wisdom of those who decided it was best to sell in the first place.[49]

The close watch in the quarters over what had been received by whom – which Ware understood as "jealousy" – defended common terms of exchange and common values. Teachers were not left altogether free to select according to their own lights the combination of want, hard work, female virtue, or classroom performance that merited a "gift."

Philbrick decided to eliminate in-kind compensation in 1863. In return for a day's labor, he proposed to pay a day's wages of twenty-five cents in cash,

48. Pearson, ed., *Letters from Port Royal*, p. 88.   49. Ibid., pp. 45, 51–52.

probably at monthly intervals.[50] That decision marked an attempt to generalize a new form of compensation; but more importantly, the daily cash wage was intended to foster a transformation of the material and moral character of slave society. The new occupants of the big house were conscious that the cent was being embarked on a proselytizing mission: "The great civilizer here is the 'dime,' " proclaimed Frederick A. Eustis, a Ladies Island planter who had left Milton, Massachusetts, to buy and organize cultivation on his deceased stepmother's plantation in 1863.[51] The new form of compensation came in the service of canons on the organization and nature of work that left freedpeople slow to adopt the new faith. Orthodoxy was short lived. Within four months, Philbrick had discarded any notion of trying to pay daily wages under conditions of "having to deal with large numbers of laborers and large acres of land, where the old organization had melted away from the sudden removal of its only stamina, the lash" and was searching for new scriptures if not a new creed.[52] What was amiss?

Quite simply, as Philbrick first saw it, it was the race of the new owners and employers that had made it "nearly impossible to employ [freedpeople] by the day or month with any satisfactory result." "The white race had thus far been known to them," he reasoned, "as a sort of natural enemy, against which it behooved every man to be on his guard." He judged that dilatory workers had not, by the spring of 1863, gained sufficient "personal acquaintance with the character of their individual employers . . . to feel any confidence in our disposition to pay for their labor."[53]

Philbrick's racial explanation for the unattractiveness of wage labor is less than convincing. Freedpeople on St. Helena had been acquainted with most of his six superintendents and with Philbrick himself for nearly a year by the spring of 1863. That had been sufficient time for them not only to observe and compare the ways of Yankee and Secesh white people, but also to make comparisons among the Yankees. When Josiah Fairfield, the former superintendent of Mulberry Hill plantation in 1862, tried two years later to persuade a Mulberry Hill resident, the driver Paris, to buy a tract of land on a plantation that Fairfield planned to lease, it

50. Edward Philbrick to AFIC, 17 Aug. 1863, Report of the AFIC, Letters Received by the Adjutant General's Office, 1861–70, M 619, r 200, 0416–27; Rose, *Rehearsal for Reconstruction,* p. 225.

51. Testimony of F. A. Eustis, Extracts of Testimony, Department of the South, Report of the AFIC, Letters Received by the Adjutant General's Office, 1861–70, M 619, r 200; William F. Allen Diary, typescript, 25 Dec. 1863, p. 70, WiM; Edward L. Pierce to Salmon P. Chase, 3 Feb. 1862, in Moore, ed., *Rebellion Record,* vol. 1 supplement, p. 305. By his claim, Eustis thereby also endorsed reducing pay from twenty-five cents to ten cents per task.

52. Edward Philbrick to AFIC, 17 Aug. 1863, Report of the AFIC, Letters Received by the Adjutant General's Office, 1861–70, M 619, r 200, 0416–27.

53. Ibid.

was what Paris knew about Fairfield, not what he did not know, that influenced Paris's decision. As Paris explained to the white Northern superintendent Charles Folsom, he "had seen something of Mr. Fairfield's pie, and didn't want to have his finger in it again."[54] What Philbrick styled the legacy of race relations under slavery obscures laborers' objections to premises that underlay his scheme of daily wages. To appreciate fully the sources of Philbrick's employees' disinclination to work six twelve-hour days per week in order to prepare the land and sow cotton during the 1863 planting season, we should take a cue from Paris and look a bit more closely at Philbrick's "pie."

Responses to Philbrick's work arrangements were not uniform. His superintendents, like other Northern wartime planters in the area, often expressed fullest satisfaction with the work routines of healthy elderly freedpeople, that is, men and women in the neighborhood of fifty years of age and older. In part, wartime planters' satisfaction stemmed from enthusiasm that people excused from labor under slavery were again at work. Some of the elderly reportedly took on duties from which they had been exempt as slaves. Limus Anders, an "old man . . . over fifty," earned the twenty-five dollars that he brought to the property auctions in 1863 by cutting marsh grass, work from which he had been "laid aside" for ten to twelve years "before his freedom."[55] Keeping in mind historian Willie Lee Rose's caution that it is a peculiar social order in which satisfaction is expressed when old people do hard work, there is good reason to accept in part the claim that able, elderly freedpeople came closest to giving that good and faithful labor that planters more widely sought in the quarters.

Frederick A. Eustis unreservedly praised the industry of elderly laborers on his mother's Ladies Island plantation: "There are twenty people whom I know who were considered worn out and too old to work under the slave system, who are now working cotton as well as their two acres of provisions." The elderly woman Deborah, who "has great-grandchildren living," reportedly cultivated three acres of cotton, three acres of corn, and an acre of potatoes in 1863 – an acreage equaled that year by only one other person on the three St. Helena plantations superintended by Charles Folsom – and told a Northern teacher that she "thanked the Lord fervently for living to see this day."[56]

54.   William F. Allen Diary, typescript, 14 Jan. 1864, p. 93, WiM. The significance of Philbrick's resort to race should be considered in light of the stimulating and insightful discussions in Fields, "Ideology and Race," pp. 143–77, and Holt, " 'An Empire Over the Mind,' " pp. 283–313.

55.   William F. Allen Diary, typescript, 23 Nov. 1863, p. 26, 19 Dec. 1863, p. 63a, WiM; Rose, *Rehearsal for Reconstruction*, pp. 302–03.

56.   Testimony of F. A. Eustis, Report of the AFIC, Letters Received by the Adjutant General's Office, 1861–70, M 619, r 200; William F. Allen Diary, typescript, 25 Dec. 1863, pp. 74–75, WiM; F. A. Eustis to O. O. Howard, 30 Nov. 1865, M 752, r 20, 0214–23; Pearson, ed., *Letters from Port Royal*, p. 126.

Agreement was widespread that, more than any other category of workers, the elderly were at least initially more likely to comply with the sunup to sundown workday in the fields, and would not singly challenge changes in work routines or attempts to punish infractions. Philbrick was certain that, on his places, refusals to observe what he had established as the length of the working day were led by young people:

> When at work by the day, some few of the older and more faithful hands began by doing a fair days work as required of all. The young and careless ones found [sic] of play, and less serious in their intentions invariably began by shirking and continued by a series of daily experiments to test the minimum of labor which would be accepted by their employers as a days work.[57]

On balance, Northerners tended to praise the industry of elderly freedpeople because they seemed to take responsibility for cultivating cotton and provision crops in the same proportions as younger workers, gave a workday that came closest to meeting the Northerners' standard for at least five of the six "working days," and all without complaint.

The work patterns that the new planters described had antebellum roots. Rewards of antebellum task work had gone to the swift. Younger and more healthy slave men and women had been best able to achieve a semi-independent management of their working time at tasked work by speeding up the pace with which they completed daily work quotas. In providing his overseer with guidelines for establishing the amount of work that should constitute a daily task, a Georgetown rice planter posited a clear relationship between the physical capacity of the slave worker and the hours of labor that the daily task should require: "A task is as much work as the meanest full hand can do in nine hours, working industriously," Plowden C. Weston instructed in 1856.[58] Weston thus expected that during the long daylight of spring and summer, the "meanest" full hands might complete their work quotas in nine hours. Somewhere between 2:00 and 4:00 P.M., provided the driver approved their work, the average low-country slave could then quit the rice or cotton fields, free to take up other work in provision grounds or family gardens, to go fishing, or to undertake whatever activities their circumstances permitted during the three to five remaining hours of daylight. It is unfortunate that connotations of "leisure" embedded in contemporary characterizations of the average full hand's twelve to fourteen hours of spring and summer daylight work in staple crop cultivation and nonplantation production com-

---

57. Edward Philbrick to AFIC, 17 Aug. 1863, Report of the AFIC, Letters Received by the Adjutant General's Office, 1861–70, M 619, r 200, 0416–27.
58. Excerpt from "Rules on the Rice Estate of P. C. Weston," reprinted in Phillips, ed., *Plantation and Frontier*, vol. 1, pp. 115–22, quoted passage at p. 117.

bined have reappeared in some accounts of slave labor in this region.[59] The more quickly full hands from the "meanest" to the "prime" completed their daily tasks, the more daylight hours they could save for other work. From its able, full hands, the slave plantation required the most intense exertion to complete daily tasks in less than nine hours.

Only when they had been permitted to receive help from younger slaves, or when several fractional hands were assigned to a full hand's tasks, could the elderly hope to complete daily quotas of field work within the work time established for full hands. The nonfield duties most commonly assigned to superannuated slave laborers – nursing the sick, weeding and tending the big house's floral and vegetable gardens, minding the youngest slave children, watching cattle and other plantation stock – did not readily lend themselves to speed-ups. From the elderly slaves who filled the plantation's work force in categories ranging from "quarter hands" to the "barely taskable," the completion of task work had exacted labor of the longest duration. Thus, by the time they reached their seniority, the old people had become ill able to defend certain key elements of task work. Their tasked work as slaves had, with age, come to be bound more closely by the hours of daylight than by a consistent daily quota in work loads. If they more readily gave the sunup to sundown labor in planting and hoeing and picking cotton that wartime planters wished to institute, it was because age had dissolved the margins between their best efforts and the hours of daylight.

There are indications that, for some elderly workers in Port Royal, the quotas that composed a full hand's daily work load might have become fuzzy. The number of elderly people living on Cherry Hill plantation made this St. Helena plantation, formerly owned by Thomas Aston Coffin, "one of the most encouraging places" that government superintendent Charles Ware was managing in 1862. At Cherry Hill, Ware reported, "The people are of a more sensible caste, old people, almost entirely, who see the sense and propriety of right measures, and display a most comfortable willingness to work and be content, though with less energy, of course, than younger men." The success of the "ingenious method" by

59. Morgan, "Work and Culture"; idem, "Ownership of Property"; Armstrong, "From Task Labor to Free Labor." Morgan and Armstrong, perhaps misled by L. C. Gray, mistakenly view task work and slave gang labor as opposed systems of cultivation. Joyner, *Down By the Riverside,* pp. 43–44, 129, appreciates the self-exploitation and long hours that task labor under slavery involved. Genovese, *Roll, Jordan, Roll,* pp. 59–61, locates slaves' hours of labor within the larger context of precapitalist work rhythms and assesses regional differences in hours of field labor from the vantages of both masters and slaves. Drawing on her study of nineteenth-century rice cultivation, Leslie S. Rowland called attention to the amount of time that most field hands required to complete their tasks during sessions at the Conference on the Study of Emancipation, University of Virginia, 4–6 May 1983.

which Tony, the driver at Cherry Hill, "induced the people to plant more cotton than they wanted" in 1862, may have turned on the by-then-remote standards that the old people applied to the quotas of task work in cotton cultivation. In staking out the quarter-acre tasks, Tony increased the number of rows within each task from twenty-one to twenty-four. To Ware's amused satisfaction, the driver succeeded in "adding twelve rows to every acre, which the people blindly tilled, never suspecting but that they were having their own way about their cotton."[60]

The apparent compliance of the elderly and the contentiousness of the young plantation workers were, nevertheless, of a piece. To be an elder on these sea-island plantation sites of wartime Northern cotton growing was more than a merely chronological affair. It was also in some sense to stand at the head of a hierarchy in the plantation quarters whose divisions recognized rank and status as commanding special privilege. The elders spoke with the strong voice of moral authority to their plantation kin – no small number on many of these plantations. The stature of age was reinforced by long-term residence on the place. The cook Phoebe, bought by her owner twenty years before the war, did not receive the fullest deference that age could command. Twenty years after Phoebe's purchase, "her family is regarded as 'interlopers' to this day."[61] The influence that age and long-term residence could exert was further compounded by honorific rank at the center of the quarter's spiritual life. Praise leaders were chosen from the ranks of the elderly, and it was from the cabin households of the elderly that one hut was selected as the site of biweekly praise meetings and less frequent "shouts."[62] Barred by their status as slaves

60. Pearson, ed., *Letters from Port Royal,* pp. 79–80. Ware himself may have been blinded by the illusion of victory on this point. It is important to note that Tony's ruse violated the letter but not the spirit of antebellum task work in sea-island cotton cultivation. The number of rows per quarter-acre task and the number of plants per row were not fixed; the latter increased in inverse relation to the fertility of the soil. See [Capers], "Reply," especially p. 403. Therefore, some flexibility with respect to the number of rows per task was built into sea-island cotton cultivation. Individual assignments were modified in terms of the number of rows and the heaviness of land, even for full hands. Had Tony increased the number of quarter tasks for which the workers were responsible, or attempted to increase the task unit beyond its customary quarter-acre size, he might well have provoked the protest that his increase in the number of rows did not trigger. Because of this built-in flexibility, task work-loads are not strictly additive or mathematically comparable when calculated in terms of acreage. It is a former sea-island driver, Harry McMillan, who correlates task units with number of rows. Field workers may have made no such calculation based on rows. Cherry Hill workers may have thus generously conceded the increase in rows based on what they knew to be customary standards of fairness. See Testimony of Harry McMillan, Report of the AFIC, Letters Received by the Adjutant General's Office, 1861–70, M 619, r 200.

61. William F. Allen Diary, typescript, 25 Nov. 1863, p. 32, WiM. This discussion has been influenced by the exploration of slaves' construction of status and authority in Blassingame, "Status and Social Structure."

62. Holland, ed., *Laura Towne Letters,* pp. 20–21; Edward L. Pierce to Salmon P. Chase,

from impassioned displays of authority that were believed by many a commentator to tarnish the aura of slaveowning patriarchs in the big house, the aged gentlemen and ladies living in the quarters perhaps gave paternalism its most gracious expression.[63] Denied the power to command, which was, after all, preeminently the prerogative of slaveowning rather than of age, the strength of the elders was to persuade. They monopolized dignity, not force. Quick to apologize for the people's "bad manners" during pointed negotiations over the terms of work, the same elders would nevertheless serve as spokesmen to present the workers' terms or lend their authority to efforts criticizing the conditions of labor on their places. They were not docile. Theirs was a sense of power that valued persuasion over confrontation. It was to this tactic that the great-grandmother Deborah turned when she intervened to calm her grandson Jimmy, who was "brandishing a ramrod" during a heated dispute with a plantation superintendent. "Peac[e], peace, patience," she "gently and sweetly" counseled Jimmy; "Peace make half the road to heaven, and patience open the gate wide."[64] The circumstances of their rank made elderly men and women most fully able to articulate the ethical sanctions of the antebellum slave community.

On adults less than fifty years of age converged the customary obligations from the old order and the fullest pressures of the new. Their rank entitled the elders to certain tributes from the younger folk. The success with which older laborers reportedly cultivated cotton in amounts equaled by younger hands probably reflects the work that younger people contributed under freedpeople's wartime revisions of cultivation to their old folks' plots. Old Grace, whose husband was a coachman and had been carried off to the mainland during evacuation, was praised by the teacher Harriet Ware in 1862 for having done "more work than any one on the plantation on cotton this year." But when, in January 1865, Grace headed a delegation of twenty women who came to Philbrick to insist on higher pay, she showed that her work in cotton had not been the result of her own unaided effort. Grace prefaced her negotiations by explaining, "I'se been working for owner three years, and made with my chillun two bales cotton last year, two more this year."[65]

3 Feb. 1862, in Moore, ed., *Rebellion Record,* vol. 1 supplement, p. 305.

63. Genovese, *Roll, Jordan, Roll,* pp. 113–23, suggestively places etiquette and courtesy within the context of relations of power on the antebellum plantation. On p. 118 he observes that "the finest, if rudest, examples of the southern lady and gentlemen were to be found in the quarters even more readily than in the Big House."

64 William F. Allen Diary, typescript, 19 Dec. 1863, p. 64, WiM.

65. Pearson, ed., *Letters from Port Royal* pp. 126, 303. Frederick Eustis reported that he allotted to the seventeen elderly people on his Ladies Island plantation "all the land for which they have asked," noting that "if they could not work it[,] it has always been charitably done for them by others." F. A. Eustis to O. O. Howard, 30 Nov. 1865, M 752, r 20, 0214–23.

Older people's rights to obligate favors from the young received fullest acknowledgment when the old people still lived in a plantation setting where antebellum sale and wartime removal had not truncated their networks of accountable kin. Apparently, the elderly freedman May could hold few kin to such duties. May, who had been owned by "a 'cracker' or mean white on one of the Hunting Islands," seemed to a teacher "a mere wreck of a man" in 1863. But by that year May, "poor broken-down old creature that he is," along with his wife, had moved to Cherry Hill plantation on St. Helena and "cultivated three acres of cotton this year, and tolerably well." He and his wife therefore made their best, if enfeebled, efforts to take on the work required of younger people. By contrast, the elderly freedman Isaac lived on Big House plantation where, as late as February 1864, none of the younger men had volunteered for service in the Union army. Isaac seemed to teacher Allen "an old broken-down man." The teacher judged him "the only negro on the place who cannot support himself" but later discovered that Isaac was "supported by his nephews – Robin and Moses."[66]

Allen thus glimpsed a redistribution of work loads and the products of family labor along fairly close kinship lines. During wartime occupation, ex-slaves reshaped antebellum task labor to help out their old folks with greater regularity, rejecting the individualized accountability that had structured antebellum tasks.[67]

Refugees from the Combahee River rice district revealed to Elizabeth Hyde Botume many ways in which cooperative work and sharing along an extended family network colored their relationships. Some valued articles belonged more to the household than to any single household member. Learning that a party of Northern visitors would stop to observe her classes in November 1864, Botume sent her students home to wash and dress before the visitors arrived. When her pupils returned, wearing clothes whose "variety and grotesqueness . . . defies description," she concluded: "No doubt each one had assumed the best thing he could find, no matter to whom it belonged. Girls had on men's coats, some of which were so big they reached to the ground."[68] During her three-year residence in Port Royal, Botume often paused to make note

66. May's circumstances are recounted in William F. Allen Diary, typescript, 19 Dec. 1863, p. 62a, WiM; the characterization of Isaac is drawn from conflated entries in ibid., 11 Dec. 1863, p. 56, and 19 Dec. 1963, p. 26. Isaac was certainly Robin's paternal uncle and probably bore the same relationship to Moses. See also ibid., 24 Feb. 1864, p. 137, where Allen reported that he told some of the men that "it is a shame to the plantation that none of its men have volunteered."

67. Certainly, the obligation to provide material support to acknowledged kin was strong enough to be tapped and made into a formal requirement by the occupying army. In 1863, an aide on Saxton's staff explained that the military governor issued rations only to those "unable to help themselves and having no relatives who can support them." [R.] Saxton through E. W. Hooper, 11 Dec. 1863, Saxton Papers, CtY.

68. Botume, *First Days*, p. 51, quotation at p. 111.

when conceptions of household property and family labor penetrated her classroom.

By and large, the new planters and their superintendents were not close observers of forms of cooperative work among freedpeople. Some mistook any form of collective labor for "gang" labor. Superintendent Charles Ware thought that, when laborers swore to him that "they will not work in gang," they referred to a system of "all working the whole and all sharing alike."[69] Such objectionable "gangs" probably did not embrace acknowledged kin. Among extended kin, it would seem that some selective sharing was tolerated and on some occasions obligatory.

Freedpeople trying to make familial what had been individualized labor obligations under slavery quickly ran afoul of wartime planters. Edward Philbrick was adamant that, without a "foreman" to ensure that his employees all worked for the same length of time and at the same pace, a system of monthly wages "would fail to call out the individual exertions of the people." As he saw it, to pay the same monthly wage to workers who did not spend equal amounts of time in the cotton fields would "be only a premium on deceit and laziness." Sharing work loads under cooperative work arrangements made it impossible, he felt, to distinguish the "industrious" from the "lazy."[70] His expectation that a "foreman" would establish a uniform time and pace of work in the cotton fields collided with workers' efforts to elaborate cooperative work arrangements. Identical workdays of uniform duration were also poised to strike directly at young adults who, under the old order, had given their best work when they worked fastest at cotton cultivation in order to raise foodstuffs in provision grounds, garden patches, and by hunting or fishing to supply articles not included in the plantation allowance.

Like Northern factory owners, Philbrick insisted in 1863 that the wage relationship precluded control of the time and pace of labor by workers themselves:

> All systems of day wages presuppose an independent, unprejudiced foreman who enjoys the confidence of the laborers and who controls the time and manner [of] doing the work; he must also keep a record of the amount of work done by each laborer and be responsible to his employer for the correct p[er]formance of the work.[71]

In order to introduce his scheme of plantation management, Philbrick hoped to call into service the driver, a remnant of the old order rechristened the "foreman," to mark his induction into the new.

69. Pearson, ed., *Letters from Port Royal*, p. 112.   70. Ibid., pp. 108–09.
71. Edward Philbrick to AFIC, 17 Aug. 1863, Report of the AFIC, Letters Received by the Adjutant General's Office, 1861–70, M 619, r 200, 0416–27; Montgomery, "Workers' Control of Machine Production," in Montgomery, *Workers' Control in America*, pp. 9–31.

Some antebellum drivers, and perhaps more often slave carpenters and boatmen, were less closely enmeshed in the internal production and exchanges of plantation life than either their families or other slave field workers.[72] Required to inspect the work of all field workers, from the fastest to the slowest, drivers more often supervised than performed the cooperative work practices that slaves developed within such limits as antebellum task organization allowed. Because they gave all of their daytime work to the plantation and therefore could seldom work in provision grounds or household patches, they often drew benefits from cooperative work without regularly swapping nonplantation chores themselves. Restitution for drivers' losses of time – in the form of increased time for nonplantation cultivation for their wives, the assignment of other field workers to labor in plots whose produce was earmarked for the driver's use, and their larger allowances of food and clothing – were all resources that depended on the master's authority.[73]

There are occasional hints that drivers tended to be less completely integrated in the cultural life of the quarters as well, particularly when their work required regular absences from the plantation.[74] Driver "managers," who traveled frequently among their owner's various plantations, had opportunity and perhaps necessity to cement their ties to slaves on several plantations by taking a wife on more than one place – a practice that seems to have been at best lukewarmly tolerated by members of plantation churches. Limus Anders, who was in his fifties when the war started, had served as driver on several small St. Helena properties owned by Martha McTureous. While teaching Anders to read in May 1862, Harriet Ware discovered that at Pine Grove plantation "He has a wife . . . and grown children, and another on the other plantation, the rascal." Anders's domestic arrangements may in part explain the amused response of the plantation's church members who, when asked whether Limus "belongs to them," would answer, " 'Not yet,' with a smile."[75] His distance

72. Reconsideration of the role of drivers in plantation and nonplantation production in long-staple and cotton and rice districts would still seem to offer rewards. Succinct analyses in Rose, *Rehearsal for Reconstruction*, pp. 80–81, 132–33, and Genovese, *Roll, Jordan, Roll*, pp. 365–88, have not been superseded by Van Deburg, *Slave Drivers*. Stone, "Black Leadership," provides an excellent point of departure for future studies.

73. In addition to the studies cited in note 72, see this volume, Chapter 1.

74. Of course some drivers, like the driver 'Siah mentioned later in this chapter, legitimated their supervisory powers over other slave laborers by taking leadership positions in slaves' plantation churches.

75. Pearson, ed., *Letters from Port Royal*, pp. 37, 77; Rose, *Rehearsal for Reconstruction*, pp. 234–35. The occasionally expressed belief that drivers and artisans were entitled to more than one wife may reflect the extent to which their work required regular long-term absences. Like Limus, the carpenter Will had been required as a slave to absent himself from his plantation while carpentering for his owner. When he had been

from the plantation church and the mobility of his antebellum work left Anders and some other drivers on the fringes of the obligations and rights of cooperative forms of labor. Multiple marriages might well have restored in the form of labor services more effectively commanded by their wives the social support that came by way of obligations to kin.

Former drivers figured prominently among ex-slave wartime purchasers of Port Royal plantation lands, cultivating between fifteen and sixty acres of cotton grown by a combination of family and hired labor.[76] For example, Limus Anders, whose antebellum work more closely approximated that of an overseer of several small plantations than that of a driver who supervised workers on a single place, placed his wartime managerial talents at the service of his families, not at Philbrick's employ. Within months of the occupation of St. Helena, Anders gave up driving. A year and a half later, he had taken on an array of enterprises. In the half acre behind his cabin he raised poultry, pigs, corn, and vegetables for Hilton Head markets; he cultivated fourteen acres of cotton with the aid of family labor from one of his wives and their daughters, and with the hired labor of a family of refugees from Edisto whose male members he paid eight dollars monthly; he ran a weekly packet carrying passengers, produce, and fish to Hilton Head; and he sold fish and venison to regular customers on St. Helena and to the army staff at Hilton Head, where he also rented out a seine, a cart, and horses. By January 1864, his enterprises employed several ex-slave men and a white newcomer to the island "whom nobody seems to know anything about."[77] Those drivers who, like Anders, had served the old order much like plantation managers, wished to put their talents to their family's use as petty entrepreneurs or small planters, not as paid foremen.

Drivers who remained at their old work were no better able than wartime superintendents to hold every plantation worker to the "stan-

away for a long time, his wife, who was not owned by the planter to whom Will belonged, concluded that Will had been sold and took another husband. Unlike Limus, however, Will legitimated the authority that he exercised as driver by becoming a church member. He therefore shaped his domestic life to conform to that plantation body's expectations. Will remarried and declined to live again with his former wife, explaining, "I consider she has done that which is unlawful and I didn't want the church to be defiled through me." See Botume, *First Days,* pp. 162–63.

76. See J. W. Alvord to O. O. Howard, 1 Sept. 1865, M 752, r 74, 0095–105; Holland, ed., *Laura Towne Letters,* p. 106; J. A. Saxton to J. J. Childs, 15 March 1864, Saxton Papers, CtY; and Rose, *Rehearsal for Reconstruction,* p. 314, all of which refer to Harry (or variantly, Henry) McMillan, whose testimony suggests that he had been a driver. Testimony of Harry McMillan, Report of the AFIC, Letters Received by the Adjutant General's Office, 1861–70, M 619, r 200. See also H. G. Judd to Saxton, 13 Oct. [1865], Correspondence Relating to the Restoration of Property, ser. 3108, Beaufort, Subordinate Field Office Records, RG 105.

77. Pearson, ed., *Letters from Port Royal,* pp. 37–38nn; William F. Allen Diary, typescript, 6 Dec. 1863, p. 46, 28 Jan. 1864, p. 111, WiM.

dard for a days work" that Philbrick tried to fix in the spring of 1863. Philbrick tried changing drivers and shifting them to new places, apparently hoping that success would come from having the drivers supervise workers on places other than their home plantations.[78] His six superintendents, who on average oversaw the labor of around a hundred people, spent the entire year on the plantations – a wartime change that on some places increased the intervention of the big house in plantation work, and on Fripp Point precipitated an early plantationwide resistance that became increasingly organized.

The people of Fripp Point plantation, owned by sons of William and Harriett Fripp, on the eve of the war had been working largely under the eye of their driver and church elder 'Siah. No plantation residence had been built there, for Fripp Point adjoined Pine Grove, one of Fripp's residential places, and the habits of Fripp's son Mass Eden, who lived alone at Fripp Point, seem not to have required that he live on the place in a "white people's house." As Tom of Pine Grove informed a teacher: "With only one meal a day, [Eden] lived on whiskey, and, beyond his own control most of the time, he used to 'lick wus 'an fire.' " As early as September 1862, Philbrick complained that Fripp Point people, in contrast to people on the other places that he was managing for the government, had "neglected" the last cotton hoeing of the season. The following year it was a resident of Fripp Point, Alec, who demanded to know why Philbrick's spring 1863 plantation purchases were exempt from the announced preemption scheme. After the fall 1863 harvest, Fripp Point residents unsuccessfully contested the claim of Philbrick's superintendent to the cotton seed, which the people used to fertilize their corn lands. Their failure was thought to have directly prompted them to buy the plantation's movable properties away from the same superintendent during the spring 1864 auctions. In 1864, the names of their driver and church elder 'Siah, Pompey, and the younger John Major, whose family had worked for Philbrick at Fripp Point while Major was working around army camps at Hilton Head, headed a petition from fifteen former slave men to Abraham Lincoln complaining of Philbrick's "oppression." That same year, in addition to demanding that Philbrick raise the task rates that he had set for work in cotton, the people countered rising costs at Philbrick's plantation stores by planting corn in two of every three cotton rows. "In one task," a plantation manager complained, "in every row they had planted corn, and as thickly as in a regular corn field." After the 1864 harvest, the peo-

78. Edward Philbrick to AFIC, 17 Aug. 1863, Report of the AFIC, Letters Received by the Adjutant General's Office, 1861–70, M 619, r 200, 0416–27. No itemization of the daily work quotas that Philbrick or other Northern planters tried to establish between 1863 and 1865 has yet been discovered.

ple at Fripp Point withheld the in-kind rent that Philbrick assessed on lands where they had been permitted to grow corn. Fripp Point was one of the first properties from which Philbrick severed his managerial ties. In January 1865, he leased it to a certain Mr. York, whose introduction to the people was greeted by chants of their now year-old demand for "A dollar a task! A dollar a task!"[79]

"A Dollar a Task!"

By the winter of 1864–65, the demand for higher pay for task work voiced by the Fripp Point people rang widely in the sea islands. Plantation disputes had taken on new intensity during 1864. The defeat of a preemption measure that had promised ex-slaves land on terms that many of them found incongruous, the sale by auction of plantation lands and movable property, and forced military conscription carried out with new vigor in the summer of 1864, formed a troubled backdrop to the disputes.[80] The broad demands for higher wages in the spring of 1864 do not seem to have been coordinated across plantation boundaries. Rather, the demands appear to have emerged from immediate struggles on the separate plantations. "A dollar a task" was a slogan around which ex-slave plantation workers rallied to assert a wage demand that actually rejected individualist features of Philbrick's notion of wage relations. The demand emerged at a time when not all protesters had agreed to make increased task rates their principal objective or to insist that task rates be uniform. On Fripp Point, for example, Pompey cautiously indicated that his primary concern was his right to buy land there; 'Siah thought "he ought to have fifty cents for what he is now paid forty for," whereas their younger fellow petitioner John Major most strongly defended the dollar amount.[81] The "dollar a task" demand probably does reflect wide agreement among plantation workers that task rates should be higher. More importantly, the "dollar a task" demand resumed in another form freed workers' earlier struggles for control of their time, of land and other productive prop-

79.   The overview of Fripp Point is drawn from scattered accounts in Pearson, ed., *Letters from Port Royal*, pp. 12, 30, 31–32, 126, 224, 261, 263–64, 300–01; William F. Allen Diary, typescript, 17 Jan. 1864, pp. 99–100; 8 March 1864, p. 146; 15 March 1864, p. 149; 24 April 1864, pp. 181–82, 186; 9 May 1864, p. 190, WiM. Harriet Ware believed that the petition had been written at Hilton Head, a circumstance that not only draws attention to the organizational role of John Major but also raises questions concerning the involvement of people working in Limus's Hilton Head packet and cooperative soldiers in Hilton Head's camps. See also Rose, *Rehearsal for Reconstruction*, pp. 312, 313n.

80.   Powell, *New Masters*, p. 101; Rose, *Rehearsal for Reconstruction*, pp. 311–14.

81.   Pearson, ed., *Letters from Port Royal*, p. 260.

erty, and of the products of their labor. The protest grew out of the mixture of victory and defeat for freedpeople and for their employers that had been part of cotton cultivation in the sea islands since 1863. Cotton continued to be grown on terms that wholly suited neither party, less a stable compromise than an ongoing struggle.

Sometime after the spring 1863 planting, Philbrick acknowledged that his foremen could not be "relied upon to render an account of the work done daily by the several hands" simply because "each hand had been at work when & how it pleased him or her to go."[82] He offered no details about how laborers thwarted his requirement that the foreman record the amount of work done daily by each worker. There survives, however, a vivid account of the opposition that an officer of the 128th United States Colored Infantry provoked after the war, in May 1866, when he tried to enforce a foreman's attempt to use the quarter-acre tasks into which the cotton lands on Bonny Doon plantation on Hilton Head Island were divided as a means of holding workers individually accountable for task work and increasing their work load in cotton.

On 23 May, the plantation's foreman, William Hodges, discovered that the forty freedpeople employed on Bonny Doon had hoed on average only one-half task (one-eighth acre) each. He then ordered them to begin work the next day in new tasks, leaving the "uncompleted work" for their employer M. J. Kirk to inspect. "The next morning," Kirk later reported to the local Freedmen's Bureau officer, "they not only refused to commence new tasks as directed, but all in a body went to work finishing the work assigned the day previous and that [too] in a gang." Though Hodges "remonstrated with them and insisted that they should obey his instructions[,] to this they paid no attention whatever and kept on working the entire day in a gang." The officer, William Wilcox, who had been "constantly in the field with the foreman" since his assignment to Bonny Doon, ordered the laborers to obey the foreman and to go to work in separate tasks. When they refused, the soldier proceeded to act according to his view of plantation management that "what knocking down, and tying up by the thumbs can't do, my revolver will." Jim Singleton had been tied for nearly an hour when his fellow workers left the fields, some carrying hoes and one person stopping to pick up an ax. They chased Wilcox toward the Big House, where, from the piazza, the soldier shouted "that if any of them came inside the gate he would shoot them." No one came through the gate, but they stood outside for fifteen minutes, the planter reported, "behaving in a most shameful manner, making use of the most

82. Edward Philbrick to AFIC, 17 Aug. 1863, Report of the AFIC, Letters Received by the Adjutant General's Office, 1861–70, M 619, r 200, 0416–27.

indecent language, and threatening and daring the soldier to come out of the house."[83]

The forty workers at Bonny Doon, much like Philbrick's employees, insisted on sharing work in the quarter-acre tasks according to their own lights. Collectively they opposed an inspection of the task units of field cultivation designed to measure and hold them separately accountable for their work. That collective forms of work implied a collective defense of their pace of work was a point that the former slave John Calhoun made to the ill-starred Wilcox. Sometime before the 24 May explosion, Wilcox had tied up Calhoun in the stable with a plow line for "neglecting his work." Upon his release fifteen minutes later, Calhoun responded to the soldier's query "if he would work better" by answering that "he would as much as any one."[84]

The wartime cultivation of cotton on Philbrick's places proceeded by attaching itself to the cooperative organization of work that the freedpeople elaborated during federal occupation. Reasoning that the amount of cotton produced could be made to show the exertions of individual families, if not of individual workers, Philbrick had portions of the planted fields assigned to families "in such proportions as they desired" and agreed to pay each family at harvest "a p[r]ice per pound" for the cotton they raised. Conceding that "the daily wants of the people could not wait for the harvest of the crop," he made interim payments for field work done before the harvest. He set the amount of those "practical payments" with a view to guarantee that the family cotton plots received the full work that they required until the harvest. The calculation seemed to him a risky matter: "It was evident that all payments of this sort must be made with great caution in order that they might be proportionate, as nearly as possible to the amount of labor actually performed." He settled on near-monthly payments of fifty cents per acre (or twelve and a half cents per task), about one-tenth the maximum task rates that freedpeople would demand the next year. That rate, he felt, would guarantee that laborers gave acceptable time to cotton. At the same time, however, Philbrick left it to family households to adjust and organize that working time as they saw fit. He ordered maps to be drawn of the cotton fields "so that riding over them I could always tell on whose patch I happened to stand at any moment."

83.   M. J. Kirk to [Martin R.] Delaney [*sic*], 24 May 1866, r 35, 0679–84; Erastus W. Everson to H. W. Smith, 15 June 1866, r 35, 0691–700; both in M 752. See also copies and supplemental documents in M. J. Kirk to [M. R. Delany], 24 May 1866, r 9; M. R. Delany to H. W. Smith, 27 May 1866, r 9; Erastus W. Everson to H. W. Smith, 15 June 1866, r 9; all in M 869.
84.   Erastus W. Everson to H. W. Smith, 15 June 1866, M 869, r 9.

August found Philbrick rather pleased with his apparent success at tying cooperative family work arrangements to a mode and rate of payment that could coerce the amount of work in cotton that he desired:

> The success of this system has exceeded our hopes. The division of the land into these temporary allotment[s] gives the laborer a proprietary interest in the crop & he feels as if working for himself. The more eff[icient?] and industrious should soon [see] the effects of their industry by the superior conditions of their crops.[85]

Wartime Port Royal's unprecedented "temporary allotment" of arable cotton land into units for household cultivation was a step toward tenancy arrangements that landless laborers on the mainland would pursue with war's end.

The household division of cotton lands did not preclude freedpeople's attempts to introduce cooperation into other stages of cotton cultivation. They turned to kinship networks to link throughout the agricultural season cultivation routines that had been atomized under slavery. People now hoed, picked, carried to have weighed, then sorted and ginned the cotton that other family members had helped to raise.

In the late fall of 1863, the teacher William F. Allen glimpsed this family cultivation in operation during the harvest season. Walking through the fields in which laborers grew sweet potatoes and patches of benne, a plant of African origin akin to sesame, Allen came to a large field of which 130 acres was planted in corn and 100 acres in cotton. The people were picking the cotton "in aprons hanging like bags before them," he noted, "piling it then in sheets which they carried to be weighed – each pile is kept separate." Two months later, Allen strolled over to the cotton house where he found the people "hard at work; ginning, moting and packing cotton" and resumed his observations:

> I described once before how they pick the cotton into great sheets, which are carried to the cotton house and weighed, and then put in heaps, each person having his own heap – a very obvious proof who has done most work. These heaps, by the way, are of families, not individuals. Next the cotton is sorted. The women take, each her own cotton, out upon a sort of shed . . . where they pick out the yellow cotton, and dry the whole in the sun.[86]

Where family members retained possession of foot gins, a fairly common wartime circumstance on the eastern portion of St. Helena that Allen most often toured, family members also ginned the same cotton that their

85. The descriptions are all from Edward Philbrick to AFIC, 17 Aug. 1863, Report of the AFIC, Letters Received by the Adjutant General's Office, 1861–70, M 619, r 200, 0416–27.
86. William F. Allen Diary, typescript, 11 Nov. 1863, p. 14, 4 Jan. 1864, p. 82, WiM.

families had cultivated. On paydays, Philbrick's superintendents handed to household representatives (often the oldest members) a collective payment for phases of cotton work that had variably claimed the time of the household's old, young, and, by 1864, largely female, members. The division of this cash income among family members was cloaked by the privacy of the quarters. However, it is important to note that in 1864, freedpeople presented their wage demands in the form of the task rates by which preharvest work was compensated, not in the form of payment adopted for picking and processing, where rates were calculated by volume. The form of ex-slaves' wage demands would have increased family pay in the more certain segment that was based on the number of tasks cultivated rather than in the segment where pay was based on the unpredictable volume that a cotton harvest would yield.

On the whole, wartime plantation workers seemed more concerned to prevent an inequality of income among households than to address the inequality of income among various family members that some historians of postwar agriculture have detected.[87] In a cotton field known as The Hill, which was regarded as "the best cotton land" on Big House plantation, Allen discovered in February 1864 that "each person has some tasks here" and tasks in inferior fields as well,[88] a measure apparently designed to minimize the very inequities in the amount of cotton each household produced that Philbrick regarded as the sharpest goad to labor.

Cotton ginning seems to have been more directly restructured by the wartime landowners than other aspects of cultivation and processing. Philbrick's employees on eastern St. Helena were somewhat unusual in possessing foot gins. Cotton grown on Port Royal Island was mostly ginned in Beaufort or in New York, slaves having perhaps marked the island's steam-operated gins for special attention during the rioting that had accompanied invasion and evacuation.[89] Wartime conditions probably facilitated a broader adoption of steam-powered ginning than had been possible during slavery.[90] Local workers seem to have been unco-

87. Noralee Frankel, "Rural Black Women in Mississippi: Their Withdrawal from the Work Force, 1865–1868," paper delivered at the annual meeting of the Organization of American Historians, April 1980.

88. William F. Allen Diary, typescript, 21 Feb. 1864, p. 132, WiM. A similar pattern of cultivation in strips in scattered fields was adopted by freedpeople in Georgetown's rice district during the absence of their owners in 1865; see Chapter 1.

89. [R.] Saxton to E. W. Canby, 9 March 1864, Saxton Papers, CtY; Rose, *Rehearsal for Reconstruction*, p. 130.

90. Steam engines had been adopted for ginning operations in the sea islands only in the 1850s. In addition to the well-known geographical constraints that restricted the scale of long-staple cotton cultivation, antebellum accounts identified constraints imposed by labor arrangements on both sides of the Atlantic as impediments to a wider adoption of steam power. Agricultural journals in the 1850s acknowledged that steam gins increased at least fivefold the amount of cotton that would have to be cleaned and

operative in repairing steam gins. Philbrick called on men from distant plantations to repair the few engines that he found. Nero, a fugitive slave who had escaped from near Edisto Island, repaired the engine that Philbrick found on Big House plantation.[91]

Overshadowing the pace of ginning, Philbrick's employees on eastern St. Helena were made to know, was the "moral stimulus" of the steam gin at Big House. When Charles Folsom, Philbrick's superintendent at Cherry Hill, decided that the laborer Jimmy had "neglected" his ginning, he confiscated Jimmy's foot gin and gave it to Morris, telling Jimmy that when Morris had finished ginning he would return the gin only for "a certain number of days; then if his cotton wasn't finished, he would send it to the steam gin." Even on eastern St. Helena plantations, family foot gins were not to set the pace of work. Schoolteacher Allen learned this lesson within a month of his arrival in the department: "This is the rule: They are paid by the pound for ginning, and the work must be done speedily so that the cotton can be got to market."[92]

If, on the whole, Philbrick accommodated the work of producing cotton to the organization and division of labor worked out in the quarters, no such accommodation was rendered to the customs that had been part of antebellum plantation work outside of staple crop cultivation. There was sound observation in an elderly freedman's lament, "The Yankees preach nothing but cotton, cotton."[93] Wartime planters identified duty, industry, foresight, and energy with labor that produced the regional sta-

---

sorted daily. It is therefore not clear that even those slaveowners able to invest in steam power would have been able to adopt it without having to enter a market for slaves in which they were poor competitors with large southwestern "nabobs." Those antebellum sea-island planters who received the highest prices for their cotton more typically exploited nontechnological innovations such as seed selection and labor-intensive processing methods that seem to have fallen primarily to the duty of female slaves. See [Allston], "Sea-Coast Crops of the South"; Edward L. Pierce to Hon. S. P. Chase, 2 March 1862, vol. 19, item 78, Port Royal correspondence, 5th Agency, RG 366 [Q-9]; Rosengarten, *Tombee*, pp. 70–73, 76; Margaret Creel, "Slave Women and the Production of Sea Island Cotton," paper delivered at the annual meeting of the Organization of American Historians, April 1980. In 1853, an annoyed correspondent to a Savannah, Georgia, newspaper attributed the market advantage that producers of carefully cleaned long-staple lots enjoyed over those who sold steam-ginned parcels to British spinners working on piece rates who were "independent enough to decline working upon illy prepared cotton out of which they cannot get as large a weight of fine yarn per day as they can out of clean lots." [Allston], "Sea-Coast Crops," quotation at pp. 597–98nn. Buoyed by unprecedented prices, wartime cotton planters shared few of the slaveowning planters' reservations about steam gins.

91. William F. Allen Diary, typescript, 4 Jan. 1864, p. 83, WiM; Pearson, ed., *Letters from Port Royal*, p. 236.

92. Pearson, ed., *Letters from Port Royal*, p. 236; William F. Allen Diary, typescript, 19 Dec. 1863, pp. 63–64, WiM.

93. Holland, ed., *Laura Towne Letters*, p. 20. See also Cooper, *Slaves to Squatters*, pp. 25–33, 45–46, 111–16.

ple for a world market; privilege, laziness, ignorance, and ease lurked in the realm of nonwage alternatives that workers undertook to produce what they could use directly.

Wartime wage arrangements quickly altered the conditions under which antebellum slaves produced supplements to the plantation allowance. Possession of what stock and draft animals they retained after the 1864 spring property auctions was limited by Philbrick's requirement, announced that same year, that employees owning horses and cows must either fence any lands that they owned and graze the animals there, or pay him for pasturage. When this termination of common pasturage rights on plantation lands was reiterated in May 1865 to the people of Coffin's Point, many of whose families had by then bought five- to ten-acre tracts of land on one of the McTureous places, they pronounced Philbrick "a thief, robber, liar, and everything else that was bad."[94]

People who had conceded the necessity if not the justice of buying land found that the terms of their employment further restricted the use that they could make of their purchased tracts. Some wartime planters stipulated that their employees grow no cotton on their own lands,[95] apparently more willing to require them to raise a portion of their own food than to tolerate their possible access to sources of cash income outside plantation work. Wartime workers continued to plant food crops on plantation lands, and many extracted from new landowners in 1864 a larger acreage for such cultivation before they would go to work.[96] Nevertheless, the terms of access to such lands underwent important changes. Philbrick's employees received no cash payments for the corn, potatoes, and vegetables that they cultivated at the rate of one and a half acres per "full hand." Moreover, an in-kind tax was levied on the food crops produced,[97] thereby abolishing the reciprocal exchanges by which masters had gained access to the produce of garden plots. Cultivation of foodstuffs was no longer a source of subsistence for which workers received token restitution. It had become a source of subsistence from which workers turned over a portion of what they had produced.

Wartime planters envisioned terms of compensation that threatened to extinguish the rewards that fitter workers had been able to wrench from task labor under slavery. Employers calculated how much to pay per task by discovering how many tasks a healthy young adult worker could perform in a workday. Antebellum tasks became wartime piecework, as

94. Pearson, ed., *Letters from Port Royal,* pp. 251, 310, 312.
95. J. A. Saxton to E. S. Philbrick, 15 June 1864, Saxton Papers, CtY; Holland, ed., *Laura Towne Letters,* pp. 122–23.
96. William F. Allen Diary, typescript, 15 March 1864, p. 149, 3 June 1864, p. 205, WiM.
97. Ibid., 24 April 1864, p. 182; J. A. Saxton to E. S. Philbrick, 15 June 1864, Saxton Papers, CtY.

wage rates made the younger workers' maximum performance the ideal measure of what every "industrious" worker should achieve.[98] If able young adults had complied – and they were the only workers whose exertions could have held to this standard – they would have given more hours to cotton cultivation as wage earners than they had as slaves. Moreover, labor in subsistence cultivation became literally free labor, since wages could be earned only for work in cotton.

The logic of piece rates seemed to stand the principles of task labor under slavery on their head. In place of the rewards that swift, able workers extracted from antebellum task work, wartime piece rates substituted a standardized time. In effect, the rewards of wartime piece rates went neither to the swift nor to the strong. Instead, the exertions of the most able defined a standard output whose time and circumstance were to be endured by all.

The elderly worker Taft deftly captured the rationale of the new arrangement. He and a woman named Flora, whose relationship to Taft cannot be established, were listing corn land one Tuesday afternoon in February while Taft's wife Tyra, "too infirm to work, sat by a little smoldering fire, to get water or cook food for them." Taft explained to an inquirer why he was now at work in the corn land when, by his reckoning, he had already done more than a day's work: "Taft said the money was for himself now and 'I work as long as I kin.' " His questioner went away, happily persuaded that "[t]hey evidently appreciate independence thoroughly,"[99] even as Tyra and Flora showed the social support such "independence" required, while the "money" restricted to cotton cultivation denied that they were working at all.

The demands for higher task rates surfaced in 1864 as part of freedpeople's general refusal to confront the conditions and products of their work as capital at the service of their employers. From the diary of the teacher Allen we glimpse the transformation of plantation properties, customary possessions, and the products of agricultural cultivation into potential sources of income for the landowner. As Allen glanced over the plantations that Philbrick had bought only a year earlier, he began to list the items for which Philbrick could justly charge his employees – the old slave cabins, provision lands, fuel gathered from the woods, pasturage,

98. William F. Allen Diary, typescript, 24 April 1864, p. 182 repeats what would become a standard defense of task rates: "[A] man can easily list three tasks in what would be at the North a working day." See the similar justification that William Towne offered in reply to Martin Delany as reported in Edw. M. Stoeber to S. M. Taylor, 24 July 1865, in M 869, r 8. The piece rates that the planters proposed were thus calculated, as Karl Marx explained, "by spreading the value of labor power over the quantity that a worker can produce in a working day." See Tom Bottomore, ed., *A Dictionary of Marxist Thought*, pp. 517–18, regarding wages.

99. William F. Allen Diary, typescript, 23 Feb. 1864, p. 135, WiM.

the use of plantation draft animals for nonplantation work, cotton seed, and barnyard manure.[100] Although Philbrick's actual charges in 1864 had not kept pace with Allen's mental calculations, plantation employees nevertheless disputed the accounting in forms as varied as the entries themselves. They tried to retain possession of the ginned cotton their families had raised; disputed what they would plant, where they would plant it, and in what amounts; and demanded higher rates for task work, launching the farm workers' long postwar struggle to control the terms of agricultural production.[101]

As early as the 1864 harvest, laborers on sea-island plantations were withholding ginned cotton from the cotton storehouses, evidently preferring to dispose of the crop themselves rather than to receive the proceeds from its sale. Such an appropriation marked a turning point in what slaveowner and postwar employer alike would denominate "theft." As slaves, plantation workers had always had their secret places for hiding some portion of the plantation staple in order to turn it more directly to their own ends. From Edisto refugees gathered at that island's eastern end in January 1862, a Union naval officer had learned "that they have small quantities of cotton hidden in various localities" on the places from which they had fled during evacuation.[102] Stealthful appropriations remained a recourse of wartime plantation laborers, particularly those women refugees who seem to have been less successful in incorporating cotton cultivation within household units than Philbrick's employees, who largely worked on the plantations where they had lived as slaves.

Elizabeth Botume accidentally encountered among the largely female refugees from the Combahee River – who had been put to work growing long-staple cotton on Port Royal Island – a successful evasion of a plantation regulation that prohibited "the colored people . . . from appropriating even a single boll of cotton to their own use." She learned that, notwithstanding the regulation, it was "a very common thing for each woman to secrete a few handfuls of the cotton she had picked when she left the field." During the first months of Botume's stay, she witnessed, though not without initially provoking some suspicion from the Combahee women, at least one use to which they put the embezzled cotton: "I saw many pairs of shapely gloves and stout stockings made of the coarse yarn spun in a tin basin and knitted on reeds, cut in the swamps. These were sent to husbands, sons, and lovers off on duty as soldiers." Gradually she came to understand the diffidence with which many women

100. Ibid., 24 April 1864, p. 182; 29 April 1864, p. 185.
101. Powell, *New Masters,* pp. 97–122, offers an important treatment of postwar plantation struggles.
102. Danl. Ammen to S. F. Du Pont, 21 Jan. 1862, in *ORN,* ser. 1, vol. 12, part 2, pp. 516–17.

greeted her enthusiastic inquiries about their spinning and knitting skills. "It was a long time," she confessed, "before I learned that the crude material used was 'contraband.' "[103]

A new spirit infused the alleged predial thefts that continued during the war. Stealth and secrecy gave way to what seems, in some instances, acts that, not only because of the larger amounts of cotton involved, had more the flavor of confiscation or rightful seizure than of pilferage. The foreman Tony at Cherry Hill refused to turn over to Philbrick's superintendent the cotton his family had raised in 1864. Instead, he stored the cotton in his cabin and spent two weeks in jail for the offense. In January 1865, when Philbrick came onto the place, Tony complained to him about the superintendent's conduct in the affair,[104] clear testimony to Tony's sense that immediate possession of the cotton crop was a free worker's right. Withholding the ginned cotton seems to have been for Tony a prelude to negotiation.

Similarly, a Freedmen's Bureau officer reported a mass seizure of picked cotton when after the war, in December 1866, he went to Rabbit Point plantation on Edisto Island to divide the workers' and employer's shares of the stored cotton crop:

> The moment the cotton house was opened the people rushed in and a number of them took forcible possession of their cotton and carried it off without division and all refused to allow any division to take place, threatened to knock my brains out and forcibly resisted me."[105]

As terms of postwar employment increasingly made the harvested crop the source of the only return to workers for the labor that they had expended in its cultivation, their moves to control the timing, amount, and form of access to the values of the crop would become more widespread. Assertions of contested rights lay behind the November 1865 complaints from Beaufort landowners that cotton storehouses had been broken into, and the simultaneous claims from St. Helena planters that one-fourth of the island's cotton crop had been "stolen."[106] Higher task rates, the planting of foodstuffs rather than of cotton, and the seizure of crops were means by which plantation workers tried to guarantee their livelihood as a precondition of their labor rather than as an uncertain outcome of expended work.

---

103. Botume, *First Days,* pp. 52–53.
104. Pearson, ed., *Letters from Port Royal,* p. 301.
105. J. C. Cornelius to Edw. W. Deane, 22 Dec. 1866, M 869, r 9.
106. Geo. Quimby to C. J. Lemen, 4 Dec. 1865, enclosed in J. E. Greene to O. S. B. Wall, 15 Nov. 1865, M 869, r 7; Wm. Beebe Jr. to J. W. Clous, 20 Nov. 1865, Letters and Reports Received Relating to Freedmen and Civil Affairs, ser. 4112, 2d Military District, RG 393 Pt 1.

War and emancipation made for important changes in the character of the freed population that came to inhabit the Carolina portion of Sherman's coastal reservation in 1865. Between January and May, some fifteen thousand of the Georgia slaves who made their way to Union territory in the wake of Sherman's armies were settled on islands off the Carolina coast.[107] By the spring, perhaps half the freedpeople living on South Carolina's sea islands and adjacent mainland had come from either the interior of Georgia or coastal counties north of Savannah. Some Port Royal planters discovered in the gaunt, haggard fugitives who began to arrive in the area of wartime occupation in January 1865, a pool of workers to replace plantation workers then holding out for better terms in the 1865 agricultural season. The Georgians came at the end of a planting year that had demonstrated that freedpeople and their employers did not measure freedom by the same gauge.

"As Hard Times as They Has See with the Rebel"

In August 1865, the former slave D. Chaplin, who perhaps had been a wartime refugee, struggled with a newly won literacy to explain to Secretary of War Edwin Stanton the price he was paying for freedom. It seemed to Chaplin that the plantation superintendent's storage of the harvested cotton, together with loss of land, inadequate task wages, and the new postwar phenomenon of eviction, demonstrated that the superintendent was trying to "kill the people." Chaplin scanned the St. Helena Island plantation where he had planted that year and found that the "quart dolers a day" that he was paid and the injunction that "[w]e all have buy land" when he had "not a of money to buy it With" meant only that "last years i plant my crop and i not have a mouthfull to eat this year me and my Wife and Children." Although Chaplin assured Stanton that "the poor peopel is glad for the war," he wrote that Stanton might "know how the poor Coled pople is surfer":

> [The superintendent] took all the land from them   can get not a pice
> to plant and if they [spaked?] then we have to run away in the Wood

107. Unidentified newspaper clipping, "Reply of General Saxton to the Report of Gens. Fullerton and Steedman, 15 June 1866," Clippings, Box 4, Saxton Papers, CtY; H. G. Judd to R. Saxton, 1 Aug. 1865, M 869, r 34, 0183–95. Both estimate that between fifteen thousand and seventeen thousand refugees from Georgia passed through Beaufort and were settled within the Carolina portion of the Sherman reserve. Cf. Williamson, *After Slavery*, p. 62. On some islands the proportion of Georgia refugees in 1865 was considerably higher than half the freed population. On the small island of Dawfuskie, "nearly all" of the freedpeople present in July 1865 said that they were from the interior of Georgia. See A. Hammond to nn, 29 July 1865, M 869, r 7.

and he took all the crops that they plant put it in the his house and
now Sir i till you the [illeg] people See a[s] hard times now . . . as they
has See with the rebel . . . he will take all the things and carry it and
trows it in the publick road . . . and they have a to sleep in the woods
with all youngs children   all the raine full down pun we and that to
pay for because they wont agree to work for him for twenty five cent
a Tays

For redress, Chaplin turned to Stanton to "please make some easement"
and in the meantime "i pray the lord might helpe the We all in the might
gite home to the famly Safe."[108] Chaplin's letter underscores the new necessities that underlay ex-slaves' assertions of new rights.

108.   D. Chaplin to Edwin M. Stanton, 15 Aug. 1865, M 869, r 7, 0229–32.

3

Restoration and Reaction: The Struggle for Land in the Sherman Reserve

By 1865, struggles for possession of land had become an undercurrent of labor conflicts in the wartime area of Union occupation around Port Royal. On Edisto, Wadmalaw, John's, and James islands south of Charleston and on the rice estates of the lower Savannah River along the border with Georgia, former slaves mounted a postwar movement in which claims to land achieved most overt and organized expression. Union general William T. Sherman's wartime Field Order 15, issued from Savannah in January 1865, stimulated this popular initiative. Setting aside territory on the mainland and sea islands lying southward from Charleston to the St. John's River in northern Florida for settlement and cultivation by former slaves, Field Order 15 has been aptly characterized as "the most far-reaching step taken toward the distribution of land from above" to emerge as wartime federal policy.[1]

Sherman's wartime measure proved as singular as it was temporary. Settlement of the islands adjacent to Charleston began after the city's surrender in mid-February, under auspices of Port Royal's wartime military governor, Rufus Saxton. Newcomers to the islands predominated among the diverse population of Georgia refugees and ex-slave emigrants from Port Royal. By the time that former slaves from the islands slowly returned coastward from the interior in July, the "terrible, swift sword" of wartime emancipation was becoming a duller, double-edged blade of peacetime occupation. Struggles for land in the Sherman reserve proceeded within limits of this transformation.

Although Sherman's field order also extended to the mainland south of Charleston for thirty miles inland, there was no effective federal resettlement of freedpeople under its terms. Instead, delayed federal occupation left the

---

1. The insights of Allen, "Struggle for Land," are in no way diminished by the author's mistaken assertion that the Sherman territory extended from the coast to Augusta, Georgia. The quoted passage appears at p. 353.

coastal strip of the Sherman reserve an embattled region until early summer. Armed bands of Confederate loyalists roamed its neighborhoods well into the spring. One such band, which at its height numbered eighty men, roamed St. Paul's Parish during much of April. Its sworn mission to "kill all the damn niggers" and to "take or kill every man who had taken the oath of allegiance [to the federal government], also to take all the property they had & burn their buildings" brought it to within ten miles of Charleston. Among the identified leaders of the band known to have murdered three former slave men on a single plantation alone, sacked Middleton Place in St. Andrew's Parish, and seized food and driven off stock from rich and poor alike, was a former "Negro catcher" and Confederate deserter of St. Bartholomew's Parish.[2] Outlaws driven more by destitution than revenge for Confederate defeat also wreaked havoc on whatever remnants of slave residents, plantation property, stock, and food the upheavals of war had left behind.

The pace of postwar occupation helped localize contests opened by Sherman's field order in South Carolina to federally controlled sea islands and the lower Savannah River. The arrival of Union troops in late spring somewhat contained the violence wreaked along the coast by the decomposition of Confederate causes. However, effective federal military occupation also introduced plantation regulations yet unknown on the adjacent islands. Army officers obligated freedpeople on the mainland's abandoned places to contract to work for the rest of the year under the direction of an appointed driver, and ejected laborers who would not comply with such terms.[3]

Labor policies of the occupying army contributed to an early tendency for ex-slaves who managed to reach the coast to strike out for the sea islands rather than mainland areas within the Sherman territory. Government agents' rough attempts to count the reserve's ex-slave inhabitants in 1865 suggest that the earliest and largest concentrations of freed settlers were to be found on sea islands closest to Charleston. Edisto Island alone contained as much as one-third of the thirty thousand freedpeople thought to have been living on the "Charleston islands" in the summer of 1865.[4] By contrast, the mainland's coastal rice and cotton plantations re-

---

2. Affidavit of J. W. Griffen [14 Aug. 1865], enclosed in Jno. P. Hatch to O. O. Howard, 4 July 1865, M 752, r 15, 0489–92.
3. James C. Beecher to Capt. Taylor, 11 Sept. 1865, M 869, r 34, 0292–302; James C. Beecher to L. B. Perry, 25 July 1865, Letters and Reports Received Relating to Freedmen and Civil Affairs, ser. 4112, 2d Military District, RG 393 Pt 1.
4. Calculations based on the various estimates of population are quite tentative. Ames, *New England Woman's Diary*, p. 16, was informed that ten thousand freedpeople were living on Edisto in May 1865. Several months later, James Fullerton estimated that eight thousand freedpeople lived on Edisto and that the freed population of the "Charleston islands" numbered thirty thousand. See J. S. Fullerton to O. O. Howard, 22 July 1865, r 14, 1370, and J. S. Fullerton to [Howard], 11 Aug. 1865, r 74, 0066–84, both in M 752.

mained sparsely settled at the end of August, populated chiefly by people who described themselves as old inhabitants, left to make their own support by masters fleeing federal invasions during the winter of 1864–65.[5]

Resistance to postwar revisions of Sherman's order therefore became largely the coordinated effort of newly constituted communities established chiefly on the sea islands under the jurisdiction of Port Royal's wartime agencies.

Even before sea-island settlers faced the dilution of Sherman's land order, ex-slave inhabitants of the mainland nominally embraced by the field order faced struggles from which no plantation product was exempt. Abolition of the ownership of humans sparked immediate contests over the disposition of agricultural products and plantation supplies. Perhaps the scarcity that wartime destruction, impressment, and loss had brought home to all plantation residents gave the outcome of these contests special urgency. Certainly, no article was too insignificant to be grabbed.

Planters returning to abandoned mainland plantations at times gained assistance from the occupying army in confiscating food, clothing, and rudiments of daily existence from slaves whom they had abandoned in the press of war. When former slaveowner S. J. Magwood, for example, returned with a federal escort to his mainland plantation in St. Andrew's Parish late in the summer of 1865, he and the soldiers not only "helped themselves" to growing food crops. Magwood also helped himself to a bit of cash, an ax, a coat, a vest, a pair of pants, and a cast net – all of which he recovered while ostensibly searching the people's cabins for ammunition. [6]

The seeming smallness of the sums or the demonstrable need of planter and former slave alike should not obscure the emerging class dimensions of what was at stake. Whether they staked their claims to plantation lands or fishing nets, ex-masters and ex-slaves had launched competitive bids for federal support. What chance or might had redistributed during the power vacuum of the last season of civil war required legitimation during the power vacuum of peacetime.

Reserved island territory near Charleston seemed to offer freedpeople the most advanced field for independent social organization. Nevertheless, circumstances under which the territory was settled imposed major constraints to ex-slaves' occupation and cultivation of island lands. Settlement of the islands proceeded in 1865 in the face of a scarcity more pervasive than slaves abandoned on their home plantations had encountered

5. H. G. Judd to R. Saxton, 1 Aug, 1865, r 34, 0183–95, and H. G. Judd to R. Saxton, 29 Aug. 1865, r 34, 0239–60, both in M 869.
6. Reuben Tomlinson to L. B. Perry, 14 Sept. 1865, M 869, r 8. See also Reuben Tomlinson to George S. Burger, 12 Sept. 1865, M 869, r 8.

around Port Royal four years earlier. In April, more than two-thirds of the reserve's population was judged destitute by the none-too-generous War Department standards that the Freedmen's Bureau's newly appointed assistant commissioner, Rufus Saxton, applied. To the earliest settlers fell some of the army's "partially broken down" animals, whose temporary use by freedpeople on the plantations had been authorized by Sherman in January; but the majority of the population, which was thought to have doubled in the reserve between April and June, lacked shelter, tools, seed, and food.[7] Only by a combination of sharing, short-term wage labor, and what incoming army officers described as "plunder," did early settlers start to farm the forty-acre tracts tenuously committed to them when Congress established the Freedmen's Bureau without an appropriation in March 1865.

Pockets of early settlers brought the basis of a rough sufficiency with them when they began to arrive on islands near Charleston in February. A companion of Mary Ames, who began her short career as a teacher on Edisto Island by throwing out into the night an "angry old woman, who said we had taken possession of her quarters, and must pay her for them," observed differences in the material well-being and comfort of Edisto's settlers.[8] Such variations generated the informal exchanges of food reported by ex-slave Baptist minister J. M. Simms, when he visited freed settlers of rice plantations on the lower Savannah River in May. It required community assistance, Simms explained, for settlers in the country simply to reach Savannah, where the bureau distributed army rations whose quality Simms thought "[m]erely sufficient to Sustain life and that is More the cause of Sickness than Strength to Labour." Boats were scarce, he explained, and so many people walked twelve or fourteen miles to Savannah

> and then Wait Around the office of genrl Saxton, as Long as one week in Most cases for their Turn to Procure their [ration] Tickets. All this time Nearly Starved having no Means to Procure food in the citty. Some of them goes the Distance Back to the farm Borrow food from those that have and return, sometimes Twice Before they can get their Rations, Loosing Nearly half their time of Labour.

7. Rufus Saxton to [E. M. Stanton?], 6 April 1865, reprinted in New Orleans *Tribune*, 19 May 1865, cited in Oubre, *Forty Acres and a Mule*, p. 47; W. L. M. Burger to R. Saxton, 22 Jan. 1865, *OR*, ser. 1, vol. 47, part 2, p. 115; R. Saxton to O. O. Howard, 4 June 1865, enclosed in Q. A. Gillmore to L. Thomas, 24 May 1865, M 752, r 17, 0024–32. Hermann, *Pursuit of a Dream*, examines the Davis Bend community.
8. Ames, *New England Woman's Diary*, pp. 12–13; extract from 26 October 1865 letter of Emily Bliss, published in *Liberator*, 1 Dec. 1865, p. 184, cols. 4–6. Fullerton explained the differences by noting that about half the people on Edisto in August 1865 had arrived too late to plant. See J. S. Fullerton to O. O. Howard, 11 Aug. 1865, M 752, r 74, 0066–84.

Simms, urging a different policy, anticipated that "[w]hen the time of Harvest comes these poor People Will be called Idlers and Lazy Because their crops is not Sufficient for their years Support."[9]

The promise of land alone could scarcely ward off the threat of destitution. Hence some settlers, largely men, stayed in the reserved territory only long enough to obtain a land warrant and settle their families. They then left to seek employment in Charleston or Savannah, but expected to return in time to make a fair start at a good crop the next year.[10]

The largest number of settlers would seem to have stayed in the reserve and set about making their living from resources closer to hand. Along the Ashepoo, Combahee, and Edisto rivers of lower Colleton district on the mainland, many rice plantations had been partially cultivated by reduced work forces until Sherman's army began its march across the state in January. These plantations' partial stores of food and cattle, as well as the abandoned supplies of Confederate encampments, attracted ex-slave settlers and white families from the pinelands alike. Men from island settlements formed parties that regularly visited the mainland after the fall of Charleston and carried back plantation supplies, especially cattle. By June, what seems to have become a fairly regular traffic between the Colleton coast and some of the islands in arms, cattle, and agricultural supplies alarmed arriving Union officer James C. Beecher. "The Dist of Colleton," he informed his commanding officer, "is in worse condition than any in which I have yet held command." The regular communication between the sea islands and the Colleton mainland convinced Beecher that ex-slave settlers "ostensibly under charge of the Freedmen's Bureau, are really supported by the plunder of Plantations in Colleton." He placed the blame on lax bureau supervision of island freedpeople and white mainland residents, "a low class of whom are in league with them."[11]

The rather surprising collusion between freedpeople and white backswoodsmen does not seem to have extended beyond plantation raiding and swapping. Members of ex-slave raiding parties from the islands, however, occasionally went on to involve themselves in internal affairs of mainland plantations. Beecher believed that four men from St. Helena and Chisholm's islands were responsible for the "complete demoralization" that he reported among workers on a plantation in lower Colleton.

9. J. M. Simms to [J. M. C. Perkins], 25 May 1865, enclosed in wrapper labeled Revd J. M. Simms, 25 May 1865, M 752, r 17, 0045–58.
10. Thomas Black to nn, 11 April 1866, r 9; W. C. Daniell to Robert K. Scott, 17 Nov. 1866, r 20, 0936; both in M 869.
11. James C. Beecher to R. Saxton, 28 July 1865, M 869, r 34, 0179–82; James C. Beecher to L. B. Perry, 25 July 1865, Letters and Reports Received Relating to Freedmen and Civil Affairs, ser. 4112, 2d Military District, RG 393 Pt 1.

Under the influence of these outsiders, Beecher charged, "The people had driven off the proprietor, beaten the negro foreman nearly to death – barred up the gates – set up an armed guard – broke open the houses – taken 100 Bushels of rice & 40 bushels of Corn & declared that no white man should come on the place."[12] Island settlers' rough tactics helped extend the terms of Sherman's field order to the Colleton mainland's inhospitable terrain.

Forceful seizure of mainland plantations did not always involve the active assistance of nonplantation residents. Similar takeovers occurred on large properties scattered outside the bounds of Sherman's field order along the rivers of Georgetown district without known cooperation from strangers.[13] Nevertheless, not even during the thwarted Vesey insurrection had island and coastal plantation residents established such effective cooperation.[14]

Island raiders found a welcome (and, no doubt, a hiding place) in exslaves' quarters on the coast. In the four months between Confederate retreat and effective Union occupation of the mainland, island bandits like Morgan Island's "Double Quick,"[15] whose nickname commends one skill on which his exploits depended, began to extend the social network of the slave quarters beyond plantation borders. They also moved ahead of bureau policy to supply island settlers with the means of working and living on their promised lands. Confiscation from below gave the assistance needed to make useful the wartime distribution of land from above.

After July, the reserve's settlements began to include larger numbers of former residents who had been moved from the coast during the war. Their return added another dimension to the popular reallocation of plantation supplies, which low-country planter Robert Chisolm unconsciously identified when he wrote in November 1866 to inform state Bureau head Robert K. Scott how more than a year of cumulative thefts had compromised his postwar planting operations. Chisolm apparently owned at least three plantations, two of which lay within the Sherman territory. He had removed his slaves to southwest Georgia during the war and in February 1866 was trying to resume his career as a planter near Orangeburg, on the one place that he owned outside the Sherman reserve. Some of his former slaves, however, had left Georgia ahead of Chisolm to establish themselves as farmers, selecting Chisolm's place in lower Colleton within the reserve. "One of my refugee negroes," Chisolm com-

12. James C. Beecher to Gilbert Pillsbury, 11 Aug. 1865, enclosed in G. Pillsbury to R. Saxton, 27 Aug. 1865, M 869, r 34, 0222–28.

13. B. F. Smith to H. W. Smith, 6 April 1866, M 869,. r 34, 0486–88; Foner, *Nothing But Freedom*, pp. 79–82.

14. Lofton, *Denmark Vesey's Revolt*, p. 138.

15. S. H. Hawkins to J. W. Clous, 13 Aug. 1865, M 869, r 34, 0196–207.

plained, had come from the Colleton plantation to the plantation near Orangeburg in August 1865, "and stole and carried off two mares that I had here." To make matters worse, the people he later brought to Orangeburg from Georgia "had deserted and gone to the coast" to settle on his plantations included in the Sherman order, four children having been "carried off" by "parents or by friends sent for the purpose."

Confiscation from below sometimes showed the influence of petty traders from the North. In Colleton, three of Chisolm's "refugee Freedmen" dismantled a cotton gin and other plantation machinery and transported two loads by flat to Beaufort, where storekeepers offered freedpeople cash or goods in exchange for scrap iron and disinterred animal bones, which they resold to Northern factories.[16] Even as Chisolm's former slaves seized the conditions thrown up by Confederate defeat to organize a new social order, they scavenged within the bounds of their old plantations.

Of course, it mattered little to planters or to military officers that this species or popular confiscation was only occasionally violent, that it was not altogether random, or that its primary object was to reallocate or trade crops, animals, and supplies. The movement to secure the food, animals, and supplies that were preconditions for freedpeople's independent farming on Sherman's reserved lands nonetheless portended expropriation of plantation properties. James Beecher, an army captain whose mainland jurisdiction included many of the islands affected by Sherman's field order, saw only that "[t]hese negroes come and go without let or hindrance, and plunder at their option." He quickly concluded that to fix ex-slaves' residence on the plantations was "a *military necessity*," expecting that at harvest time "a determined endeavor will be made by freed persons on many plantations, incited and assisted by the proteges of the Freedmen's Bureau and by certain low whites to seize all the crop made."[17] In the summer of 1865, Beecher and military officers elsewhere in the lower districts therefore pieced together a contract labor code enforced by written passes to authorize travel or trade, vagrancy punishments, armed pickets, and military arrests,[18] many of whose features reappeared in the more elaborate state measures adopted in late November.

Such military regulations not only impeded the scavenging of plantation refuse and the dismantling of plantation machinery for scrap, but

16.   Robt. Chisolm to R. K. Scott, 1 Nov. 1866, r 20, 0815; Benjamin S. Pardee to Robert K. Scott, 9 Dec. 1867, r 14; M[artin] R. Delany to J. M. Crofut, 26 Nov. 1865, enclosed in Pardee to Scott, 9 Dec. 1865, r 14; all in M 869.

17.   James C. Beecher to R. Saxton, 28 July 1865, M 869, r 34, 0179–82.

18.   James C. Beecher to R. Saxton, 28 July 1865, r 34, 0179–82; James C. Beecher to Gilbert Pillsbury, 11 Aug. 1865, enclosed in G. Pillsbury to R. Saxton, 27 Aug. 1865, r 34, 0222–28; Special Orders No. 15, 5 Aug. 1865, enclosed in James C. Beecher to Capt. Taylor, 11 Sept. 1865, r 34, 0292–302; all in M 869.

also placed virtually all ex-slaves' efforts at local marketing under a cloud of illegitimacy. Although military attempts to monitor trade between freedpeople and petty river traffickers focused largely on the lower mainland, freedpeople traveling from the islands to sell wood and hay in city markets were also often stopped.[19] In Charleston, Freedmen's Bureau agent Gilbert Pillsbury discovered that planters and factors were relying on a cooperative civil government rather than the federal army to nourish many a lean plantation account: "If colored persons come into the city with rice, corn, wood[,] a horse, mule, or any property, they are almost sure to be seized, their property to be confiscated, and they sentenced to prison for theft." In August, Pillsbury found the city jail "crammed with these poor, dumb, helpless victims." His legal assistance successfully enabled an unspecified number of ex-slave clients to recover some eight hundred bushels of rice, "quantities" of corn, as well as wood, forage, horses, mules, and carts whose total value he placed at a mere $1,500.[20]

The army measures probably enjoyed uneven success; but the military occupation of the coast further restricted the direct disposition of plantation supplies and products that freedpeople had begun during the planters' absence. By the time that bureau commissioner Oliver Otis Howard came to South Carolina in October to announce the executive ruling that federal confiscation extended only to abandoned plantations that had been sold by 12 September,[21] the weight of military force had already been mobilized on the planters' side.

Local movements to hold onto reserve lands organized, while congressional legislation, presidential amnesty, and encroaching military jurisdiction narrowed the terms by which freedpeople could claim portions of a progressively shrinking territory. There had always, perhaps, been a fictional aspect to the promise of lands abstractly granted to former slaves on the eve of Northern victory in the March 1865 bureau act. Bureau commissioner O. O. Howard sensed the illusion. In later years, he employed a rough calculation to explain why the land-distribution scheme had been more mirage than oasis. The largest amount of land under bureau supervision, Howard recalled, would have awarded no more than one acre of land to each freed family.[22] His rough ratio merely illustrates the generally accepted weakness of the agency's access to land. When

19. James C. Beecher to Geo. W. Hooker, 6 Nov. 1865, Letters and Reports Received Relating to Freedmen and Civil Affairs, ser. 4112, 2d Military District, RG 393 Pt 1; D. T. Corbin to H. W. Smith, 1 Feb. 1866, r 9; F. W. Leidtke to O. D. Kinsman, 31 March 1866, r 21, 0284; both in M 869.

20. G[ilbert] Pillsbury to R. Saxton, 27 Aug. 1865, M 869, r 34, 0233–38.

21. McFeely, *Yankee Stepfather*, p. 134; Oubre, *Forty Acres and a Mule*, p. 38; Howard, *Autobiography*, vol. 2, p. 235.

22. Howard, *Autobiography*, vol. 2, p. 229.

presidential amnesty was added to the latitude that the March bureau act granted to military jurisdiction in bureau matters, even the agency's limited reallocation of land soon tapered off.

The closing session of the Thirty-eighth Congress left the confiscatory implications of Field Order 15 in abeyance. Whether Southern economic development should proceed through punitive government confiscation of rebel estates and the creation of a class of small commercial farmers was most explicitly debated two years later, when Thaddeus Stevens aired his confiscation scheme in the spring of 1867.[23] By that time, however, national legislation had already prepared the means to wed Sherman's wartime land measure to a market system of peacetime land distribution. The first Freedmen's Bureau Act of March 1865 proposed that ex-slaves pay a three-year rent of 6 percent assessed value to the United States government for plots of a maximum size of forty acres. In July 1866, the second Freedmen's Bureau Act restricted government-sponsored purchases of twenty-acre plots to unsold Direct Tax lands in the South Carolina parishes of St. Helena and St. Luke's, suspending for the moment national seizure of the entire extent of coastal lands.[24]

Former landowners in the two parishes where Congress upheld wartime seizure and sale of lands under the Direct Tax Act of 1862, scarcely appreciated that the Freedmen's Bureau Act of 1866 drew back from acting on Sherman's wartime field order. A former slaveowner who had taken refuge in Greenville during the war grumbled loudly when he returned to St. Helena in November 1865 to find that "[t]he Government took his cotton, and somebody, Government or niggers, got everything else that was left. Then in the spring of 1863, they sold his plantation. Some Massachusetts man bought it, and he didn't know when he'd get it back."[25] Elsewhere, in the reserve lands unaffected by Direct Tax auctions, military enforcement of presidential amnesty mortally wounded ex-slaves' land claims even before Congress declined to embrace larger confiscations in the 1866 bureau act.

Military authorities on the South Carolina coast were somewhat slower than their Georgia counterparts to restore abandoned estates embraced by the Sherman field order to their antebellum owners. In September 1865, Freedmen's Bureau commissioner Oliver Otis Howard issued as Bureau Circular 15 a letter drafted by President Andrew Johnson, which ordered

---

23. Cox, "Promise of Land"; Foner, "Thaddeus Stevens," in Foner, *Politics and Ideology,* pp. 128–49.
24. *Statutes-at-Large of the United States,* vol. 13, p. 508; vol. 14, pp. 174–75.
25. *Nation,* 30 Nov. 1865, p. 682. Congressional provisions for sale of confiscated lands in St. Helena and St. Luke's parishes would not seem to have precluded the postwar reconstitution of large estates by purchases from the area's debt-strapped small farmers. See Rose, *Rehearsal for Reconstruction,* pp. 396–98; Botume, *First Day,* p. 259.

that Sherman lands be restored to pardoned landowners.[26] Restoration along the Georgia coast had anticipated Circular 15 by several months. As early as July, the provost marshal's court in Savannah had authorized restoration in several instances, notably on the Georgia sea island of St. Catherine's. Bureau protest temporarily halted these actions. It was a district officer's opinion that "no real or permanent harm has been done, beyond the alarm spread among the negroes concerning the tenure of the lands."[27]

Army commanders in South Carolina soon made amends for their delay. Military jurisdiction over government transportation became after October 1865 an important weapon in the arsenal of tactics used to support restoration and to compel written contracts. On the heels of Howard's visit to Charleston and Edisto in October, the authority that commanders outside the reserve exercised over government-assisted transportation helped to undermine the sea-island movement to resist restoration.

Officers stationed at major points of transit for rail connections to Charleston authorized transportation to the coast only when parties could prove that they would be self-supporting.[28] The timing of such measures was critical, for they coincided with what may have been the largest seasonal movement coastward in the first year of emancipation. Large numbers of former coastal residents, who had postponed journeys home until crops that they had cultivated on interior plantations had been harvested and divided, were joined by streams of newcomers, drawn by the insistent popular expectation that a reconvened Congress would distribute lands on the coast. In dispensing government transport, interior officers favored workers who had signed agreements to work for a coastal landowner, encouraging all others to sign contracts and remain where they were.

In December, E. A. Kozlay, the military bureau agent stationed sixty miles north of Charleston in Orangeburg, advised freedpeople as far west as Barnwell district to remain and work for landowners in the neighborhood rather than head for the Sherman reserve. His lectures were to little avail: "Nearly all seem to be bound to travel to the Islands, where they expect to get a better future."[29]

26. McFeely, *Yankee Stepfather*, p. 134; Oubre, *Forty Acres and a Mule*, p. 38; Howard, *Autobiography*, vol. 2, p. 235.
27. Edw. A. Wild to R. Saxton, 14 July 1865, M 869, r 34, 0168–77.
28. E. A. Kozlay to H. W. Smith, 28 Nov. 1865, r 20, 0291; C. H. Howard to R. Saxton, 29 Nov. 1865, r 36, 0217–28; E. A. Kozlay to H. W. Smith, 29 Jan. 1866, r 34, 0416–14; all in M 869; Ralph Ely to J. A. Clark, 25 Jan. 1866, Letters and Reports Received Relating to Freedmen and Civil Affairs, ser. 4112, 2d Military District, RG 393 Pt 1.
29. E. A. Kozlay to T. D. Hodges, 5 Dec. 1865, Letters and Reports Received Relating to Freedmen and Civil Affairs, ser. 4112, 2d Military District, RG 393 Pt 1.

Not to be outdone after they had been denied government transportation from Orangeburg, at least seven hundred people "sold all their scanty crop, hired a car, and went down" to Charleston in January 1866. In other instances in Orangeburg district, men "started on foot" and "left their families behind," forcing Kozlay to contemplate the prospect of a labor force largely composed of women and children. He reported that "of a necessity I was compelled to send their wives and children after them; being assured, that they will be no burden upon the Government after joining their husbands and male protectors." In late January, Kozlay made the regulations governing transportation absolute; he suspended all government transportation from his district. Even then, small numbers of people continued to leave, "bound for the Sea Islands, disregarding the contracts made since New Years day, – alleging that Congress has already passed a bill giving them title to lands on the sea coast, and that they intend to go there to secure a portion for themselves."[30]

On reaching the coast, the travelers encountered additional regulations that further restricted travel to the sea islands. A January 1866 department order required district commanders to permit only army officers and bureau agents to land on Edisto, James, John's, and Wadmalaw islands without a written pass.[31] No doubt some people managed to evade the order, for in February, the local commander James Beecher reported in frustration that "many freedpeople have smuggled themselves on the islands," thereby, as he saw it, "preferring to starve upon 40 acres of land which they have no means of working rather than to lay up from $100 to $200 by working for fair wages on land restored to its former owner."[32]

The secrecy of the means by which ex-slaves "smuggled" themselves onto the sea islands remains unbroken. What is certain is that the 1866 "smugglers" gained little advantage for their efforts. In March 1866, the Freedmen's Bureau ruled that no freed person who arrived after 17 October 1865, the date of Howard's arrival in South Carolina to announce restoration, could claim title to land in the Sherman reserve. [33] No matter that many successfully circumvented increasingly stringent regulations governing transportation to the coast. The large postharvest migrations became an important source of workers who signed yearly contracts in the reserve.

30. E. A. Kozlay to H. W. Smith, 29 Jan. 1866, M 869, r 34, 0406–14.
31. M. N. Rice to J. C. Beecher, 8 Jan. 1866, M 869, r 11.
32. James C. Beecher to M. N. Rice, 7 Feb. 1866, enclosed in wrapper labeled Headquarters, Military District of Charleston, 16 Feb. 1866, Letters and Reports Received Relating to Freedmen and Civil Affairs, ser, 4112, 2d Military District, RG 393 Pt 1; A. P. Ketchum to [O. O. Howard], 19 Jan. 1866, telegram, M 752, r 21, 0592.
33. H. W. Smith to [E. W.] Everson, 17 March 1866, M 752, r 29, 0803–06.

Settlement in the territory described in Field Order 15 before 17 October did not become the final test by which freedpeople could gain standing to pursue on the reserve's lands "such title thereto as the United States can convey."[34] On the eve of the 1866 planting season, commissioned officers and a bureau staff drawn increasingly from army ranks invented a retroactive formulation of what constituted valid possession. From ingredients part writ, part quantification, and part geomancy, administered in a medium of absolute property rights, James Beecher devised in early February a restoration procedure to "bring the various so called [possessory] land titles to a test, and without further delay."[35]

To be recognized as valid, the claim of a reserve settler had to be described in a written possessory certificate that "state[d] a specified number of acres"; in addition, the plot "must have been duly measured and staked out" and have been occupied by the claimant or his family. Certificates that met these tests confirmed their holders' right to claim mere soil, since Beecher further instructed his officers that "[n]o land claim or warrant includes any buildings upon the ground claimed or upon the plantation, or right to occupy the same except by permission of the proprietor unless such right is stated in the warrant."[36]

By Beecher's measures, eleven valid possessory titles emerged from the more than four thousand settlers on John's and Wadmalaw islands. He began early in February 1866 to restore to antebellum owners the full extent of island plantation lands dotted with "anomalous 40 acre tracts of land," making "no provision . . . for claims of freedpeople which claims consist of four pine stakes & the freedmen's word and possibly a certificate locating him on the spot or somewhere else." In mid-February, squads from his Thirty-fifth United States Colored Infantry began to "clean out" settlers who refused contracts after their claims had been judged invalid. This forced removal proceeded by carrying people in flats to the mainland near Rantowles village. There guards awaited the people to "march them up" the twenty-odd miles to Beecher's headquarters at Summerville, where, since August, he had maintained an employment bureau for the neighborhood's pardoned planters.[37]

34. The language quoted is that of Section 4 of the March 1865 BRFAL Act, *Statutes-at-Large of the United States*, vol. 13, p. 508.
35. Circular No. 7 [James C. Beecher] to Officers comg. Johns, Wadmalaw, and Edisto islands, 11 Feb. 1866, enclosed in wrapper labeled Headquarters, Military District of Charleston, 16 Feb. 1866, Letters and Reports Received Relating to Freedmen and Civil Affairs, ser, 4112, 2d Military District, RG 393 Pt 1.
36. Ibid.
37. James C. Beecher to M. N. Rice, 19 Feb. 1866, Letters and Reports Received Relating to Freedmen and Civil Affairs, ser. 4112, 2d Military District, RG 393 Pt 1; James C. Beecher to Capt. Taylor, 11 Sept. 1865, M 869, r 34, 0292–302.

Restoration under Beecher's guidelines had been underway on the islands for a month before the state bureau headquarters instructed its agents about possessory titles. Bureau guidelines issued on 17 March 1866 differed from Beecher's instructions in two respects. Bureau provisions modified the written requirements of a valid possessory title. If a settler had erred while finding his way through the maze of written procedures that federal authority brought to largely illiterate slaves, and had mistakenly equated a written travel pass to select land with a possessory certificate, his claim would not be disallowed. The regulations also required that ex-slave settlers be paid cash for any buildings they had constructed during their residence.[38]

Both Beecher's guidelines and the bureau's regulations placed a premium on terms of possession that were least characteristic of the conditions under which freedpeople had settled and cultivated the reserve's abandoned lands. Those who had farmed jointly were ill able to meet the requirement that settlers must have resided and worked on the plantation described in the possessory title. Those who had worked in Charleston or Savannah, a likely recourse for adults in the many families that arrived too late to plant a full crop, were disadvantaged by the stipulation in favor of continuous occupation of the lot. [39] Those rare settlers who had arrived early enough to plant; who had brought or acquired adequate seed, tools, food, and farm animals; who had settled on and exclusively cultivated the lands described in their certificates; and who had built dwellings or stipulated that the dwellings that they occupied were rightfully included within the terms of their possession, were likely to establish the full validity of their possessory titles. Only by backdating and issuing new certificates to claimants who could at least establish that they had lived on the sea islands in 1865 did bureau agents identify about 450 valid claims on the islands and a similar number in the Savannah River area. [40]

Although the bureau's reckoning substantially increased the number of valid claimants over what the army's accounting would have yielded, the agency's methods probably established valid claims for scarcely one-fifth of the families on Edisto, John's, Wadmalaw, and James islands in the

38. H. W. Smith to [E. W.] Everson, 17 March 1866, M 752, r 29, 0803–06.
39. Erastus W. Everson to H. W. Smith, 30 May 1866, r 9; Thomas Black to nn, 11 April 1866, enclosed in J. E. Cornelius to nn, 27 March 1866, r 9; John A. Alden to R. Saxton, 18 Oct. 1865, r 7; all in M 869; J. S. Fullerton to [O. O. Howard], 11 Aug. 1865, M 752, r 74, 0066–84.
40. R. K. Scott to O. O. Howard, 29 May 1866, telegram, M 752, r 35, 0322; James C. Beecher to M. N. Rice, 13 Feb. 1866, enclosed in wrapper labeled Headquarters, Military District of Charleston, 16 Feb. 1866, Letters and Reports Received Relating to Freedmen and Civil Affairs, ser. 4112, 2d Military District, RG 393 Pt 1.

spring of 1866.[41] Charges that the army evicted people whose claims bureau agents had reassessed as valid[42] and Oliver O. Howard's March 1866 instructions that valid claims be consolidated and ex-slaves' settlements be rearranged "with a view to the working of the plantations, so as to relieve the planters as much as possible"[43] may explain why an even smaller number of possessory titles was to be found when Johnson's inspectors James Steedman and James S. Fullerton visited the area in June 1866. At the time of their visit, the inspectors reported, 141 possessory titles had survived to "encumber" thirty-two plantations – only one-tenth of the 310 plantations that bureau agents had reported as abandoned on Edisto, John's, Wadmalaw, and James islands in August 1865. In July 1866, the second Freedmen's Bureau Act extended to holders of valid possessory titles a first option to purchase tracts in St. Helena and St. Luke's parishes.[44] Nevertheless, valid claimants had by that time been reduced to a shadow of the settlers of the Sherman lands.

South Carolina movements to resist restoration centered on the sea islands closest to Charleston and on the abandoned rice estates of the lower Savannah River. A close analysis of the latter movement is outside the scope of the present study. But resistance to restoration in the sea islands bears re-examination if not retelling.[45] A comparison of the tactics and organization of the sea-island movement with rural organizations elsewhere in the state forms an important chapter in the early history of freedpeople's social movements. Summer military occupation of the mainland

41. The rough calculation, which assumes that six thousand people lived on John's, James, and Wadmalaw islands, and that seven thousand lived on Edisto, allows five members per household represented by each valid claim. Population estimates appear in J. E. Cornelius to H. W. Smith, 14 July 1866, M 752, r 36, 0056–59, an extract of which appears in *Nation*, 16 Aug. 1866, p. 123, and in Endorsement of J. E. Cornelius, 27 April 1866, on Charles Devens to R. K. Scott, 4 April 1866, M 869, r 9.

42. James C. Beecher to W. L. M. Burger, 20 March 1866, enclosed in R. K. Scott to D. E. Sickles, 16 March 1866, r 11; James C. Beecher to H. W. Smith, 16 March 1866, r 9; R. K. Scott to [D. E.] Sickles, 20 March 1866, r 11; Charles Devens to R. K. Scott, 15 March 1866, r 9; J. E. Cornelius to H. W. Smith, 27 April 1866, r 9; all in M 869; J. H. Long to R. K. Scott, 16 March 1866, r 29, 0845–48; R. K. Scott to Chas. Devens, Jr., 14 March 1866, r 29, 0826–27; James C. Beecher to J. W. Clous, 10 April 1866, r 29, 1073–78; R. K. Scott to James C. Beecher, 26 Feb. 1866, r 29, 0855–57; Endorsement of Charles Devens, Jr., 20 March 1866, on wrapper labeled BRFAL, Assistant Commissioner of South Carolina, 26 March 1866, r 29, 0828; R. K. Scott to D. E. Sickles, 26 March 1866, r 29, 0832–34; all in M 752.

43. O. O. Howard to R. K. Scott, 6 March 1866, M 752, r 29, 0853–54.

44. James B. Steedman and J. S. Fullerton to E. M. Stanton, 4 June 1866, M 752, r 39, 0464–92; *Statutes-at-Large of the United States*, vol. 14, p. 175.

45. Accounts of Howard's visit to Edisto and of the freedpeople's resistance to restoration appear in Hoffman, "From Slavery to Self-Reliance"; McFeeley, *Yankee Stepfather*, pp. 141–45; Oubre, *Forty Acres and a Mule*, pp. 52–55; Powell, *New Masters*, pp. 99–100; Williamson, *After Slavery*, pp. 80–86; and Rose, *Rehearsal for Reconstruction*, pp. 352–58.

impeded communication between mainland and island settlers and thereby detached mainland plantation communities from participation in the organized opposition to restoration of the Sherman lands. Hence, in the area of the reserve below Charleston, coordinated resistance to restoration was primarily a sea-island movement.

The movement to hold sea-island lands arose directly from Howard's announcement of restoration at Edisto in October 1865. It was, however, rooted in an understanding of emancipation widespread outside the area as well. Virtually all former slaves expected the possession of land to be the material basis of their emancipation.[46] At times, ex-slaves approached the possession of land by measures that seemed to draw upon what one historian has characterized as the quietest millennial tradition of the antebellum slave community.[47] Insistently, if quietly, they waited for a superior authority to demonstrate its justness by granting them land. For nearly three years, from federal occupation in the summer and fall of 1865 to the assembly of the first legislature elected under the Reconstruction Acts, the convocation of federal or local assemblies, with the notable exception of the reconvened 1865 state legislature, stimulated an endemic hunger for land to assume more open expression. The assembly of the Thirty-ninth Congress, a November 1865 black state convention in Charleston, and the deliberations of the 1868 constitutional convention and the first Reconstruction legislature, were regarded as preludes to an imminent division of land.[48]

Outside the centers of resistance to restoration, popular agitation for land often spoke in an indirect protopolitical idiom of song, dance, religious enthusiasm, and the interpretation of omens. Admittedly scant documentation suggests the broad range of symbols incorporated into these popular festivals. As though to summon the just order whose arrival seemed imminent on the eve of the November 1865 black state convention in Charleston, freedpeople in an unidentified county in the eastern part of the state planned to gather to raise a liberty pole.[49] Earlier that same year, women rice workers of Guendalos plantation ceremonialized in dance the tension with which plantation workers awaited the arrival of a squad of soldiers who were to determine whether a recently returned landowner was authorized to take keys to a storage house from the plantation's ex-slave foreman. Women "revolved around us," so the planter's

46. A fuller discussion of freedpeople's expectations of land appears in Chapters 2 and 5.
47. Genovese, *Roll, Jordan, Roll*, pp. 272–79.
48. A. J. Willard to George W. Hooker, 19 Nov. 1865, Letters and Reports Received Relating to Freedmen and Civil Affairs, ser. 4112, 2d Military District, RG 393 Pt 1; E. A. Kozlay to H. W. Smith, 29 Jan. 1866, M 869, r 34, 0406–14; R. K. Scott to O. O. Howard, 26 March 1868 [summary of reports for February 1868], M 752, r 55, 0446–60.
49. Charleston *Courier*, 25 Nov. 1865, p. 1, col. 4.

sister later recalled, "holding out their skirts and dancing – now with slow, swinging movements, now with rapid jig-motions, but always with weird chant and wild gestures."[50]

Instruction in the theatrical display that figured in these rituals began early. Elizabeth Botume sensed that dramatized storytelling served as an important means of communication in the quarters during her wartime residence in Port Royal. On observing the studied gesturing of her pupils outside the classroom, she reflected,

> I wish to ask why so many well-intentioned people treat those who are poor and destitute and helpless as if they were bereft of all their five senses. . . . Visitors would talk before the contrabands as if they could neither see nor hear nor feel. If they could have seen those children at recess, when their visit was over, repeating their words, mimicking their tones and gestures, they would have been undeceived.[51]

It is no easy matter for the historian dependent on written records to explore the meaning of the unwritten expressive forms traditional to largely nonliterate rural folk. Their messages were perhaps clearer to members of the 1865 state legislature in the wake of the popular celebrations that blossomed on plantations, market villages, and larger urban centers after emancipation. A section of the state's Black Codes placed fortune tellers, unlicensed musicians, and unlicensed performers of any public or private "tragedy, interlude, comedy, farce, play or other similar entertainment" under the ban of criminal law.[52]

Processions and festivals were only the most public and celebratory occasions at which freedpeople shared their understandings of emancipation. Regular meetings and discussions, particularly on the eve of a new planting season, were an important empirical tool in the attempt to collectively regulate working conditions. It seems likely that, at least at the outset, these embryonic agricultural associations included the bulk of the plantation community. However, male members early played a specialized ceremonial role. Coordination of the meetings and dissemination of news also fell to male plantation representatives, whose special offices were designated by titles most often adapted from the newly introduced organizational structures of the army or the Freedmen's Bureau; or less frequently, from the lay organization of the Methodist church.[53] Even out-

50. A terse description of the dance and chant appears in Pringle, *Chicora Wood*, p. 273.
51. Botume, *First Days*, p. 107.
52. *Statutes of South Carolina*, 1865, p. 303 (hereafter cited as *SC Statutes*). Williamson, *After Slavery*, appreciates the significance of such festivities. Cf. Foner, *Nothing But Freedom*, p. 50. Hobsbawm, *Primitive Rebels*, offers a pioneering assessment of early social organization among European peasantries.
53. James C. Beecher to [O. D.] Kinsman, 7 Oct. 1865, M 869, r 7; R. K. Scott to O. O. Howard, 23 Jan. 1867 [summary of reports for Dec. 1866], M 752, r 44, 0177–97. Fuller discussion of sources, timing, and forms of popular mobilization appears in Chapter 5.

side the areas where resistance to restoration centered, freedpeople expressed awareness of a corporate identity advanced in comparison with other agricultural workers of the time.

The organization and structure of the agricultural associations that emerged in the sea islands were not peculiar to the region. The distinctiveness of the sea-island associations lay in their goal of resisting restoration of the Sherman lands. The land movement incorporated and developed patterns of association widespread among freed communities in the wake of emancipation.

Attempts to resist restoration drew on the experiences of older bodies organized to regulate plantation affairs. We know little about how such postwar plantation councils worked, but the existence of some type of self-government was suggested whenever federal agents or teachers encountered in a plantation community people whom they readily identified as local spokesmen. Erastus Everson, detailed as a bureau agent for the sea islands in January 1866, coined a term to designate these leaders, who seemed by agreement to speak on behalf of the people of a particular plantation. "There are men among them who are 'oracles,' " Everson concluded after his first trip to James, John's, and Wadmalaw islands in January 1866, "and as *they* go, so go the whole without stopping to consider."[54]

Because outsiders were not parties to their deliberations, a nonplantation resident often encountered the results achieved by these discussions even when the decision-making process itself remained obscure. For example, when the teacher Elizabeth Botume went to visit a settlement on Port Royal Island's Battery plantation that was composed of former Battery slaves who had recently returned from the interior, as well as of refugees from Georgia, she discovered that the settlement had somehow reached an agreement about how to divide the plantation dwelling houses. She found the former slaves from Battery occupying the old slave quarters, "delighted to see again the familiar places and the cabins where they were born," whereas the Georgians had taken up residence in the big house.[55]

Such problems were especially likely to arise on the Charleston sea islands, where returning residents were apt to find their places occupied by Georgia refugees and other freedpeople drawn to claim land in the reserve. Attempts to resolve such disputes were underway in January 1866.

54. Erastus W. Everson to Henry W. Smith, 30 Jan. 1866, M 869, r 9. Everson offers a brief autobiographical statement in *Ku-Klux Conspiracy*, vol. 1, p. 330, and is identified as sub-assistant commissioner for the islands in H. W. Smith to Everson, 17 March 1866, M 752, r 29, 0803–06.
55. Botume, *First Days*, p. 84.

At the time of his January tour, Everson observed, "In most cases, the Freed people who now occupy these plantations, are not those who were formerly in bondage upon them, and I found discontent, and quarreling, because the original workers of these places, upon their return, find that they are now being occupied by other Freedmen who have come from up the country."[56] For all their frequency, however, such disputes do not seem to have been brought to bureau agents for adjudication. Rather, they formed part of the hidden agenda of internal plantation affairs that the people ordered by their own counsel.

Such direct management made for a decorum in freedpeople's community life that surprised Emily Bliss, a resident of Springfield, Massachusetts, who taught school on Edisto Island in 1865. "I can hardly realize that we are living in the midst of a people who have so lately been slaves, and been so suddenly thrown into freedom," Bliss wrote home in June 1865, "[f]or everything is as quiet and orderly as if they had always been accustomed to it, and they take care of themselves as readily and handily as if they were always free."[57] Edisto Island's "simple police" system, of whose existence James Beecher became aware when he visited Edisto in December 1865 to assess a report that freedpeople intended to employ force to defeat restoration,[58] had its origins in the expansion of bodies of internal governance to a field of social organization beyond the plantation village.

In its origins, the Edisto freedpeople's "simple police" probably resembled a similar organization that freed men on St. Helena Island had formed by the summer of 1865.[59] The local body, formed principally of ex-slave soldiers, administered matters of public welfare in the quarters. "The rules in regard to their cleaning plantation streets are such as returned soldiers would make," reported a Northern resident on St. Helena about that island's association. To matters of public concern such as sanitation and the protection of growing crops against vandalism by Northern troops stationed in the area, the St. Helena association added the functions of a beneficial society, collecting dues to be used for burial expenses or relief for members' families in time of need. Public drills and ceremonies and keeping watch at island landings became more frequent as former owners returned to inquire about gaining possession of abandoned lands. The associations' vigilance quickly embraced dispossession of land as the community's major peril.

56. Erastus W. Everson to Henry W. Smith, 30 Jan. 1866, M 869, r 9.
57. *Liberator,* 1 Dec. 1865, p. 184, cols. 4–6.
58. James C. Beecher to T. D. Hodges, 2 Dec. 1865, Letters and Reports Received Relating to Freedmen and Civil Affairs, ser. 4112, 2d Military District, RG 393 Pt 1.
59. W. E. Towne to [Rufus Saxton], 17 Aug. 1865, M 869, r 8.

The depth of the concern that restoration provoked is suggested by the assembly of eight hundred ex-slave men to meet with Beecher in early December. Although he regarded the assembly as a "very pleasant meeting," it is worth noting that the male party probably represented every household among the roughly five thousand freedpeople who then lived on Edisto.[60] At that meeting, freed households would not seem to have delegated authority, even to their "simple police."

The alarm of the loss of land called into existence new councils whose coordinated meetings and discussions played an important role in broadening the particularism of organized plantation life. Little can be learned about how the audience of former slaves assembled at Edisto Island's Episcopal church on 19 October to hear Oliver Otis Howard's address came to select the three men who formed the "committee" to whom Howard's brother Charles explained details of the government's restoration policies. There is no clue whether they had been among the eighteen "oddly mounted" men who formed a cavalcade and saluted the general and his traveling party when they arrived on Edisto.[61] It is nevertheless clear that the Edisto committee members, Henry Bram, Yates Sampson, and Ishmael Moultrie, later took an active role in organizing committees on other islands to coordinate discussions and represent the views of island settlers concerning restoration.

Shadrack Seabrook of Wadmalaw Island eagerly anticipated the coming of the Edisto committee to his island in early December 1865. Discussions on Wadmalaw had convinced him that "[t]his is the Idea of the Peopels of the Islan not to work for there Former owners but b[u]y land." At the time that Seabrook wrote to Rufus Saxton, people on Wadmalaw had begun to consider what they would do in the event of restoration. As Seabrook explained to Saxton, "[I]f the President and if the Goverment Cant sell ous land and cant Compell the Origanal ow[n]ers to sell some of there lands do wish you to incorage the Goverment to take ous out the state   we would of Perfer living in south but Rather then live as slaves agin to leave the state." With so many matters to arrange, Seabrook was concerned that on Wadmalaw "we haven now Committee on the Islan to see Justos" and evidently was relieved that "the Committee at Edisto Prommis to be here on Thousday to Point a Committee."[62] The sponsorship of the Edisto committee promised to

---

60.   James C. Beecher to T. D. Hodges, 2 Dec. 1865, Letters and Reports Received Relating to Freedmen and Civil Affairs, ser. 4112, 2d Military District, RG 393 Pt 1.
61.   Contemporary accounts of the freedpeople's meeting with Howard appear in *Liberator*, 1 Dec. 1865, p. 184, cols. 4–6, 15 Dec. 1865, p. 198, cols. 1–2, and p. 198, cols. 2–3. See also Ames, *New England Woman's Diary*, pp. 95–99.
62.   Shadrack Seabrook to R. Saxton, 8 Dec. 1865, M 869, r 20, 0404.

give added authority to the resolutions that had already been adopted during discussions and meetings on Wadmalaw.

From the many discussions and meetings generated during the movement to hold sea-island lands emerged a historically informed consciousness that plantation spokesmen now acted on behalf of a larger collectivity. Shortly after Howard's visit, Edisto's committee of three took up the question of restoration in a letter to Andrew Johnson on behalf of "Wee the freedmen of South Carlina."[63] Lest the significance of the committee's phraseology be overlooked, an equally extraordinary document jointly composed by former slave men outside the Sherman territory underscores the expanding social context in which ex-slaves consciously attempted to place their emancipation. The terminology appropriate to their enlarged civil domain puzzled the eleven men in Georgetown district who, in January 1866, wrote Howard "to give you information as regards to the present state of affairs in this D C." Perhaps the men had been influenced by the division of the state into military districts, or imperfectly rendered the state custom to refer to legislative units as districts rather than as counties, or possibly even endorsed their new ties to Washington, DC. However ambiguous their intent, it is clear that "D C," as they used it, designated the specific area embraced by their report.

These Georgetown committee members wished to report on a general social condition, not their particular circumstances: "We a fue Names of the Colard Citasin of Georgetown So Ca have taken upon our Self to make inquirey of you for those roundabout us who are not Able to do it for them Self." They wrote in full confidence that no faithful account of plantation labor in Georgetown district could proceed without their testimony: "Sir we See it published in the newspapers that the freed [people] in S C wont work. . . . *Hon* Sir it is Not so in this D C." Indeed, the question seemed to them of global significance. They did not want "the reports to continare to spred through the whorld that the freedman wont work."[64]

The passions and judgments that compelled the eleven-member committee in Georgetown to address history in their people's behalf was compactly expressed by the Edisto committee. In a surviving draft of their letter to Andrew Johnson in October 1865, Edisto's committee explained, "We have for the last four yars ben studing with justis and the best of our

63. The quoted passage appears in the excerpt from a draft of the committee's letter to Johnson published in Ames, *New England Woman's Diary*, pp. 99–103. The author of the draft petition is uncertain. However, the additional letters of Henry Bram that are scattered throughout the BRFAL records suggest that he had not written the draft that Ames transcribed in her diary.
64. J. H. Sheckelfod and others to [O. O. Howard], 17 Jan. 1866, enclosed in wrapper labeled J. H. Shackleford and others, 17 Jan. 1866, M 752, r 24, 0513–15.

ability what step wee should take to become a people."[65] An appreciation of the historic significance of emancipation was central to the attempt to coordinate the organization of their domestic and working lives.

Written expression played a surprisingly significant role during the organization of the public life of what was still a predominantly illiterate adult population. The freedpeople's determination to penetrate the mysteries of reading and writing has been widely reported.[66] The social and political significance that ex-slaves attached to literacy was symbolically demonstrated at a gathering in an interior market town in the eastern part of the state. An unsympathetic observer witnessed with disgust a mid-November 1865 rally in which "a crazed negress harangued the public, avowing herself the bearer of a commission to revolutionize this country."[67] Even those who did not fully conquer its mysteries saw literacy as empowerment. A potential power reposed in a body of written national laws, written bureau and army orders, and even written work agreements that they could wield against the old order. "We have no master now. We is come to the law now," was the reply that James Fullerton frequently received in July 1865 from ex-slaves in the track of Sherman's army.[68] The written word marked a path by which they could appeal to a less personal and more accountable authority.

It was not unknown for freedpeople individually to seek redress by presenting their employers and former owners with written bureau orders. Wade Adams's former owner reminded him that the authority of written orders was potential rather than actual. Taking Adams and his three children from the field where they had been at work with other hands, the Edgefield farmer John Adams "[s]triped our clothes off us and whiped us Severely at the same time saying that if I brought any paper to him from the damn Yankees he would blow my damned head off."[69]

The organized public life of freedpeople on the sea islands early linked written expression to the strength of a popular movement by adapting writing and reading to social processes by which the written word could provide even the illiterate with information and a means of collective expression. Illiteracy did not prevent people from reading and writing. At least some of the meetings at which restoration was discussed in the winter of 1865–66 concluded with the people signing or marking written

65. Quoted in Ames, *New England Woman's Diary*, pp. 99–100.
66. Ames, *New England Woman's Diary*, p. 55; Holt, "Negro Legislators," pp. 233, 241; Powell, *New Masters*, pp. 93–96; Berlin et al., eds., *Black Military Experience*, p. 28; Rose, *Rehearsal for Reconstruction*, pp. 85–88; Ripley, *Slaves and Freedmen*; Litwack, *Been in the Storm So Long*, pp. 472–74.
67. Charleston *Courier*, 25 Nov. 1865, p. 1, col. 4.
68. J. S. Fullerton to O. O. Howard, 28 July 1865, M 752, r 14, 1363–64.
69. [Affidavit of Wade Adams], 18 Sept. 1865, M 869, r 20, 0004.

pledges to stand together.[70] A featured item of the business conducted at these meetings was the reading of newspapers and bureau and army regulations. The significance of reading as a public activity was spelled out in October 1866 when "The People of Edisto Island S.C." petitioned Howard to remove Robert K. Scott as assistant commissioner after "Genl Scott contrary to all law and order and even the Articles of the Constitution, & Civil Rights Bill has commanded us on the penalty of threats to hold no mass meetings or conventions of the people on this Island":

> This is to stop in a great measure all important public news as this is the only method by which the people can obtain the news of the country. We having no public Journals or Newspapers, and if we had very few could read them. In an interview with your honor, you specially advised us to hold conventions of the people as that was the proper mode of enlightening the minds of the people on general news and political topics.[71]

Reading and writing became public activities, collaboratively structured to overcome the bar that illiteracy posed to informed discussion of common concerns. Assemblies at times drew up documents in a form intended to indicate their public origins. Henry Bram, a member of the original Edisto committee of three, headed a list of more than sixty names attached to a letter that explained why an earlier petition demanding Scott's removal had carried no personal signatures: "[T]he only reason of our witholding the names from the petition was, that it was thought by the majority unnecessary, as it was the sentiments of not a few, but the *People of the island.*"[72]

We can glimpse, if often only by inference, how a broad community opinion guided the work of the Edisto committee as its members composed letters to Howard and Johnson to protest restoration in October 1865. Dates on the surviving draft of one of the committee's letters indicate that at least some of the work of composition was done on weekdays[73]—an allocation of time that was in part possible because hours of employment had not yet absorbed the daylight portion of these days as "working time" owed to an employer. Memorization, a skill that teachers reported to have been keenly developed in emancipated adults and children alike, is as evident as literacy in the composition of these letters.

---

70. James C. Beecher to T. D. Hodges, 1 Dec. 1865, Letters and Reports Received Relating to Freedmen and Civil Affairs, ser. 4112, 2d Military District, RG 393 Pt 1.
71. "The People of Edisto Island, S. C." to O. O. Howard, 2 Oct. 1866, M 752, r 37, 0404–09.
72. [Henry Bram et al. to O. O. Howard], 3 Nov. 1866, M 752, r 37, 0460–69. The same letter withdraws their request for Scott's removal.
73. Ames, *New England Woman's Diary*, p. 103, gives the date on the draft petition to Johnson as Wednesday, 25 Oct. 1865.

When read together, the committee's letters directly respond to Howard's address and to the remarks of William Whaley, an Edisto planter who frankly if somewhat mysteriously informed the bureau agent appointed to superintend the restoration of Sherman lands "that he took a personal pride in his enterprise with regard to these lands, and that if he succeeded he should secure to himself individual benefits and advantages of no ordinary moment, while a failure would interfere with his purposes and be a sore disappointment."[74] Whaley, who had spoken at Howard's request, apparently made his remarks while the committee was conferring with Charles H. Howard. When the committee's formal petitions turned to Whaley's remarks, they probably drew on the memory of others who had remained in the audience.

If the process of composing the letters remains at best speculative, the letters themselves establish that restoration provoked the most forceful written assertion of the national government's obligations to former slaves. The committee rebuked Johnson, gently to be sure, because they were "well aware of the many perplexing and trying questions that burden your mind," for what Howard told them had been the president's decision to order restoration. Their emancipation, they reminded Johnson, drew its force from divine justice, government policy, and their wartime services. It was, they expostulated, "god (the preserver of all)" acting "through our Late and beloved President (Lincoln) proclamation and the war" that had "made Us A free people." Lest Johnson prove blind to how "that wisdom that Cometh from above" required him to "settle these great and Important Questions for the best interests of the country and the Colored race," the committee claimed loyalty to the Union as the ex-slaves' peculiar cause in a state "where secession was born and Nurtured":

> [W]e were the only true and Loyal people that were found in possession of these Lands. we have been always ready to strike for Liberty and humanity yea to fight if needs be To preserve this glorious Union. Shall not we who Are freedman and have always been true to this Union have the same rights as are enjoyed by Others? Have we broken any Law of these United States? Have we forfieted [sic] our rights of property in land? – If not then! are not our rights as A free people and good citizens of these United States To be considered before the rights of those who were Found in rebellion against this good and just Government (and now being conquered) come (as they Seem) with penitent hearts and beg forgiveness For past offences and also ask if

74. Like Ketchum, we are still "entirely in the dark with regard to the object to which [Whaley] thus obscurely alluded." See A. P. Ketchum to O. O. Howard, 6 Nov. 1865, M 752, r 21, 0466–69.

thier lands Cannot be restored to them[?] . . . God forbid, Land mo-
nopoly is injurious to the advancement of the course of freedom.[75]

The committee's appeal to Johnson framed a historical basis for what a
freed man contemplating restoration in tidewater Virginia characterized
as "a divine right to the land"[76] in the moral terms of evangelical antislavery, the political terms of Republican unionism, and the social terms
of an antimonopolist critique of nineteenth-century America.

As the government emissary who had announced restoration, Howard
received the committee's most extended reasoning on why they could not
agree to restoration in exchange for employment by pardoned landowners. To explain why "we want Homesteads," the committee elaborated on the succinct notice given Johnson that said, "This is our home,
we have made these lands what they are."[77] Land, they explained to
Howard, was not like other property. They claimed land by the prerogative of birth and by the franchise with which free people defend themselves from the obligations of servitude. Their compound claims
established possession of land as an inalienable heritage without which
"we cannot feel our rights Safe":

> We are at the mercy of those who are combined to prevent us from
> getting land enough to lay our Fathers bones upon. We Have prop-
> erty in Horses, Cattle, Carriages, & articles of furniture, but we are
> landless and Homeless   from the Homes we Have lived In In the
> past   we can only do one of three things   Step Into the public *road
> or the sea* or remain on them working as In former time and subject
> to thire will as then. We can not resist It In any way without being
> driven out Homeless upon the road. You will see this Is not the con-
> dition of really freemen [78]

The reasoning that underlies these petitions to Johnson and Howard
becomes more apparent if we keep in mind that the letters were not literal descriptions of the circumstances of sea-island settlers or autobiographical accounts of the direct experiences of the committee members
written as historical explanation. The committee emphasized claims derived from the historical experiences of an emancipated people who, having rendered the Union critical assistance, were then working lands where
they had formerly been slaves. Henry Bram, the one committee member
about whom we can gain additional information, was by some accounts

75. Henry Bram, Ishmael Moultrie, and Yates Sampson to "The President of These United
    States," 28 Oct. 1865, M 752, r 23, 0435–41.
76. Speech of ex-slave Bayley Wyatt, delivered to a meeting of freedpeople in Yorktown,
    VA, in the winter of 1866, in *Pennsylvania Freedmen's Bulletin* (March 1867): 15–16.
77. Henry Bram et al. to [Johnson], 28 Oct. 1865, M 752, r 23, 0435–41.
78. Henry Bram, Ishmael Moultrie, and Yates Sampson to "General" [O. O. Howard]
    [Oct. 1865], M 752, r 29, 0838–42.

freeborn, had maintained an inn in Charleston and Boston before the war, and until he headed an expedition of homesteaders from the sea islands to public lands in Florida in January 1867, had leased or otherwise cultivated several plantations on Edisto and marketed the cotton raised on them.[79] The petitions nonetheless speak of injustice done the former slave when he was expected to work for "[t]he man who tied me to a tree & gave me 39 lashes & who stripped and flogged my mother & my sister."[80] They speak to the interests of working people who require "land of my own" if they are to ward off a "Condition of Helplessness,"[81] not to the commercial interests of petty cotton merchants. One of the October petitions pronounced, "Here is w[h]ere we have toiled nearly all Our lives as slaves"[82] well before former island residents came to compose a sizable portion of the population, and before the large postharvest exodus of Georgia refugees made actual the course expressed in a song sung at the meeting with Howard: "We'll camp awhile in the wilderness/Then we'll be going home."[83]

An earlier draft of the petition to Johnson insisted "man that have stud upon the feal of battle & have shot there master & sons now Going to ask ether one for bread or for shelter or Confortable for his wife & children sunch a thing the u st should not aught to Expect a man (to do)."[84] It thereby emphasized the significance of military service of former slaves, whose families were well represented on the islands (if not in the state); but it probably did not describe the personal experiences of all the committee members, since none of the South Carolina black regiments had been mustered out by October 1865. In brief, the committee's petitions culled regional and national developments of wartime emancipation to establish the justice of ex-slaves' characteristic expectation that on emancipation they would agree "to work for no one but themselves."[85]

Because the relationship between the surviving draft of the petition to Johnson and the formal petitions cannot be established, it is not possible to isolate the contributions of Northern antislavery sympathizers with any certainty. Both formal petitions did, however, excise indemnification as a basis for claiming land. The draft had insisted that a slaveowner who had enjoyed the "labers & the Profet of there yearly [early] youth"[86] by right owed land to former slaves. To Johnson, however, the formal peti-

79. New York *Herald*, 23 May 1866, p. 5, col. 3; R. K. Scott to O. O. Howard, 13 Oct. 1866, M 752, r 39, 0604–07. His name variantly appears as Braun, Brahm, and Bram.
80. Henry Bram et al. to [Howard] [Oct. 1865], M 752, r 19, 0838–42.   81. Ibid.
82. Henry Bram et al. to [Johnson], 28 Oct. 1865, M 752, r 23, 0435–41.
83. The song is quoted in *Liberator*, 15 Dec. 1865, p. 198, cols. 2–3.
84. Ames, *New England Woman's Diary*, p. 101.
85. Erastus W. Everson to Henry W. Smith, 30 Jan. 1866, M 869, r 9.
86. Ames, *New England Woman's Diary*, p. 102.

tion asserted, "We are ready to pay for this land When Government calls for it."[87] This alternative would seem to have been ahead of the slave constituency in whose name it was raised. In his visits and conferences with former slaves on the sea islands in the winter of 1865–66, James Beecher found fullest evidence on Edisto that ex-slaves "will gladly pay any reasonable or unreasonable price" for land. After later trips to John's, James, and Wadmalaw islands, he was, by February 1866, complaining, "I have not yet found a freedman who has an idea that he is to pay rent for the 40 acre tracts."[88]

Freedpeople's understanding of the lease provision of the 1865 bureau act and their agreement to purchase land were the special results of the educational work of the Edisto committee. The committee's written declaration that purchase of land was an option that the government should justly extend to former slaves may also reflect the editing services of the sympathetic local bureau agent John Alden, who "revise[d] and correcte[d]" the committee's draft petition. The Springfield, Massachusetts teacher Emily Bliss, who intended to "copy" Alden's revised petition, pronounced the committee's draft "very well expressed, but in their peculiar manner."[89] Whatever the source of the formal petition's reference to buying land, the alternative did not faithfully represent the judgments that island bureau agent Everson also found popularly expressed on John's, James, and Wadmalaw islands in January 1866. There, Everson reported, "They have generally the idea that the Islands are theirs"; at the same time, "those who are not so sanguine in this" were, under the influence of plantation "oracles," "firm in their declarations that no one shall prevent them from occupying and cultivating there, as they see fit."[90]

The organizing work of the Edisto committee achieved mixed results. Under its auspices, freedpeople extended the organized framework of making decisions beyond the social unit of the plantation to a wider regional field. As a consequence of its consultations with former slaves and sympathetic government agents and teachers, the committee's formal petitions came to bear the imprint of Northern abolitionists' and former slaves' assessments of the significance of war and emancipation. In its tendency to seek government endorsement, the committee perhaps encouraged the inclination that its emancipated constituency shared with precapitalist peasantries – the belief that the principles of a distant, "good and just" state authority were in harmony with their own. The army's

87. Henry Bram et al. to [Johnson], 28 Oct. 1865, M 752, r 23, 0435–41.
88. James C. Beecher to T. D. Hodges, 2 Dec. 1865; James C. Beecher to M. N. Rice, 6 Feb. 1866; both in Letters and Reports Received Relating to Freedmen and Civil Affairs, ser. 4112, 2d Military District, RG 393 Pt 1.
89. *Liberator*, 1 Dec. 1865, p. 184, col. 6.
90. Erastus W. Everson to Henry W. Smith, 30 Jan. 1866, M 869, r 9.

forced removal of people with "invalid" possessory titles, carried out by squads from the Thirty-fifth United States Colored Infantry (because company and district commanders agreed that black soldiers "would exercise a more favorable influence" than white troops),[91] encountered no broadly organized resistance. People evacuated from the islands reportedly told Beecher that "the Government had a place for them, and that they would go with my guards wherever I ordered them to do so."[92] What opposition the evacuations encountered came from holders of "valid" titles on several plantations who, Beecher believed, intended to "*invite all the people to locate on it.*"[93]

The success with which the public meetings kept people apprised of official policy is perhaps reflected in some settlers' informed but vain attempts to defend their possession of land within government guidelines that were becoming progressively more narrow. People variously said that they would sign contracts if their possessory titles were deemed invalid; one man, in keeping with the three-year lease provision of the 1865 bureau bill, requested government assistance for two additional years, after which time he would purchase his tract; others resignedly said that they would contract only with Northern planters.[94] Such offers show that familiarity with changing government options ran deep in the quarters. Nevertheless, the effort to realize popular desires to hold land within the terms of postwar government policy was doomed.

Freedpeople's island police squads maintained forceful direct action against restoration between November 1865 and January 1866. Parties of returning planters or visiting Northerners were driven away altogether or detained and marched to a local government post.[95] However, the open organization and public drilling of these island associations had largely ceased by the spring of 1866, a victim of disbanding by the occupying army. The military flavor of the popular island patrols was still evident on Wadmalaw Island in March 1866, when a hidden watchman commanded a Northern superintendent of Osmar Bailey's plantation, "[Y]ou

91.   Charles Devens to W. L. M. Burger, 30 Nov. 1865; Charles Devens to W. L. M. Burger, 1 Dec. 1865; both in Letters and Reports Received Relating to Freedmen and Civil Affairs, ser. 4112, 2d Military District, RG 393 Pt 1.
92.   James C. Beecher to M. N. Rice, 19 Feb. 1866, in ibid.
93.   Ibid.
94.   Endorsement of R. K. Scott, 23 March 1866, on Constantine Bailey to O. O. Howard [March 1866]; Constantine Bailey to O. O. Howard [March 1866]; Erastus W. Everson to Henry W. Smith, 30 Jan. 1866; all in M 869, r 9; James C. Beecher to T. D. Hodges, 2 Dec. 1865, James C. Beecher to M. N. Rice, 7 Feb. 1866, enclosed in wrapper labeled Headquarters, Military District of Charleston, 16 Feb. 1866, both in Letters and Reports Received Relating to Freedmen and Civil Affairs, ser. 4112, 2d Military District, RG 393 Pt 1.
95.   Powell, *New Masters*, pp. 99–100.

God damned Son of a bitch, halt" and discharged a musket in the superintendent's direction. The concealment of the speaker and the superintendent's belief that the voice was that of a "white man" suggests the
degree to which indirection and anonymity had reclaimed the once open
and public island police.[96] The challenge was in form, if not in spirit, far
removed from the January 1866 occasion when nearly fifty men had provided public escort on Wadmalaw to three men from Edisto "calling
themselves 'Commissioners,' " as the "commissioners" carried to the post
commander on Wadmalaw Island Saxton's written order overruling the
army's ban of their announced meeting.[97]

After the spring of 1866, as direct action against restoration again de-
volved onto plantation communities, defense of claims to land that contemplated the use of force was localized, largely spontaneous, and overtly
involved women to a greater degree. An encounter between Freedmen's
Bureau agent Erastus Everson and the largely female portion of a settlement of Georgia refugees, rallied by their "oracle" Mary Ann, illustrates
the ritualized shaming, denunciation, and physical assault that ex-slave
women employed in collective demonstrations. In May 1866, Everson
went to explain to the Georgia refugees who remained cultivating John
Townsend's Sea Cloud plantation on Edisto Island that they would have
to contract with Townsend or move out of the house because their claims
were invalid and Townsend had been pardoned.

> I was beset by the women on this place in a very serious manner, and
> was obliged to use decisive measures for the preservation of the prop-
> erty as well as for my own head. After I had made known my errand,
> and told them who I was, and what I came for, and being also in uni-
> form, they absolutely refused to give me any information. . . . They
> then said I wouldn't have durst come there had not part of the men
> gone to the city. . . . They said they would not make any arrangement
> whatever, for me or anybody else; that they cared for no United States
> officer: the Govt brought them to the island & 'they would burn
> down the house before they would move away' or 'farm it themselves
> until put out.'

Everson next tried to arrest Leah Jenkins and her daughter Jane because
they had threatened to set fire to the house. As he led them off, he reported, "The people followed me about a half a mile with hoes and sticks,
and I got sick of this business, and said to them 'this is the last time I tell
you this this'　they refused to obey, and I drew my revolver faced my
horse about and charged them back to camp." Everson insisted that Leah

---

96.　J. E. Cornelius to H. W. Smith, 30 March 1866, M 752, r 29, 0911–13.
97.　James C. Beecher to [H. W.] Smith, 31 Jan. 1866, M 869, r 9; S. W. Saxton, 17 Jan.
　　1866 [Special Order], Saxton Papers, CtY.

and Jane Jenkins, as well as Mary Ann, "the oracle," should be brought to trial. He explained his options to the district commander with chilling frankness: "I do not think I can unaided arrest them, but if you order it, I will try, begging to be excused from any consequences arising from the attempt."[98] The short-lived sea-island land movement therefore organized but was not to supplant the common regulation of work by the plantation community.

Organized resistance to restoration on the sea islands enjoyed remarkable success in coordinating informed action among newly constituted plantation settlements. It nevertheless remained a geographically circumscribed movement, drawing virtually no support from freedpeople in Charleston, with the possible exception of a series of printed petitions against restoration that were circulated in November.[99] By contrast, resistance to restoration on the abandoned rice estates of the lower Savannah River gradually assumed a broader geographic and social character. Under the harassed leadership of Aaron Bradley, South Carolina's fugitive slave shoemaker and self-styled lawyer who later was active in Georgia Reconstruction politics, rice workers on the South Carolina and Georgia lands along the Savannah River sustained a two-year struggle against restoration. Their land movement climaxed in early 1867 when an estimated three hundred freed men, women, and children, refusing to exchange their possessory certificates for warrants to land in St. Helena and St. Luke's parishes, succeeded in occupying two Savannah River rice plantations under armed fire from a detachment of the Sixteenth United States Infantry.[100] The sea-island land movement coordinated attempts to hold land within the narrow terms of federal policy, whereas its Savannah-based counterpart gradually mounted a campaign to seize land and was thereby drawn into more explicit conflict with the federal military and bureau staff.

In September of 1867, on the eve of Georgia's constitutional convention assembled under the Reconstruction Acts, Aaron Bradley addressed a Savannah rally, where placards demanding "homesteads for all men of families in the county and town in which they belong (paying the state in seven years) to stop pauperism and dignify labor" joined with slogans demanding "relief from Debt," the "Eight Hour Day," "Reduction of

98.   Erastus W. Everson to H. W. Smith, 30 May 1866, M 869, r 9.
99.   The printed petitions appear in M 752, r 20, 0081–84, and r 24, 0320–27.
100.   See compiled file labeled H. C. Brandt, "Papers relating to Savannah trouble" [Jan. 1867], M 869, r 22, 0050–60; Horace Neide to Howard, 4 Feb. 1867, r 43, 0477–85, and H. Neide to Edw. L. Deane, 15 Feb. 1867, r 44, 0290–98, both in M 752. Reidy, "Aaron A. Bradley," pp. 281–308, revises judgments advanced by Coulter, *Negro Legislators in Georgia*, pp. 37–120.

Rents," and "Equal Political Rights."[101] The slogans reflected Bradley's broad relations with urban workers, particularly longshoremen in Savannah, and rice workers on the Savannah and Ogeechee rivers.

In Charleston, the sea-island agitation for land found no mass base.[102] With the collapse of the sea-island movement, the terms of postwar planting came more closely to resemble the conditions that William Whaley had announced to Edisto's freedpeople in October 1865. Addressing some of his former slaves in the audience, Whaley thought to encourage them to accept "some arrangement to secure their services" by announcing that "*[h]e* had capital, and *they* [had] labor."[103] Unwittingly, Whaley had announced the basis of a new opposition.

101. Gottlieb, "Land Question," quoted passages at 376.
102. Holt, "Negro Legislators in South Carolina," pp. 239–40, 242.
103. *Liberator,* 15 Dec. 1865, p. 198, cols. 1–2.

4

The Reconstruction of Work

Remaking Family Life and Labor in the Interior

Freedpeople living inland in 1865 confronted circumstances of residence and labor that made their agenda at emancipation differ in important respects from that of former slaves on the coast. Slaves owned by the small planters and middling farmers who predominated in the Piedmont had seldom lived on the same place among all members of their immediate families. In areas where slaves had been owned in small lots, the dispersion of kin among neighboring owners was common. Although ties of kinship and marriage had linked them as a people, they had remained dissociable as property by a master's lawful authority. Consequently, ex-slaves in interior districts often needed to reclaim even those family members who could be found living in the same neighborhood. Under such circumstances, asserting claims to particular persons preceded claims to particular lands.

As a slave, Allan Quick had been worked as a field hand in Marlboro district, where he lived three miles from his wife and their ten children. Quick later recalled how he had supplemented his family's allowances by nighttime overwork:

> I had several hogs in the yard at their quarters – and I built a smoke house there to keep such provisions in as I could buy or raise for my family in case they should not get enough from their master. I worked at night at shoemaking and making horse collars and chair bottoms– matts &c – for which I was paid – I raised hogs & chickens – and corn – with my own money I bought the "quilts" and "spreads"[1]

Even before emancipation, Quick began to close the rift between "home place" and "wife place" and to expand his parental and marital roles. "During the war," he later recalled, "I went to see my family twice every week and all day Sunday."[2]

1. Testimony of Allan Quick, 22 May 1876, claim of Allan Quick, Marlboro County SC case files, Approved Claims, ser. 732, Southern Claims Commission, 3d Auditor, RG 217 [I-82].
2. Ibid.

Like Quick, other adults in formerly dispersed households seized free status as an entitlement to reorganize residence on the basis of kinship rather than antebellum ownership. Short visits with scattered kin proceeded in the face of threatened dismissals for negligence during the remainder of the 1865 crop year. As the first planting season after emancipation rolled around, many sought to give their newly reconstituted households a more secure standing. Contracts negotiated in interior and up-country cotton districts for the 1866 planting season began to stipulate that the landowner had agreed "to receive {the parties} as one family."[3]

Observers noticed the trend to consolidate familial households, even if they did not always endorse it. Early in 1866, a family of seven turned down employment by a Richland district farmer "only needing three 3 to fill out my number (10) and the family not wishing to separate."[4] Freed men often quit their "home places" to join wives and children on lands owned by the former owners of their families, thereby making no small contribution to the women's widely noted "disposition to keep out of the filds [*sic*] as much as possible."[5] A Freedmen's Bureau agent stationed in Greenville who noted freedpeople's opposition to apprenticeship of children concluded, "These freedmen appear to have ambition to live in a patriarchal manner by getting as many of the children of their kinsmen around them as possible; evidently with the intention of being supported by their labor."[6] Narrowly construing their motives and perhaps imposing a conception of kinship alien to that of the freedpeople themselves, the agent nevertheless glimpsed the importance that ex-slaves soon attached to reconstituting their households.

Ex-slaves' attempts to concentrate kin in one place not only reflected the strength with which affective ties were sustained during slavery, but also underscored the inescapable compromises that had tortured even the closest of bonds among men, women, and children who were property in the households of their masters.

Freed adults' competing claims to children offer testimony to the strain on families that the old order had imposed.[7] The freed in-laws Henry Cal-

3. Joseph F. Bell, Dec. 1866, Labor Contracts, ser. 3037, Abbeville, Subordinate Field Office Records, RG 105.

4. John A. Smith to L. B. Meunard, 7 Feb. 1866, vol. 128, pp. 217–20, Registers of Letters Received, ser. 3155, Columbia, Subordinate Field Office Records, RG 105.

5. John A. Smith to L. B. Meunard, 7 Feb. 1866, vol. 128, pp. 217–20, Registers of Letters Received, Columbia, ser. 3155, Subordinate Field Office Records, RG 105; W. T. Lesesne to Gen. D. E. Sickles, 28 June 1867, M 869, r 14; the quoted phrase appears in A. E. Niles to H. W. Smith, 13 July 1866, Letters Received, Office of the Commissioner, RG 105 [A-7323].

6. A. E. Niles to H. W. Smith, 13 July 1865, Letters Received, Office of the Commissioner, RG 105 [A-7323].

7. For a suggestive exploration of the interrelationship between such family conflicts and apprenticeship laws, see Fields, *Slavery and Freedom*, pp. 155–56.

houn and Sarah Gillebeau both claimed custody of Calhoun's sons, who were also Gillebeau's nephews. In January 1867, Calhoun, "an aged and now decreped freedman," returned to his onetime home in Abbeville district on the upper Savannah River from the expanding plantation region around Dougherty County, Georgia, to which he had been sold in his prime. Renewing personal contacts in his old neighborhood while he recruited workers for a planter in southwest Georgia, Calhoun also used the occasion to recover his sons as well. By that time, however, the boys' mother had died. Before her death, she had tried to reinforce her sons' claim on a residence in the neighborhood by placing them under their aunt's care. Calhoun's return probably prompted the boys' aunt to strengthen her claim to Calhoun's sons by apprenticing the eldest boy to a neighboring farmer. When Calhoun arranged to ferry his sons to the Georgia side of the Savannah River, the farmer took the boys off the ferry and later defended his act against Calhoun's charge of kidnapping by appealing to the dying mother's charge to the boys' aunt.[8] The final disposition of the boys' custody is unknown, although federal and state guidelines made recognition of kinship secondary to the economic consequences of particular living arrangements.[9] In contrast, all parties in the dispute between Calhoun and Gillebeau had expressed preferences for particular work arrangements in the idiom of kinship.

Former slaveowners proved versatile in the tongue. The Black Codes dressed the old crime of running away in the garb of "abandonment of husband or wife."[10] Planters were keen to petition bureau agents to hold absent husbands and wives to the fulfillment of familial obligations when the offending party's absence diminished the number of able hands in their labor force.[11] Perhaps few excelled the Abbeville landowner J. S. Chipley, who condemned the independence with which older adolescents often made arrangements to work apart from their families. Chipley was

8.   C. H. Howard to C. C. Sibley, 19 April 1867; Endorsements of C. H. Howard, 1 June 1867 and C. R. Becker, 10 May 1867, on C. H. Howard to C. C. Sibley, 19 April 1867; both in Letters Received, ser. 3028, Abbeville, Subordinate Field Office Records, RG 105; Sarah Gillebeau and J. L. Bouchillon, Jan. 1867, Labor Contracts, ser. 3037, Abbeville, Subordinate Field Office Records, RG 105.

9.   The state code of 1866 had envisioned children over two years of age, who had lost either a mother or a father by the parent's death or sale out of the district in which the children currently resided, as candidates for apprenticeship. Ignoring the interests of other kin, the code vested the right to indenture minors under ten years of age first in a resident father and second in a resident mother. *SC Statutes,* 1866, pp. 292, 293. The role of the Freedmen's Bureau in custody disputes merits separate study, although it seems clear that the bureau chiefly endorsed custody arrangements that promised to avert the necessity of government relief. Calhoun's debility might well have kept him from gaining the bureau's support.

10.   *SC Statutes,* 1866, p. 292.

11.   Jesse Telford (freedman) to Maj. Wm. Stone, 10 April 1866, Unregistered Letters Received, ser. 3067, Anderson, Subordinate Field Office Records, RG 105 [A-7223].

outraged when a neighbor hired a sixteen-year-old boy in a freed family of nine people after the youth's father had signed a contract to work on Chipley's place. The neighbor's hiring conveniently conformed to arrangements supported by the Black Codes, which had held fathers responsible for supporting children less than fifteen years old. Nonetheless, Chipley charged that his neighbor was "teaching the boy to show disrespect to his farther," and defended his own claim to the labor of the entire household as a guarantor of the integrity of the freed family as an economic unit: "[A]ll from plowboys up will leave their payrents and set up for themselves," he fumed, "& a white man should be punished for persuading boys to leave their payrents."[12] Notwithstanding their fluency, however, ex-masters proved inept spokesmen in behalf of ex-slaves' familial rights.

Political overtones attended the reconstitution of families in the wake of emancipation. The consolidation of households animated those challenges to the master's authority that had reposed in slaves' networks of kin associations.[13] In reorganizing their family life, freedpeople on smaller places initially expressed the terms and conditions of labor that they considered implicit in emancipation. Kinship provided the primary means by which ex-slaves on smaller places first articulated resistance to postwar working arrangements.

The reconstitution of families brought to the fore challenges to the master's personal sovereignty lurking behind abolition. Former slaves most readily defended social obligations carried by ties of blood and marriage. When Edgefield farmer Thomas Price beat his employee Fannie Price with limbs from a plum tree in October 1865, her father refused to hold her down. For her father's passive resistance, the daughter later reported to a commander of a local military post, the farmer "did break the arm of her Father (Sam Price) with a club."[14]

Direct action on farms and small plantations in the immediate postwar period often proceeded along ties created by blood or marriage. Hence, when the freedman Ben "had some words" with his Aiken county employer James Martin on his way to the fields to hoe, it was Ben's wife (who notably was *not* heading for the fields that spring morning in 1868) who took up the issue, whose substance, unfortunately, remains undisclosed. Hearing her cries for help when Martin began beating her, Ben ran back

12. J. S. Chipley to C. C. Perry, 11 Jan. 1868, Letters Received, ser. 3028, Abbeville, Subordinate Field Office Records, RG 105; *SC Statutes*, 1866, p. 292.
13. Gutman, *Black Family*, offers a pathbreaking investigation of slaves' family life.
14. Affidavit of Fannie Price, *United States* v. *Thomas Price*, 19 Oct. 1865, Letters Received, ser. 631, Office of the Assistant Commissioner for Georgia, RG 105 [A-366]; *Sally Clayburn* v. *Duck Boozer*, 26 June 1868, vol. 103, p. 21, Register of Complaints, ser. 3034, Abbeville, Subordinate Field Office Records, RG 105.

to the house only to be shot in the face by Martin, who had apparently been armed during the encounter. Ben's brother-in-law then rallied the other hands (unidentified in the complaint), who pursued Martin to a nearby house and killed him.[15] Drawing on ties of kinship that extended from marriage, the family had coordinated a retaliation that ultimately exacted the fullest vengeance as the dispute escalated from heated argument to physical coercion to lethal assault.

Family members assumed primary responsibility for defending one of their own against the corporal punishment that freedpeople generally regarded as the most patent violation of their new condition. Wielding a solidarity initially expressed as kinship, the freed family became an immediate agency for defending rights that they held fundamental to emancipation.

The reunion of once-scattered families introduced, in the person of the new arrivals, parties who stood outside the particularized ties of command, power, and sentiment by which masters had established personal dominion over household affairs. When freed men came to work at the "wife place," landowners found these male newcomers a troublesome presence. John Smith, a farmer in Richland district, was certain that the arrival of the freedman Ephraim, who joined his wife and child on Smith's place sometime during 1865, had hastened rejection of the 1866 contract that Smith had announced in the quarters over the Christmas holidays.

> I am influenced to believe that Ephraim was in instrumental [*sic*] in his Brother in law Simon leaving me as he (Ephraim) told them that they had [not] entered into a written contract and were not bound. To use Ephraim's own words to his brother in law Thomas, he Ephraim said to Thomas that he would suck sorrow thro his teeth if he remained on the place.[16]

Ties of collateral kinship established by marriage channeled the course of Ephraim's counsel about working arrangements. Nevertheless, the recency of shared work experiences with in-laws and the intimacy characteristic of daily contact between small slaveowners and their slaves impeded Ephraim's efforts. Ex-master John Smith was not alone in regarding Ephraim as something of a newcomer. Ephraim's brother-in-law Thomas rejected for the moment Ephraim's advice to seek better terms elsewhere, telling him "that he had lived on the place longer than he (Ephraim) had and was willing to try it for the year." Having for the moment chosen his ties to Smith's place over his brother-in-law's counsel,

15.   William Stone to L. Walker, 20 April 1868, vol. 88, pp. 116–17, Letters Sent, ser. 3052, Aiken, Subordinate Field Office Records, RG 105.
16.   John A. Smith to L. B. Meunard, 7 Feb. 1866, vol. 128, pp. 217–20, Registers of Letters Received, ser. 3155, Columbia, Subordinate Field Office Records, RG 105.

Thomas also armed Smith's son Whiteford with advance notice that Ephraim intended to leave.[17] Thomas's doubts illustrate that acknowledgment of common kin was not sufficient to generate consciousness of common interests.[18] The reconstitution of families remained a somewhat unpredictable basis for organizing collective action beyond the immediate family.

Where the labor of children was at issue, familial interests spoke with unaccustomed, albeit precarious, authority. Mothers and fathers only gradually retrieved parental discipline from the plantation discipline that slavery had vested in the master.[19] The freed father Moses Scott acceded to the demands of his employer, Jackson Dooly, that Scott's fifteen- and seventeen-year-old sons, whom Dooly also employed, be punished for "some alleged improper conduct on [Dooly's] plantation." Knowing that a day earlier the farmer had "struck and kicked one of the boys," Scott determined that on this occasion he would whip his sons himself. Nevertheless, as Scott delivered the first blows, Dooly, "declaring that the father was not whipping them properly, snatched a hickory out of his hand," and "proceeded to beat them very severely." Although the father's mode of correction had borne more than a trace of the old plantation discipline, he nevertheless protested his employer's intervention to the Freedmen's Bureau agent in Abbeville.[20] Corporal punishment was to be a family affair.

Ex-slaves' elaboration of spheres of familial, marital, and parental prerogative opened a direct contest over the power relations implicit in daily work routines. Matthew Gray appealed to the chief officer of the state Freedmen's Bureau when, by simply renting a cabin, the ex-slave couple Coleman and Amy Circuit found their parental authority brought within the reach of plantation discipline. According to Gray, the Circuits had rented a house from Newberry landowner John G. Lipford but "they was not employed to him," since Circuit, a blacksmith, "worked about thought [throughout] the day and came home at night." The couple objected when they learned that Lipford's overseer had given their eleven-year-old son fifty lashes after having "ordered this womans Child to assist in doing some work which they boy refuse to do being as his mother Left him in the Charge of the house" while she carried her husband dinner. In

17. Ibid.
18. Mintz, "Rural Proletariat," and Hahn, *Roots of Southern Populism,* suggestively explore the social contexts in which kinship mediated class consciousness among rural workers and landowners.
19. Rose, "Domestication of Domestic Slavery," and "Childhood in Bondage," in Rose, *Slavery and Freedom,* pp. 18–36, 37–48.
20. W. F. DeKnight to Bvt. Maj. H. Neide, 3 July 1868, vol. 98, p. 481, Press Copies of Letters Sent, ser. 3025, Abbeville, Subordinate Field Office Records, RG 105.

the midst of the dispute that ensued, Lipford denied that his overseer had transgressed, swearing, "Do you suppose I'll have a man on my place unless he does as I say. . . . by God! if I have a man on my place he has got to do as I say if I tell him to kill a man." The landowner's oath became near prophecy when Amy Circuit was fatally wounded as she fought to wrest the gun away from the overseer.[21] Freed families intruded long-suppressed claims of kinship into the domain of power that masters had described as "my family white and black."[22]

Conditions of slaveholding in South Carolina's lower Piedmont had permitted regular association and intermittent contact among slaves who did not share a common owner or a common residence. Even small holdings of slaves in this region tended to be large by the standards of other states.[23] Typically owning close to ten slaves, the region's yeoman slaveowner, when pressed to supplement his labor force at seasons of peak agricultural activity, exchanged or occasionally hired other slaves from a neighbor (who was often a kinsman), but did not regularly resort to the seasonal services of free workers.[24] Hence, save for their erratic interactions with other slaves, slaves of small and middling owners typically endured intrusive contact with an owner who was present even when they were at work. Common surnames offer striking, if scarcely conclusive, testimony to the depth of character of the small slaveowner's imprint on slave life: Luke Rogers dashed a plank across the face of his former slave Carolina Rogers because she would not make her daughter keep pace with them in the field; J. H. Telford probably wrote the letter in which the freedman Jessie Telford appealed for bureau assistance to "bring [his wife Mary] to her senses" when she quit Telford's place after her husband struck her; the slave Allan Quick lived on the place of his owner Trustin

21. Matthew Gray to Robert K. Scott, 12 March 1868, vol. 98, p. 481, Press Copies of Letters Sent, ser. 3025, Abbeville, Subordinate Field Office Records, RG 105.

22. Quoted in Fox-Genovese, *Within the Plantation Household,* p. 101, which insightfully explores the fundamental limits that the power relations of antebellum slavery posed to slaves' family life.

23. Fields, *Slavery and Freedom,* examines the significance of small slaveholdings for slave community life and the course of emancipation.

24. For instances in which smaller slaveowners obtained the services of a kinsman's slaves, see David Golightly Harris Farm Journals, 8 Oct. 1860, UNC; Thomas B. Chaplin Journal, 29 Jan., 23 March 1852, SCHS. State districts in which the most frequent slaveholding was a unit of between ten and fifteen slaves include Abbeville, Edgefield, Fairfield, Laurens, and Newberry districts, five of the seven districts of the lower Piedmont. See U.S. Bureau of the Census, Eighth Census, *Agriculture,* p. 237; Ford, *Origins of Southern Radicalism,* pp. 46–47. Calculations from 1860 manuscript census returns showed that owners of fewer than twenty slaves in Laurens, Orangeburg, Colleton, and Georgetown districts held an average of six to seven slaves. U. S. Bureau of the Census, Eighth Census, population schedules for Laurens, Orangeburg, Colleton, and Georgetown districts.

Quick three miles away from his wife and ten children, who were owned by Benjamin Quick.[25]

At times, slave communities on smaller places bore the features of this resident ownership in a most literal sense. As a result, freedpeople occasionally appealed to ties of kinship with white landowners formed during slavery in attempts to ward off objectionable working arrangements. Women with young children and bereft of acknowledged ties to other freedpeople were perhaps most likely to resort to such measures. The course pursued by the freed woman in Richland district who called herself Eliza Cloud (though her former owner F. D. Cloud insisted "Delilah is her name") is illustrative. In July 1867, Eliza, mother of at least four children, lacked food to last the summer when her employer, who was also her former owner, proposed that she sign an agreement "to make [her children] work faithfully from this time forth or pay the propieter fifty cents for every day their [*sic*] fail to do so." She sought help from her employer's brother, Austin Cloud, who by F. D. Cloud's admission was "the Father of four" of Eliza's children. According to F. D. Cloud, his authority crumbled when his brother Austin "backed [Eliza] and offered to supply her with provisions":

> [T]his made mother and children very inslent to me   I saw it would
> be impossible for me to get along with them so I went to see Austin
> I mentioned the matter before his wife   I found she was ingnorant
> [*sic*] of the matter   this caused a row between them and put Austin
> in a rage with me   he swore that he would make Delilah [i.e., Eliza]
> sue me[26]

Unlike the freedwoman Eliza, most freedpeople customarily tapped their kinship to other ex-slaves in order to forge resistance to postwar work arrangements, reaching for a shield that had once held somewhat at bay the intrusive intimacy of daily contact with a resident master.

Emancipation thus heightened the protopolitical implications of slaves' kinship. Moves to concentrate once-scattered kin on a single place reversed the tendency to disperse kinship networks across different properties that had been a key feature of slave life where small holdings

25. Affidavit, Carolina Rogers, 9 Nov. 1865, M 869, r 20, 0393; "Jesse Telford (freedman)" to Maj. Wm. Stone, 10 April 1866, Unregistered Letters Received, ser. 3067, Anderson, Subordinate Field Office Records, RG 105 [A-7223]; Testimony of Allan Quick, 22 May 1876, claim of Allan Quick, Marlboro County SC case files, Approved Claims, ser. 732, Southern Claims Commission, 3d Auditor, RG 217 [I-82]; Affidavit, Wade Adams, 18 Sept. 1865, M 869, r 20, 0004; J. N. Carpenter et al. to Officer in Charge, 21 Aug. 1866, Unregistered letters Received, ser. 3067, Anderson, Subordinate Field Office Records, RG 105.

26. F. D. Cloud to Wm. J. Haikirheimer [*sic*], 17 July 1867, Letters Received, ser. 3156, Columbia, Subordinate Field Office Records, RG 105.

predominated.[27] Reconstituted families served as the chief bargaining units in establishing work arrangements with employers; relatives accompanied each other to bureau offices to demand redress, or carried complaints on a relative's behalf.[28] Even before employers' lands were subdivided for cultivation by working households, groups of freedpeople working on smaller places were increasingly associated by kinship.[29]

The reconstitution of family households was a precondition for the establishment of a household economy through whose development ex-slaves pursued economic independence. Their ambition to produce for their households proved antagonistic to their employers' claims on family labor under the free labor reconstruction of agricultural work. This contest between work for an employer and work for the household gave underlying unity at an at-times bewildering variety of postwar labor arrangements.

Control of the Crop

The written planting agreements compiled and recorded between 1865 and 1868 by bureau agents, army officers assigned to bureau service, and the latter's civilian appointees almost defy ready categorization. An attempt to sort the approved labor contracts in Orangeburg district merely according to their terms of compensation pressed the area's subdistrict commander to the point of grammatical innovation. After reviewing the contracts that had been filed in his office by early January 1866, E. A. Kozlay reported to his district commander, "I find great ununiformity."[30] From his survey at the onset of the 1866 agricultural year, Kozlay judged that agreements that promised compensation in fractional shares of har-

27.   Gutman, *Black Family*, pp. 135–43; Fields, *Middle Ground*, pp. 25–27.
28.   Wm. Stone to L. Walker, 27 Dec. 1866, Narrative Reports of Operations, ser. 3043, Aiken, Subordinate Field Office Records, RG 105; H. G. Judd to Major [S. W. Saxton], 16 Sept. 1865, M 869, r 20, 0214; W. T. Lesesne to D. E. Sickles, 28 June 1867, M 869, r 14; G. Lephard to Wm. J. Harkisheimer, 10 June 1868, Letters Received, ser. 3156, Columbia, Subordinate Field Office Records, RG 105; J. E. Lewis to Capt. Geo. E. Pingree, 21 Dec. 1867, M 869, r 13; R. H. Clarkson to Wm. J. Harkisheimer, 17 Jan. 1867, Letters Received, ser. 3156, Columbia, Subordinate Field Office Records, RG 105.
29.   Ford, "Rednecks and Merchants," 304n, found in his sample of upcountry labor contracts "only one contract . . . that could be interpreted as a squad contract." From an analysis of a larger sample, Jaynes, *Branches Without Roots,* pp. 172–90, similarly concludes that "the collective contract and squad organization of the labor force was mainly a plantation phenomenon." See also Shlomowitz, "Origins of Southern Sharecropping." Kinship probably also underlay the "squads" that work groups on larger places formed.
30.   Col. E. A. Kozlay to Lt. M. N. Rice, 5 Jan. 1866, Letters and Reports Received Relating to Freedmen and Civil Affairs, ser. 4112, 2d Military District, RG 393 Pt. 1.

vested crops tended to predominate in his district. He nevertheless noted that such share agreements existed alongside contracts that arranged for postharvest compensation in combinations of money and produce, whereas other agreements promised workers a monthly cash wage. The diversity persuaded him that "an uniform system is an impossibility; it has to be regulated according to circumstance, and sometimes to the gratification of both contracting parties."[31]

The variety in compensation that Kozlay reported was not peculiar to Orangeburg district. Varying shares of harvested crops seem to have been the most frequent form of wage payment represented in bureau contracts.[32] To the proffered shares of harvested crops, interior and up-country contracts at times added articles of clothing or a small cash bonus, whereas coastal agreements included provisions for the rent-free cultivation of a portion of the plantation's arable lands. Money wages were most common on the sea islands around Charleston and Port Royal, and on scattered large rice and cotton estates on the coast and in the interior, where wartime purchases, early postwar leasing agreements, or occasional loans made it possible for landowners and lessees to jingle ready cash as a boon of free labor.[33] At the outset, the diversity of such written agreements reflected the outcomes of immediate, on-the-spot bargaining shaped by the want of cash among all but the largest landowners or most recent northern immigrants; this diversity was also the result of the course of wartime military operations and the social organization of slave communities.

To catalog labor contracts – even by more refined attention to their proposed terms of labor organization and provisions for nonmonetary awards such as rations, medical care, or fuel – is not to establish their significance.[34] Postwar contracts gain fullest significance chiefly by discovering the sequence in which particular work arrangements developed, and when we examine the political and social contests associated with the emergence of different work arrangements, thereby reconstructing the historical experiences of parties whose separate interests the contracts attempted to join.

31. E. A. Kozlay to H. W. Smith, 29 Jan. 1866, M 869, r #34, 0406–14; the quotation appears in Kozlay to Lt. M. N. Rice, 5 Jan. 1866, Letters and Reports Received Relating to Freedmen and Civil Affairs, ser. 4112, 2d Military District, RG 393 Pt. 1.
32. Jaynes, *Branches Without Roots,* pp. 48, 50–53, 142, judges that South Carolina's postwar labor arrangements represented "probably the most extensive adoption of share payments in the South." Cf. Ransom and Sutch, *One Kind of Freedom,* pp. 57–61.
33. The characterization of postwar contractual arrangements is based on a survey of up-country labor contracts in the subordinate field office records of Abbeville, Aiken, Anderson, and Barnwell districts in RG 105. A discussion of wartime labor arrangements in Port Royal appears in this volume, Chapter 2.
34. Shlomowitz, "Origins of Southern Sharecropping," especially pp. 561–64.

From an apparent diversity in forms of compensation, employers nevertheless fashioned wage relationships fairly uniform in character.[35] Wedded to both in-kind and cash wages in the immediate postwar period were terms of work that expressed an explicitly hierarchical relationship between labor and capital. "It is a fixed fact," opined a Northern planter on St. Helena Island in October 1865, "that Capital must Control labor."[36] Landowners premised their earliest free labor reconstruction of agricultural routine on this hierarchy. Through overseers and drivers or close supervision by resident owners, with occasional reinforcement from military personnel, landowners claimed the right exclusively to direct planting operations.

Rights claimed by management varied little on the basis of the compensation proffered. Although wartime cotton planters in Port Royal had touted regular, moderate cash payments as an important goad to wage labor,[37] the timing of postwar cash payments more and more resembled the delayed settlements that evolved in share wages. Postwar proponents of cash wages increasingly stipulated that pay for daily work be delayed – chiefly by retaining a portion of weekly or monthly wages until the end of the year. The change is illustrated by modifications in Assistant Commissioner Robert K. Scott's endorsements of cash wages. In 1866, Scott endorsed daily, weekly, or monthly wage payments as "the labor system of the agricultural districts of the North and West."[38] Two years later, on the eve of his election as the state's first Republican governor, Scott issued a circular that expressed his "unqualified approval of the system of paying wages in money, . . . giving preference to payments at the end of the year as the plan best calculated to insure the laborer a portion of his pay at the termination of his contract, and it also gives the planter opportunity to at once discharge an idle or disaffected employee upon payment of wages due to date of discharge."[39] Delay in compensation, reliance on workers' advances of labor as one of the sources of credit for planting operations, and provisions for close inspection and supervision of work by employers' managerial agents (which some writers have variously attrib-

35. For analysis of the evolution of sharecropping arrangements and the social transformations that underlay their emergence, see essays by Thavolia Glymph, Harold D. Woodman, and Barbara Jeanne Fields in Glymph and Kushma, eds., *Postbellum Southern Economy*; Hahn, *Roots of Southern Populism*; Woodman, "Post–Civil War Southern Agriculture"; idem, "Postbellum Social Change"; idem, "Sequel to Slavery"; and Fields, "Nineteenth-Century American South."

36. H. L. Tafft to Colonel [Clitz], 19 Oct. 1865, Letters Received, ser. 4109, Department of South Carolina, RG 393 Pt 1 [C-1361].

37. See Chapter 2.

38. [Circular letter], Robert K. Scott, 1866, SCL.

39. [Circular letter], Robert K. Scott, 1 Jan. 1868, SCL. See also *United States* v. *Joseph W. Seabrook and Others,* 5 Nov. 1866, Case # 5, Provost Court Records, ser. 4257-A, Department of the South, RG 393 Pt 1 [C-1525]; E. W. Everson to Bvt. Maj. Horace Neide, 13 Nov. 1868, M 869, r 16.

uted either to money wages or to share wages), seem to have been features of both arrangements.[40] Whether landowners promised compensation in cash or in kind, they envisioned a scheme of centralized management by which workers could be obligated to perform a full range of general chores, both in-crop and out, as features of a wage relationship.[41]

Freedpeople's understanding of the social relations implicit in wage agreements acknowledged no such subordination in the organization of agricultural routine. Rejecting the supervision that landowners claimed as a prerogative of management, emancipated workers expected to organize agricultural production directly. In response to declarations that the harvested crop embodied the sole value to which they could assert a claim, rural laborers refused to perform any service unrelated to the crop that they had been hired to cultivate without additional compensation.

To a limited extent, ex-slaves drew upon antebellum circumstances to devise their new work routines. They attempted at the outset to establish as common features of free labor what had been seasonal or conditional privileges under slavery. Saturday, the day that had been most consistently awarded to all slaves in slack seasons, and a portion of which had been frequently turned over to many slaves except at harvest time, was reclaimed for the household. Where trading off the plantation had once been delegated to the most mobile members of the plantation community such as artisans, boatmen, or drivers, most households now tried to market some articles of local consumption directly.[42]

In contrast to slaves, however, freedpeople did not propose to produce supplements to subsistence by overwork. Complaints that workers arrived in the fields well past sunrise or periodically absented themselves from assigned daytime chores suggest that many now claimed for daytime activity the labors that field workers under gang labor had once performed chiefly after sundown. Some simply took a morning meal before beginning the day's work. Workers also often quit the fields at the same

40. Fields, "Advent of Capitalist Agriculture," in Glymph and Kushma, eds., *Postbellum Southern Economy*, especially pp. 86–89, draws attention to how sharecropping arrangements extracted advances of labor from share workers and appropriated the value of draft animals and tools from tenants. See also Jaynes, *Branches Without Roots*, p. 53. Cf. Ransom and Sutch, *One Kind of Freedom*, pp. 56–61 and idem, "Sharecropping."

41. In addition to the studies cited in this chapter, notes 35 and 40, see Ford, "Labor and Ideology."

42. [P?] Townsend to H. L. Shields, 13 Feb. 1866, enclosed in wrapper labeled Agriculture Department of, 11 April 1866, M 752, r 26, 0168–82; A. L. M. Crawford to Bvt. Col. B. F. Faust, 11 April 1866, M 869, r 9; E. T. Wright to Lt. Col. H. B. Clitz, 6 Oct. 1865, Letters Received, ser. 4109, Department of South Carolina, RG 393 Pt 1 [C-1361]; Wm. H. H. Holton to Harkisheimer, 26 Nov. 1867, Letters Received, ser. 3156, Columbia, Subordinate Field Office Records, RG 105; Lt. W. M. Wallace to Bvt. Maj. E. W. Read, 8 Jan. 1867, Letters Received, ser. 2273, Department of the South, RG 393 Pt 2 No 132 [C-1619].

time, suggesting that all now claimed a time for household production that had been arbitered by strength under the task organization of slaves' field labor.[43] In brief, freedpeople accepted neither money nor share wages as precluding their control of production.

Driven forward by freedpeople's persistent and open assertions of their right to work when, how and for whom they pleased, employers justified what was perhaps the most extreme subordination of hired workers that American employers would openly endorse for two decades. Landowners rejected ex-slaves' bids to become "partners" in production,[44] insisting that to recognize such claims would be to grant freedpeople effective proprietorship of their lands. In December 1866, the pseudonymous correspondent "Fairfield" pointedly explained to the governor that formal control of workers was inherent in the wage relationship:

> The hiring of the negro as a partner in the crop will in the end impoverish any farm and ruin the owner of the soil. They manifest no desire to do any work on the plantation, except to plant cultivate and harvest the crops, notwithstanding the contract may bind them to do everything necessary to keep the plantation in a thorough state of repair and advance the interest of the employer. They should by all means be hired for wages – *so much per month payable at the end of the year*, thereby keeping them from being partners in the crop or working of the lands on their "own hook". We could then make them labor all the year and perform any kind of work necessary for the care and preservation of the plantation.[45]

To gain the control that "Fairfield" envisioned, landowners would require more than his peculiar mode of compensation, in which employers calculated wages monthly and paid workers yearly, presumably from the proceeds of the marketed crop. Impeding the course at every turn were ex-slaves' efforts to establish share wages as a form of tenancy and to hold money wages to regular, immediate, and higher returns. Their contests renewed agitation over the control of productive property.

Landed employers and freedpeople struggled to define laborers' legitimate claims at a time when the physical climate was as brittle as the social setting. Local crop failures in 1865, 1866, and 1867 – generated by Confederate levies on men, stock and produce, and compounded by

43. Ralph Izard Middleton to General [E. R. S. Canby], Dec. 1867, Letters Received, ser. 4111, 2d Military District, Department of the South, RG 393 Pt 1 [SS-73]; J. G. McKim to Gen. Runkle, 6 Aug. 1866, Letters Received, ser. 3156, Columbia, Subordinate Field Office Records, RG 105; Edward Philbrick to AFIC, 17 Aug. 1863, Letters Received by the Adjutant General's Office, 1861–70, M 619, r 200, 0416–27; John Hair, 9 Feb. 1866, vol. 128, Registers of Letters Received, ser. 3155, Columbia, Subordinate Field Office Records, RG 105.

44. Glymph, "Freedpeople and Ex-Masters," in Glymph and Kushma, eds., *Postbellum Southern Economy*, pp. 53–54.

45. "Fairfield" to James L. Orr, 14 Dec. 1866, Governors' Papers, SCDAH. Italics added.

wartime destruction from military campaigns that spared only the most westerly Piedmont districts – lent the situation unwonted harshness as South Carolina's landowners and former slaves struggled for social advantage. In the aftermath, sharecropping began to emerge in interior and up-country cotton districts, whereas labor rents began to evolve in low-country cotton and rice districts. Both arrangements incorporated forms of the household organization of agricultural production once associated with antebellum tenancy. However, work on shares and labor rents were fundamentally wage relationships stripped of the essence of antebellum rental arrangements.[46]

Customary practices by which slaves had produced a marketable surplus for local consumption became an early focus of landowners' and freedpeople's struggles to define the meaning of emancipation. Owners of men had gained advantages from the direct production of a surplus above subsistence that mere lords of acres could not extract. Landowners in Barnwell and Orangeburg districts reportedly excluded "corn, beans, potatoes and other produce used for feeding the laborers" from ex-slaves' 1865 shares.[47] Although the commander at Orangeburg overruled such contractual provisions, other officers countenanced centralized storage and rationing of workers' daily necessities. The post commander in Pickens district, according to his successor, ordered employers to deliver freedpeople's "produce" to his headquarters in December 1865 and then used the supplies to relieve destitution in the area:

> The Freed people whose corn and other provisions had been delivered here to Capt. Bray come to get their hard [ear]nings of the past year   Capt Bray made a speech to them, and told them that he would have to keep a portion of their corn to give to those who had none.[48]

46.   In addition to the studies cited in this chapter, notes 35, 40, and 41, see Reidy, *Slavery to Agrarian Capitalism*; Roark, *Masters Without Slaves*, pp. 172–73; Foner, *Nothing But Freedom*; Weiner, *Social Origins of the New South*, pp. 35–73, 93–96; and preeminently, Woodward, *Origins of the New South*, especially pp. 175–234.

47.   Gavin Wright, *Old South, New South*, pp. 18–19, emphasizes the changed postwar circumstances of the Old South's "laborlords." Bvt. Maj. Gen. Chas. Devens to Bvt. Lt. Col. W. L. M. Burger, 23,29 Oct. 1865, both in Letters Received, ser. 4109, Department of the South, RG 393 Pt 1 [C-1361]; Lt. Col. F. H. Whittier to Lt. [Chas.] Fillebrown, 4 Oct. 1865, Letters and Reports Received Relating to Freedmen and Civil Affairs, ser. 4112, 2d Military District, RG 393 Pt 1 [C-1440]. See also Testimony of Rufus Saxton, *Report of the Joint Committee on Reconstruction*, Part 2, p. 222, where Saxton interprets reports that planters in Barnwell district were withholding produce, to refer only to cotton.

48.   Chas. W. Ferguson, 11 April 1866, vol. 128, Registers of Letters Received, ser. 3155, Columbia, Subordinate Field Office Records, RG 105. The effects of Bray's policy may well have been evident in the report from Pickens district in May 1866 that "want appears to be general among all but extensive land holders." See Henry A. Shorey to E. A. Lowe, 12 May 1866, M 752, r 31, 0379–82.

Bray's selective levies to relieve distress in the upper Piedmont enforced the peculiar dictum, "Pauvresse oblige."

In the central cotton region of eastern South Carolina, which had been planted largely corn in 1865, the commander at Darlington supplied his department commander with an explicit lesson about the potential dangers of the independence conferred upon the former slave who received at once "the means of sustenance for himself and family for the Ensuing year":

> What guarantee has his Employer that he will so employ it, or that they will not become a charge upon him, and Eventually upon the state. Would it not be advisable to have the laborers share of the crop deposited in a specified place, where under charge of one of their own number, or some competent party, it could be delivered as required for their needs, at least until their ability and desire to hoard their earnings and provide for themselves, manifests itself. There would in addition be some inducement for the laborer to remain with his Employer, whereas if his entire share should be delivered to him, the probabilities are, he is taken advantage of by some of the numerous sharpers and unprincipled men enfesting [*sic*] the country.[49]

The relationship that his subordinate established between labor discipline and the availability of daily necessities impressed the district commander. In October 1865, he recommended that officers assigned to duty in his command of the Military District of Eastern South Carolina not divide harvests before January in order "to keep the Freedman true to his agreement until the close of the term."[50] Military supervision helped ensure that in the eastern districts of South Carolina, emancipation transferred no immediate "share of output" from former masters to former slaves.[51]

On some plantations, previously unmonitored phases of the distribution of food crops were brought under supervision. On the cotton plantation of C. Y. Davis in Beaufort district, it seems that people had at one time gathered ripened ears of corn from the fields as required for their allowance. A visit from the local post commander investigating Davis's complaint of idleness in September 1865 secured from the driver the re-

49. J. P. S. Gobin to Maj. Gen. Gillmore, 9 Aug. 1865, enclosed in wrapper labeled South Carolina Department of, 15 Aug. 1865, M 752, r 17, 0124–30; Lt. Col. F H. Whittier to Lt. Fillebrown, 19 Sept. 1865, Letters and Reports Received Relating to Freedmen and Civil Affairs, ser. 4112, 2d Military District, RG 393 Pt 1 [C-1440]; Bvt. Brig. Genl. W. P. Richardson to Bvt. Lt. Col. W. L. M. Burger, 26 Nov. 1865, Letters and Reports Received Relating to Freedmen and Civil Affairs, ser. 4112, 2d Military District, RG 393 Pt 1 [C-1506].

50. George L. Beal to W. L. M. Burger, 9 Oct. 1865, Letters and Reports Received Relating to Freedmen and Civil Affairs, ser. 4112, 2d Military District, RG 393 Pt 1.

51. Cf. Ransom and Sutch, *One Kind of Freedom*, pp. 3–5.

port that "the people never worked better," and that "as to breaking corn there has been no corn been broken only that for their allowance just as they always have done." Nevertheless, the officer extracted a pledge that the people would not break corn "untill the foreman came so as to see that all was right."[52]

Planters' determination to store ex-slaves' shares of provision crops constituted more than an attempt to establish a form of the allowance system under military oversight. Viewed within the context of antebellum productive relations, centralized housing of some food crops had the mark of a reactionary toppling of slaves' customary rights. Landowners now stood to gain outright many crops that slaveowners had customarily acquired in exchange for domestic articles such as soap, tobacco, molasses, coffee, and occasionally, buttons, needles, or pieces of flatware, which slaves did not produce. From the ex-slaves' vantage, the new terms more resembled expropriation than remuneration.

Freedpeople countered the erosion of customary rights to defunct privileges by raising the standard of a new right conferred by share contracts. Insistently, wherever share contracts appeared, ex-slaves demanded to supervise the cultivation, processing, and marketing of their shares of the plantation staple.[53] Planters' pleas that the demand was tantamount to a claim against their rights of property seem apt. Unlike food crops, antebellum commercial staples had been only rarely included within the network of internal exchanges accepted by the masters. Some large cotton planters had, on occasion, designated a particular tract of land whose entire crop was to be sold on behalf of slaves, who then distributed the proceeds among themselves.[54] Generally, however, no precedent in the master–slave relationship nourished freedpeople's demand for "control of the crop."

Their claim had its most immediate origins in emancipation's betrayal of slaves' labor theory of value, and was their maxim from the bitter lesson that emancipation would be landless. A pardoned Combahee rice

52. Capt. C[aleb] B. White to Lt. S. Baker, 29 Sept. 1865, Letters Received, ser. 2384, RG 393 Pt 2 No 141 [C-1591].

53. Wm. H. H. Holton to Harkisheimer, 26 Nov. 1867, Letters Received, ser. 3156, Columbia, Subordinate Field Office Records, RG 105; B. G. Smith to Bvt. Maj. H. W. Smith, 21 Jan. 1866, M 869, r 11; Glymph, "Freedpeople and Ex-Masters." Jaynes, *Branches Without Roots,* pp. 149–57, argues that freedpeople achieved "a remarkable success" in securing possession of crops.

54. Testimony of Sam'l B. Smith, Esq. before the AFIC, 19 Nov. 1863, Letters Received, ser. 12, RG 94 [K-90]. The important work of Campbell, "'A Kind of Freeman?'" in Berlin and Morgan, eds., *Cultivation and Culture,* pp. 243–74, documents the emergence of slaves' independent production of short-staple cotton in South Carolina and the simultaneous erosion of their marketing privileges. See also the pathbreaking investigations of Reidy, "Obligation and Right" pp. 138–54, and Miller, "Plantation Labor Organization," pp. 155–69, ibid.

planter established the connection between landlessness and control of the crop when a former slave stated the precept on which his claim to the plantation lands rested. "The other day," planter Edward Barnwell Heyward informed his wife in May 1867, "a negro told me that the land ought to belong to the man who (alone) *could work it*. That I couldn't do more than sit in the house and lay my foot on the table and write on the paper, &c." Congressional action on confiscation being somewhat unresolved that spring, Heyward anticipated his most immediate worry. "Now if the land," he deduced, "why not the *present crop*."[55] "Control of the crop" admitted challenges to proprietorship through the back door that earlier declarations of the unreality of confiscation had driven from the front gate.

Gaining immediate possession of the harvested crop formed the core of ex-slaves' attempts to establish share wages as a form of tenancy. In the most strict formulation of the demand, freedpeople urged that the cotton harvest be divided daily, as the bolls were plucked.[56] By insisting on daily divisions, they attempted to ensure that landowners' and laborers' shares included both the best and the worst of the season's pickings. Although no instance where this procedure was observed has been discovered, a Freedmen's Bureau agent in Berkeley district thought to achieve a similar end by dividing cotton only after the entire crop had been ginned. "[I]f *not all the cotton is ginned prior* to its *division*," the agent reasoned in June 1866, "very few planters *will gin out* their *best* cotton for the freedman's share and retain for themselves the cotton of lower quality."[57] Notwithstanding the agent's unusual attempt to preserve a qualitative equality in the shares, his scheme postponed settlements five months beyond the mid-August date when cotton picking generally began. Not until the first of January, when he expected ginning to be completed, would he divide laborers' shares. Freedpeople had not proposed to sacrifice immediate possession in order to create shares identical in quality.

Rights of storage were inseparable from the most stringent insistence for control of the crop. More than fifty people, who identified themselves simply as "The Colored People of Edisto," spelled out for the benefit of the bureau's assistant commissioner, Robert K. Scott, why they objected to housing their shares of the 1866 cotton crop "in buildings furnished by

55. Edward Barnwell Heyward to Tat, 5 May 1867, Edward Barnwell Heyward Papers, SCL; Jaynes, *Branches Without Roots,* pp. 282–84, where the author perhaps too strongly insists that freedpeople's "notion of property was private."

56. Summary of reports from the subdistrict of Edisto in H. W. Smith to O. O. Howard, 6 Aug. 1866, M 752, r 39, 0329–45.

57. Summary of reports from the subdistricts of St. James, Goose Creek, St. Johns Berkeley, and St. Stephens, in R. K. Scott to O. O. Howard, 20 June 1866, M 752, r 35, 0518–31.

the landowner, who are authorized to put it under *lock* and *key* until all the crop be gathered in":

> [T]his is *no part* of *any* of our *contracts*; and the unfairness of the [bureau] order may be plainly seen by the following illustrations. A man wishes to procure necessary clothing or provision for his destitute family. He has no money or means to procure them unless he sell a portion of *his* share of cotton. But this he can not do, for it is under lock and consequently his family must suffer until the whole crop is collected which may take months. . . . Most honorable Sir, we consider when we have divided our cotton, we are as capable of taking care of our own part *as well*, if not *better* than our *foes*.[58]

When, like "The Colored People of Edisto," freedpeople farmed designated household-sized tracts of their employers' lands, they stored the picked cotton in their cabins and insisted on their right to pay rent plus any outstanding debts to their landlords rather than to receive their wages from their landlords after the crops had been sold. An Abbeville freed couple, though hired by landowner John C. Childs for money wages in 1867, had nevertheless stored the harvested crop in their cabin. Childs decided to dismiss the husband Henry in November after the laborer had defended his intermittent absences by insisting "that he would go when he wanted to and come when he wanted to and ask no one any odds." Childs learned from his brother, who kept the books, that the dismissed man "had gone above his wages" and that a doctor whom the farmer had promised pay had attended Henry's wife. He then decided "to secure some cotton Henry had in his house" during the family's absence one night. No sooner did Childs draw the staple from the cabin door than Henry's returning wife "came chargeing and saying if she had been there I would not have gone into that house unless I did it over her corpse." To the bureau officer who investigated the couple's complaint, Childs pointedly justified his seizure: "I considered the cotton mine made on my own land plowed by my own mules and was only taking it at a fair price to satisfy a debt I was responsible for."[59]

Freedpeople's demand to control the harvested crop did not surmount the power of claims rooted in the ownership of productive property, but it did alter the means by which claims of proprietorship were defended. Landowners tried to forestall demands for immediate possession of the crop through contractual agreements that brought storage, processing, and marketing under their jurisdiction. In 1867, contracts began to require that workers deliver their shares to employers' ginhouses, that they

---

58. The Colored People of Edisto to O. O. Howard, 2 Oct. 1866, M 752, r 36, 0404–09.
59. Jno. C. Childs to Maj. C. S. Allen, 6 Nov. 1867, Letters Received, ser. 3028, Abbeville, Subordinate Field Office Records, RG 105.

accept a marketing agent selected by the employer, and that they accept a share of the proceeds from the sale of the crop rather than a share of the actual crop.[60]

Freedmen's Bureau policy perhaps unwittingly bolstered landowners' ultimately successful bid to sever legal possession of the crop from laborers' entitlements. Under the bureau's enforcement of a laborer's lien, claims for wages took precedence over those for rent or to satisfy advances of food and agricultural supplies. The bureau measure thus overturned the 1866 legislative provision that, in according crop liens statutory recognition, had granted landlords' claims for rent, and merchants' claims for loans for agricultural purposes, prior standing to workers' claims for wages.[61] However, bureau enforcement of the laborer's lien most strongly defended workers' prior access to the proceeds of a marketed crop, not immediate possession of a harvested one. Agents supervised divisions of the crop no earlier than November, and settlements of claims often lasted well into the following spring. During the interval, processing, storage, and marketing of the harvested crop were excluded from laborers' independent management. In effect, bureau agents ensured that laborers secured first claim to a postharvest wage already consumed by indebtedness when accounts were settled.[62]

The bureau's implicit rejection of laborers' right to any interest in the crop apart from wages was made explicit by the first Republican legislature. In March 1869, the legislature enacted a laborer's lien that signaled a fundamental distinction between the status of laborers and tenants. Tenants alone were vested with legal interest in a crop that would permit

60. See, for example, the contract between Larkin Barmore and Sam, Jan. 1867, Labor Contracts, ser. 3037, Abbeville, Subordinate Field Office Records, RG 105; *Aaron et al.* v. *H. H. Easterby*, 13 Sept. 1866, Letters Received, ser. 3053, Aiken, Subordinate Field Office Records, RG 105; Agreement, Thomas B. Ellis and Sam Murry [8 Feb. 1876], Ellis Family Papers, SCL.
61. *SC Statutes*, 1866, p. 380; Ford, "Rednecks and Merchants," 307–08.
62. Capt. Woodbury C. Smith to B. F. Smith, 20 April 1866, M 869, r 11; summary of reports for subdistricts of Charleston and Lawtonville, in R. K. Scott to O. O. Howard, 23 Jan. 1867, M 752, r 44, 0177–97; summary of reports from subdistrict of Darlington, R. K. Scott to O. O. Howard, 20 July 1867, M 752, r 48, 0449–66; summary of reports from subdistrict of Charleston, R. K. Scott to O. O. Howard, 25 Sept. 1867, M 752, r 51, 0055–68; summary of reports from subdistrict of Columbia, R. K. Scott to O. O. Howard, 20 Dec. 1867, M 752, r 51, 0443–55; Bvt. Lt. Col. L. R. Bliss to Bvt. Lieut. Col. H. W. Smith, 3 July 1866, Letters and Reports Received Relating to Freedmen and Civil Affairs, ser. 4112, 2d Military District, RG 393 Pt 1 [C-1430]; W. W. White to Gen. Green, 15 Dec. 1866, Letters Received, ser. 3156, Columbia, Subordinate Field Office Records, RG 105; O. H. Hart to Maj. L. Walker, 14 March 1868, Press Copies of Letters Sent, vol. 98, p. 347, ser. 3025, Abbeville, Subordinate Field Office Records, RG 105. Cf. Jaynes, *Branches Without Roots,* pp. 149–55; Foner, *Nothing But Freedom,* pp. 60–61.

them to secure credit and make marketing arrangements independent of a landowner's control.[63]

Ex-slaves' open bids to gain "control of the crop" became diluted even before state law impaired their efforts, however. As early as 1867, freed-people in some areas demanded possession of ginned cotton, not the unprocessed seed cotton of the harvest.[64] In other instances, former slaves succeeded in getting planters to instruct factors to remit money from crop sales directly to a fellow worker whom they themselves selected.[65] Notwithstanding the increasing degree of local organization that the latter arrangement suggests, "control of the crop" had either been displaced to a point in time remote from the harvest or had become attached to crop sales rather than to the crop itself.

Efforts to control the crop survived in the form of embezzlements, which clandestinely sustained the immediate possession that laborers had once declared their right. In September 1868, when Frank Green and Plenty Grant were arrest for "stealing" cotton from the Wadmalaw Island plantation where they had contracted to work "on shares," the account of their arrest noted that the two men had initially "called for a division" at the beginning of the harvest. Their call rejected, the men made off with "a bag full of cotton" to Charleston, where they were arrested.[66] Embezzlement, by immediately securing small amounts of a harvested crop, became a tactic to limit rather than to transform share wages. When successful, laborers gained immediate possession of a small part of the crop, which they then traded for ready cash. In the end, however, their clandestine pilferage and trading became detached from collective efforts to transform share wages into tenancy arrangements that would concede laborers' right to market the crop themselves.

Control of Supplemental Plots

Concurrent with ex-slaves' demand for control over the crop were arrangements in which they gained the right to cultivate tracts of land on their own account. Under these arrangements, landowners granted plots

63. *SC Statutes,* 1869, pp. 227–29; Ford, "Rednecks and Merchants," pp. 307–08; idem, "Labor and Ideology," p. 33, where the author too hastily pronounces the postwar "furor over labor" of secondary importance to the rise of a rural bourgeoisie rooted in control of credit and agricultural advances.
64. Summary of reports from subdistrict of Columbia, R. K. Scott to O. O. Howard, 20 Dec. 1867, M 752, r 51, 0443–55; Geo. E. Pingree to Bvt. Lt. Col. H. W. Smith, 5 Nov. 1866, M 869, r 11.
65. Summary of reports from subdistrict of Columbia, R. K. Scott to O. O. Howard, 20 Dec. 1867, M 752, r 51, 0443–55.
66. Charleston *Daily Courier,* 30 Sept. 1868, p. 2, col. 2.

separate from the undivided lands that laborers worked for share or cash wages. Cultivation of supplemental plots had some semblance of antebellum precedent on low-country plantations, where slaves had cultivated at times extensive provision grounds. In interior districts, such allotments sometimes antedated emancipation; the practice may have become more widespread in response to slaves' wartime demands. A former slave who, in 1868, recalled that in Abbeville district "at the time of the surrender" he "had a patch, which I worked at night" may have described a wartime concession extracted from his owner.[67] Certainly, by the end of the war, the arrangement appeared widely in the interior. An officer whose command embraced Barnwell and Orangeburg districts in November 1865 noted that crops raised by freedpeople in these districts included "produce, on small lots, assigned to them for their benefit."[68]

Whether supplemental tracts were created from lands long set apart for separate cultivation or from lands to which distinct access had been newly granted, the existence of the arrangement during slavery was no harbinger of postwar success. Ex-slaves attempted to exploit both older plots and more recent allotments in order to produce a surplus unconstrained by evolving wage relationships. Landowners regarded supplemental tracts as incentives to labor discipline on undivided plantation lands. The postwar allocation of additional plots intensified rather than reconciled contradictions between freedpeople's organization of a household economy and the regimen of free labor.

Suggestive of the importance which ex-slaves attached to these supplemental parcels are the exacting terms and strain by which they managed to cultivate them. In order to have the use of a tract of land above one he worked together with an Orangeburg district landowner in 1867, the freedman Samuel Berg consented to let the landowner "have" his seventeen-year-old son for "three months to pay for the rent of some land wich [sic] I rented from him" and had further agreed to forgo his one-third share of the potato crop because he would plant potatoes on the additional plot.[69] The use of work animals did not always accompany such allotments, and ex-slaves struggled to share draft animals, carts, and farming implements among themselves rather than secure them from employers at the cost of incurring additional labor services.[70] In February 1867, an Abbeville freedwoman who insisted that she had been "rouged out of my

67.   Meredith Dixon to Agent, 3 Jan. 1868, Letters Received, ser. 3028, Abbeville, Subordinate Field Office Records, RG 105.
68.   Col. E. A. Kozlay to Capt. George W. Hooker, 5 Nov. 1865, Letters and Reports Received Relating to Freedmen and Civil Affairs, ser. 4112, 2d Military District, RG 393 Pt 1 [C-1449]. The officer may, of course, have referred to garden patches.
69.   Sam Berg to R. K. Scott, 16 April 1867, M 869, r 12.
70.   George W. Gile to General, 27 July 1868, M 752, r 58, 0048–54.

rites," explained to a Freedmen's Bureau agent how she and her husband came to grief during their attempt to share between two households a cow that had been jointly purchased from the woman's former owner:

> we let my son bring the cow here   my Husband told me to come here
> & live where the cow was   i done as he told me   now he has sent
> & taken the cow a way & i have no support whatever.[71]

In interior and up-country areas, cotton planters typically allotted marginal tracts entangled in customary uses that were not compatible with ex-slaves' intent to stake the well-being of their households on intensive cultivation of marginal lands. The "open range" grazing or common pasturage rights practiced on unimproved lands wreaked predictable havoc on freedpeople's crops.[72] When the freedman Jack Clarkson complained that stock belonging to Richland district planter R. H. Clarkson was destroying corn that his employer Edward Clarkson had permitted him to plant on swampland on the east bank of the Wateree River, the planter insisted that his kinsman's employee must plant according to neighborhood tradition:

> [A]s this swamp on the east bank of the River is used by us all neighboring planters in common as a pasture we each try to protect whatever little we may plant on this side the river (where it is a general pasture for stock, and all our fences are bad) as best we may by having our fields minded, etc. and hold no one but ourselves (each for himself) responsible for our crops. Freedman Jack's corn is on this east side of the River and planted under the above circumstances.[73]

Thus, planters attempted to concede the short-term use of marginal land without conceding its management. They brooked no interference in prior customs that governed the land's use. Similarly, in 1867, Aiken landowner John Seigler rented a tract of land to freedman Stephen Marshall for one-third of Marshall's crop. The landowner nevertheless refused to turn his hogs out of the field that Marshall had planted in potatoes.[74] Conflicting land uses are perhaps most apparent in specialized plantation regions of the Piedmont because the allotments on which laborers staked their production of a marketable household surplus were initially carved from marginal tracts rather than from improved acreage.

71. Nancy Patten to Mr. Allen, 11 Feb. 1867, Letters Received, ser. 3028, Abbeville, Subordinate Field Office Records, RG 105.
72. Hahn, *Roots of Southern Populism,* offers a provocative analysis of the significance of common pasturage rights within the context of nonspecialized farming of the Piedmont yeomanry.
73. R. H. Clarkson to W. J. Harkisheimer, 9 Oct. 1866, Letters Received, ser. 3156, Columbia, Subordinate Field Office Records, RG 105; vol. 254, p. 31; Register of Complaints, ser. 3309, Orangeburg, Subordinate Field Office Records, RG 105 [A-7272].
74. Wm. Stone to John Seigler, 5 Sept. 186[7], vol. 87, p. 254, Letters Sent, ser. 3052, Aiken, Subordinate Field Office Records, RG 105.

Bureau agents assessed the burden of conflicting land uses unevenly, if the decisions of an agent in Orangeburg district reflect a more general trend. When a former slave complained that a landowner's hogs had damaged his corn, the agent instructed the laborer to obtain the landowner's permission before repairing the fence that enclosed his crops and then to mend the fence only "at such hours as are not employed in the regular work of the plantation." When another worker complained that his hog had been shot when it wandered into a "neighbor's" lot, the same agent advised the former slave to pen his hogs.[75] On their small allotments in marginal tracts, ex-slaves seldom enjoyed the full advantages of either fenced crops or common grazing.

Defense of crops planted on marginal tracts drew freedpeople and landowners into assaults and counterattacks that at times threatened to engulf all crops, stock and buildings on the premises. J. Cork, a landowner in Fairfield district, rued the day "that I was so unfortunate as to alow [*sic*]" Billy Kincaide "to Plant a corn patch for himself over & above his contract thinking that it would make him do well & mind his work." Kincaide's efforts to protect his growing corn against depredations by his employer's stock climaxed when the laborer set his dog on the planter's grazing cows and gave the overseer's mare a beating to which the planter attributed her death. In retaliation for the death of his mare, the overseer shot Kincaide's dog. "[T]his enraged the Negro," the landowner reported, charting the storm of Kincaide's fury. Kincaide's rage coursed from his allotted corn land through the cotton fields, swept up the plantation stock, and ultimately hovered at the landowner's very door:

> he went the following night & threw down between 50 & 100 panel of his fence   he went into his corn field & cut Down a large Quantity of his corn   he cut Down a part of his growing cotton & he has threatened to kill every cow & hog [found] on his place before the end of the year & the man is afraid to lie Down at night not knowing but his house may be on fire before the morning[76]

The explosive chain of events on Cork's farm exposed a deeper antagonism that underlay landowners' and freedpeople's conflicting land uses.

Competing land uses were not easily reconciled when ex-slaves attempted to bring marginal tracts into more regular cultivation precisely in order to escape full-time employment on a landowner's more inten-

75. Vol. 254, p. 31, 10 Aug. 1866; p. 45, 18 Aug. 1866; p. 67, 24 Aug. 1866; all in Register of Complaints, ser. 3309, Orangeburg, Subordinate Field Office Records, RG 105 [A-7272].

76. J. Cork to Sir, 12 Aug. 1866, Letters Received, ser. 3156, Columbia, Subordinate Field Office Records, RG 105. In a postscript, the overseer assured the bureau agent that he and his brother were not without remedy: "[I]f I find [Billy Kincaide] in the place Puting any of his threatenings into Practice of Destroying fences Cuting Down Crop Killing Stock Burning Houses or Stealing I will Shoot him as Shure as the Sun Shines."

sively cultivated fields. By laboring less regularly on undivided lands and by obtaining contractual provisions for time to work their allotments, laborers attempted to produce crops independent of landowners' claims.[77] Nevertheless, as wage laborers, ex-slaves encountered a form of exclusive-use rights even on common lands. Their resistance to the dependent terms to which planters held allotments of marginal tracks strained the network of less than absolute property rights in which marginal lands were enmeshed. Pitched battles stemming from competing uses of marginal tracts and demands so insistent in 1867 as to persuade one up-country planter that ex-slaves had gone "rent crazy" helped push Piedmont planters toward those agreements to subdivide improved, arable lands into units for household cultivation that became increasingly common after 1868.[78] In the process, exclusive rights of proprietorship over land had gained sanction from those who would be renters.

Working on Shares

The conflicts that erupted from ex-slaves' attempts to organize household production on marginal tracts were an opening skirmish in share workers' long-term struggles to raise an independent surplus on someone else's land. On improved acreage rather than on marginal tracts were born the social relations of sharecropping, the postwar South's deformed analogue to antebellum tenancy.[79]

General farmers, many of them widows or nonslaveholders, earliest acceded to former slaves' attempts to establish a secure tenure in the face of landlessness. Their agreements to rent land often attracted laborers away from large landowners unwilling to offer rental tenures at the onset of the first agricultural year after emancipation. A Williamsburg planter scarcely concealed his contempt for both the freedpeople and their new landlords when he explained to John Dennett in the fall of 1865 how "a class of white folks . . . meaner than the negroes" disrupted plantation labor in his neighborhood. "One man just over the creek," the Connecticut-born planter illustrated, "who never earned a dime in his life, has got more than forty negroes on his farm; if you can call it a farm – he never made corn enough to feed himself three months."[80] Assaults in 1866 by armed bands organized to force freedpeople to return and work for their

77. See, for example, the contract of Andrew Agnew, Jan. 1867, Labor Contracts, ser. 3037, Abbeville, Subordinate Field Office Records, RG 105.
78. Ford, "Labor and Ideology," especially pp. 30–33, where the quoted phrase appears on p. 31.
79. In addition to the studies of the emergence of sharecropping in the nineteenth century, the changing character of work on shares in the twentieth century is explored in Daniel, *Breaking the Land*; and in Woodruff, *As Rare As Rain*.
80. *Nation*, 23 Nov. 1865, p. 651.

former owners lingered in the memory of a female Unionist in Pickens district. "The first spite the Rebel party showed," she later informed a Republican governor, "was that no Lowel [loyal] persons should hire a Freedman to work for them."[81] By 1868, freedpeople's landlords increasingly included both large and small landowners.

As an arrangement by which landless farmers gained tenure to family-sized farms, freedpeople's rental agreements superficially resembled antebellum rentals. However, the specificity of the crop mix, and landowner's attempts to gain exclusive rights to market the harvested crop, sharply distinguished postwar share rentals from antebellum tenancy.[82] Remnants of antebellum tenancy and newer rental agreements coexisted in 1866 and 1867 on Spartansburg district lands owned by David Golightly Harris. Black "tenants," among whom were some of Harris's former slaves, generally lacked horses and means of conveyance. Unlike Harris's white "tenants," his ex-slave renters built their own cabins and contracted to perform noncrop work. Therefore, in addition to raising particular crops in proportions implicitly set by Harris's contractual requirement of fixed amounts of cotton, corn, and other unspecified produce, freed men and boys cleared new land, hauled wood, built a new stable, sheared sheep, and performed some work on Harris's new gin for which no additional compensation was offered. Along with their own crops, they also hauled to Harris's central storehouses and processed at his central gin the shares of cotton and corn that Harris's white "tenants" paid as yearly rents. During the freed men's noncrop work, their wives and daughters sustained cultivation of the cotton, corn, and whatever household gardens the families raised. Although Harris's white "tenants" did not initially rely on him to sell them corn during the agricultural year, he hesitantly sold corn to the one black "tenant" who owned a horse but was unable to procure corn on credit from local merchants. By mid-June 1866, Harris informed the man that "his horse must die & our crop must be lost rather than give him any more corn from my crib." While one white "tenant" went off to seek work in a nearby cotton mill after the crops were laid by, freed male "tenants" received cash for work not included within the three months of noncrop work that Harris's contract required of them, at daily rates lowered by the late-summer surge in rural unemployment. By November 1867, Harris's earlier reluctance to "risk the negro the first year of his

81. Miss Amie L. Young to Robert K. Scott, 8 July 1869, Governors' Papers, SCDAH; E. M. Burkett et al. to W. [P.?] [Berry?], 21 Feb. 1866, M 869, r 9; Capt. A. Coan to Capt. J. A. Clark, 8 Feb. 1866, Letters Received, ser. 4109, Department of the South, RG 393 Pt 1 [C-1391]; A. Coan to J. A. Clark, 8 Feb. 1866, Letters and Reports Received Relating to Freedmen and Civil Affairs, ser. 4112, 2d Military District, RG 393 Pt 1; W. E. Leighton to R. K. Scott, 5 March 1866, M 869, r 10.
82. Hahn, *Roots of Southern Populism*; Glymph, "Freedpeople and Ex-Masters."

freedom" as a "tenant" had mellowed. To his journal he confided that "negroes are more reliable as regards their working contracts than white men." By 1869, the eight "tenants" on Harris's farm worked mostly for fixed rentals, their crops mortgaged to Harris for provisions that he sold them on credit during the year. Vanished in 1869 is the title of "Mister" that had often prefixed Harris's references to white "tenants" in 1866.[83] Whether Harris's 1869 "tenants" were former slaves or nonlandowning whites, most now worked for freedpeople's wages under the diluted tenancy arrangements that increasingly, though unevenly, developed in the postwar South.[84]

Postwar shares did not become a form of wage labor through arrangements that applied to ex-slaves alone. In the late 1860s, landless Piedmont tenants who resisted the postwar transformation of antebellum tenancy by arrangements similar to those David Golightly Harris adopted often found themselves evicted and their places given out to newer "tenants" who had once been slaves. A freed woman, Charlotte Fowler, attributed the 1871 murder of her husband by a Klu Klux Klan band in Spartanburg district to landless whites' hostility to a new landowner's employment practices:

> There is a parcel of [black] men who were on the plantation working Mr. Jones's land, and my old man was one of them that tended Mr. Jones's land. Mr. Jones had had a whole parcel of poor white folks on the land, and he turned them off, and put all these blacks on the premises that they had from Mr. Jones, and I don't know what it could be [why her husband was killed], but for that and the [ex-slaves' and former white tenants' undisclosed dispute about] the watermelons. That was the cause why my old man is dead, and I am left alone.[85]

Antebellum tenancy and ex-slaves' household production disintegrated in explosions of violence that marked the profundity with which work on shares transformed the antebellum orders of slave and free.

Freedpeople could not be held to subsistence wages by arrangements that applied only to agricultural workers. Eager to tap the profits of a trade in Southern staples while the postwar price boom lasted, itinerant

---

83. David Golightly Harris Farm Journals, UNC, particularly 22 Oct., 5, 24 Nov. 1865; 2, 4, 6, 11, 23 Jan., 20 Feb., 21 April, 2 May, 2, 9, 20 June, 22 Aug., 20 Nov., 6 Dec. 1866; 25 March, 24 May, 11, 13 July, 5 Aug., 17 April 1867; 4 Jan., 20 June 1868; and 5 June 1869.
84. Woodward, *Origins of the New South*, p. 211; Fields, "Ideology and Race," pp. 143–78.
85. *The Ku-Klux Conspiracy: Testimony Taken by the Joint Select Committee to Inquire into the Condition of Affairs in the Late Insurrectionary States, Part 3: South Carolina*, 3 vols. (Washington, DC: 1872), vol. 1, pp. 388, 402 (hereafter cited as *KKK Testimony*; Trelease, *White Terror*, pp. 349–82.

peddlers, seasonal storekeepers, and small traders stood ready at each harvest to buy crops in small lots.[86] Petty riverine traders coursed low-country rivers while, as the decade closed, a local trade in cotton took to the land. Rural stores, dubbed "grog shops" by their opponents, penetrated interior and up-country cotton districts. According to an irate Abbeville planter, "These groceries are owned & conducted entirely by the Southern white man."[87]

Restriction of local trade proceeded by a combination of military, statutory, and extralegal intervention. Military officers issued passes to traders authorized to trade in recently reopened ports, post commanders prohibited trade during the harvest or proposed to limit the number of storekeepers licensed within their commands, the state office of the Freedmen's Bureau proposed to penalize storekeepers who bought produce from freedpeople "without making any inquiry as to the ownership thereof," and the Black Codes placed criminal sanctions on buyers and sellers of agricultural produce who traded without landowners' written approval of an ex-slave's permission to sell.[88] Although state ordinances establishing license fees and bond requirements for traders did not emerge until after Reconstruction, the state's Republican legislature in 1872 prohibited the sale of any property on which a lien existed.[89] Since liens encumbered virtually all the staples and most of the corn that nonlandowning laborers raised, the statute by implication required landowners' approval of any local trade in produce. The measure's ineffectiveness is reflected in the conflicts that erupted, as vigilantes rallied to suppress local markets that continued to operate after law had denied them legitimacy.

Woes of the struggle to secure a form of tenancy from the evolution of share work converged during the harvest at small neighborhood grog shops, whose unpopularity among planters is perhaps to be sought in the spirit of independent proprietorship that the establishments brewed on

86. Summary of reports from subdistrict of Charleston, R. K. Scott to O. O. Howard, 20 Dec. 1866, M 752, r 39, 0895–911; James C. Beecher to Geo. W. Hooker, 6 Nov. 1867, Letters and Reports Received Relating to Freedmen and Civil Affairs, ser. 4112, 2d Military District, RG 393 Pt 1; Proceedings of a Commission convened at Rockville, Testimony of Guy Small, enclosed in R. K. Scott to O. O. Howard, 12 Dec. 1867, M 752, r 51, 0393; R. K. Scott to O. O.Howard, 18 April 1866, M 752, r 29, 1014–21.

87. W. Miles Hazzard to Robert K. Scott, 12 Aug. 1868, E. Willingham to Scott, 30 July 1869; Thos. H. Zimmerman to Scott, 25 Jan. 1869; J. L. Wright to Scott, 1 Dec. 1869; all in Governors' Papers, SCDAH; Ben Huger et al. to General, 1 Sept. 1866, M 869, r 10.

88. Capt. [J. J. Upham] to Lt. J. W. Clous, 17 Oct. 1865, vol. 154/309 DS, pp. 24–26, Letters Sent, ser. 2383, Department of the South, RG 393 Pt 2 [C-1591]; Wm. Griffin to Bvt. Brig. Gen. E. W. Hinks, 15 Dec. 1867, Letters Received, ser. 4111, 2d Military District, RG 393 Pt 1 [SS-65]; *SC Statutes,* 1866, p. 274.

89. *General Statutes of South Carolina,* Chapter 35, section 1338, p. 391.

the plantation rather than in the brewed spirits to which the trading centers owed their name. Outlets where workers could directly exchange produce and staples sustained a local trade that confounded when it did not ignore altogether the competing claims to agricultural produce grown on a landlord's land.

Postwar agriculture's wage relationship sapped the strength of direct trade between small storekeepers and former slaves. A Confederate veteran who kept a small store in Sumter district was jailed for receiving stolen cotton, which he had purchased in October 1866 from a freedman who insisted that he was not under contract and that "everything he had for sale was his own property."[90] Even traders licensed by military officers in the immediate postwar period fell under suspicion. A bureau agent thought that the "theft" that was "common" in Georgetown district during the 1867 harvest was "indirectly encouraged by one or more Jew Merchants in town" who bought rice from plantation workers by "paying a larger than the market price . . . in goods." Accordingly, the agent reported, the "two most prominent dealers are now under surveillance."[91]

With the re-establishment of civil government after the state elections of 1868, unofficial surveillance of trade became a matter to which local vigilantism also devoted its efforts during the harvest season. Patrols stopped wagons on the road to inspect their contents and carried warnings of the hazards of a trade in seed cotton to recalcitrant storekeepers.[92] A former Confederate soldier who bought a plantation and went into the furnishing business in Sumter district in 1868 began two years later to receive intermittent visits from a mounted patrol. By 1870, what had begun as a country store, extending credit to farm laborers and landowners alike, had also become a meeting place for neighborhood Republicans and the site of a school – "nothing more than a shelter" – for black children. Notwithstanding the masks, paper hats, and robes of calico and homespun in which the visiting party was outfitted, the merchant recognized the neighborhood's "young bloods," or planter's sons, as the organizers of Klu Klux Klan activity in his section. Within a year, the party had stopped the traffic in seed cotton along its circuit. "I do not believe," the merchant informed a congressional committee in June 1871 that "there is a store in my section of country that touches a pound of seed-cotton."[93]

Vigilantism targeted the marginal independence that freedpeople wrested from productive relations of the early share system by embezzle-

90. Anton F. Bruggerman to James L. Orr, 22 May 1867, Governors' Papers, SCDAH.
91. Summary of reports from subdistrict of Georgetown, R. K. Scott to O. O. Howard, 20 Dec. 1867, M 752, r 51, 0443–55.
92. Anton F. Bruggerman to James L. Orr, 22 May 1867, Governors' Papers, SCDAH.
93. KKK *Testimony*, vol. 1, pp. 45, 124.

ment, nighttime trade, and the cultivation of unappropriated patches of land. An ominous portent of later events, masked riders who took to the roads at harvest time would ride in other seasons on raids broadly aimed at local political and social institutions of the Republican rank and file.[94]

Holding onto Land and Time in the Low Country

In the low country, on plantations where slaves had long produced a good portion of plantation subsistence, ex-slaves' attempts to organize a household economy did not leave the old productive relations unaltered. No sooner did ex-slaves on the coast acknowledge their landlessness than they began to enhance subsistence cultivation on former provision grounds and house gardens. Few postwar planters mistook freedpeople's efforts as an attempt to retain or restore antebellum practices. From the outset, it was clear that ex-slaves did not intend to work provision grounds and gardens under constraints that the work load of slavery had imposed. Edward Barnwell Heyward, who in 1867 was planting Combahee River rice lands inherited from his father, found that these former sites of subsistence cultivation had become centers of household production in which women played an expanded role not compatible with the antebellum labor regimen:

> The women appear most lazy, merely because they are allowed the opportunity. They wish to stay in the house, or in the garden all the time. If you chide them, they say "Ehch! Massa, ain't I mus mind de fowl, and look a' me young corn   aint I must watch um," and to do this the best hands on the place will stay at home all day and every day, and litterally [sic] do nothing.[95]

The expansion of domestic production drew heavily on the labor of women and children. On Heyward's plantation, as on many other coastal estates, freedpeople elaborated sexual divisions of labor in order to limit the household's full obligations to plantation duties. The men of the household became the chief contract workers, performing the daily labors required by contracts. Others, largely women, children, and the elderly, agreed to be available at periods of peak seasonal demand.[96] Such seasonal arrangements left coastal planters uneasy, and, like planters who hired workers by the day or week, they envied the greater certainty about the

94. *KKK Testimony*, vol. 1, p. 51.
95. Edward Barnwell Heyward to Tat, 5 May 1867, Edward Barnwell Heyward Papers, SCL; Foner, *Nothing But Freedom*, p. 84.
96. Edward Barnwell Heyward to nn [1867?] [incomplete], Edward Barnwell Heyward Papers, SCL.

availability of harvest labor that they thought share payments ensured.[97] Heyward worried that the withdrawal of able women workers diminished family daily work groups. "I really have a well regulated gang," he explained to his wife in May 1867, "but it is in many respects a *weak* one, so much volunteer force if the women get mad I am gone."[98] Planter's fears were not without remedy.

Planters exploited their possession of land to regulate freedpeople's domestic production. A Delaware Quaker who had launched a wartime planting venture on St. Helena Island complained to a journalist at war's end because, in 1865, his workers cultivated more land in food crops than they would work in cotton: "For every acre that his people planted for him for wages," Dennett reported, "they planted precisely two acres for themselves, and it was hard to induce them to take up more cotton ground than would supply them with spending money. Their living they expected to make off their own land."[99] Postwar planters seem to have enjoyed greater success in restricting domestic production. To the approximately forty people working on his Hilton Head Island plantation, Northern planter E. T. Wright allowed "one acre to every *four 4* they cultivate for me." The owner of Boone Hall plantation outside Charleston allowed "each [full] hand" one half-acre. Freedpeople on the Jehossee Island rice plantation of former governor William Aiken, who in 1866 had been permitted to plant as much land as they could tend without interfering with their daily labor, found that in 1867 Aiken's contract allowed them to cultivate but half an acre of rice land without paying rent, and further required that the rice sown on their domestic plots be of a variety distinct from and probably commercially inferior to the plantation's. Some planters seem to have attracted workers by initially offering larger household plots, only to reduce the plots in subsequent planting years. William Hazzard attracted workers to his Santee River estates in 1867 by offering five acres to each household. The next year, Hazzard's contract offered but a single acre of rice land.[100]

97. Lt. S. Baker to Bvt. Lieut. Col. H. W. Smith, 2 Sept. 1868, vol. 154/304 DS, pp. 75–76, Letters Sent, ser. 2383, Department of the South, RG 393 Pt 2 No 141 [C-1598].

98. Edward Barnwell Heyward to Tat, 5 May 1867, Edward Barnwell Heyward Papers, SCL.

99. *Nation,* 30 Nov. 1865, p. 683, 14 Dec. 1865, p. 747.

100. E. T. Wright to H. B. Clitz, 6 Oct. 1865, Letters Received, ser. 4109, Department of South Carolina, RG 393 Pt 1 [C-1361]; E. W. Everson to R. K. Scott, 3 May 1866, M 869, r 9; J. M. Johnston to R. K. Scott, 17 Aug. 1867, M 869, r 13; Wm. Hazzard to R. K. Scott, 29 July 1867, M 869, r 13; W. M. Hazzard to R. K. Scott, 11 March 1868, M 869, r 17, 0171–73. Hazzard clearly reduced the amount of rice land that he offered his employees in 1868; he continued to make available "what high land" the working households desired and a small garden patch.

The appearance of such regulations reflects the extent to which emancipation had transformed the antebellum relationship between plantation labor and domestic production. Slaveowners had tried to guarantee that slaves produced a minimum portion of their subsistence requirements and did not limit the surplus beyond subsistence that exertion might permit slaves to generate. Postwar planters, by contrast, formally discouraged their workers from producing a surplus that threatened to supplant rather than complement plantation production. Contractual restrictions, reinforced by reductions in work stock that the 1866 South Carolina legislature initiated by enacting a fence law that ended open grazing on the sea islands, permitted freedpeople to maintain only as many animals as they could pen on their tracts. A committee of former slaves in Georgetown district pronounced restrictions on subsistence, by which "they must not have poltry of eny kind a beast or anamal of eny kind, the[y] must not plant a seed of eny kind for themselves" among features that rendered 1866 contracts "to[o] intollarable to comply – worst than slavery."[101]

Freedpeople at times honored such requirements chiefly in the breach. In 1866, a bureau inspector discovered that many workers on Boon Hall plantation, whose contracts allowed only half an acre of land for their own use, actually tended "over 5 acres which is generally under pretty good cultivation." They accomplished the additional cultivation by reducing their efforts on plantation lands, as when they would "report themselves as sick – and then go to work in their own field." They also augmented household labor by subcontracts, in which resident workers granted other freedpeople lodging in the quarters in return for assistance in the cultivation of the household plots. Thus, the bureau inspector who visited Boon Hall in May 1866 reported in surprise that, although twenty-seven workers were under contract, some fifty-seven adults actually resided on the plantation. Resident workers not under contract supplemented their return from labor on the contract workers' plots by day labor and jobbing. The vigorous community life that the inspector glimpsed at Boon Hall that spring reflected in part the expanding social contacts that day laborers had brought to the plantation. "The plantation is a kind of resort for the Negroes all around the vicinity as also from Charleston,"

101. *SC Statutes*, 1866, p. 414; *United States v. Jos. W. Seabrook and Others*, 5 Nov. 1866, Case No. 5, Proceedings of Provost Courts, Military Tribunals, and Post Court-Martial Cases Tried in North and South Carolina, ser. 4257, Department of the South, RG 393 Pt 1 [C-1525]; J. H. Shecklefod and others to O. O. Howard, 17 Jan. 1866, enclosed in wrapper labeled J. H. Shackleford and others, 17 Jan. 1866, M 752, r 24, 0513–15; [contract], E. M. Burkett and [ten freedmen], 13 Jan. 1866, enclosed in wrapper labeled A. M. L. Crawford, 24 Feb. 1866, M 869, r 9; [contract], Friendfield Plantation, Dr. A. M. Foster and [seventy-two] freedmen, Jan. 1866, enclosed in S. Willard Saxton to Bvt. Lt. Col. Smith, 10 Jan. 1866, M 869, r 11.

he noted, "as boats run up to it every day," and many freedpeople in the area attended the plantation's Sunday church services.[102]

Peculiar to the sea-island cotton and rice regions were arrangements by which freedpeople gained contractual recognition of their regular claim to a portion of their time throughout the agricultural season.[103] In return for labor on a specified number of "contract days," – usually two or three in the early postwar period – workers acquired the right to reside on and cultivate particular tracts of plantation lands. Their demarcation between "planters' time" and "laborers' time" adopted the classic peasant tactic of claiming time from obligations to landlords in order to expand household production. The Freedmen's Bureau discouraged the arrangement, refusing to lend provisions to planters who adopted it. Planters reported that they agreed to the arrangement only when they could obtain labor on no other terms, omitting to note that the arrangement released those who had not set up a plantation store from the necessity of securing credit in order to furnish provisions.[104] In 1868, a planter on Yonge's Island near Charleston reported that eleven men had insisted on working on "the *so called* 2 days System a most miserable system for both parties":

> [T]hese eleven men . . . would give me no peace until I would agree to allow them to come down to the Island and work two (2) days in each week for the use of my land and houses. I reluctantly agreed to their proposition. I wanted nothing to do with the so called 2 days system, as the only true system in my opinion to Farm is to hire for *wages* and find them in *provision*[105]

Such contractual divisions of time, however, proved poor guarantors of freedpeople's household economies. Labor rents were individualized as they became more widespread in 1866 and 1867. That is, each resident adult worker within a household was obligated to fulfill a stipulated quota of workdays in return for the right to cultivate a fixed acreage, typically one-half acre, of land. In consequence, few adult women could continue to devote their labor exclusively to household production, ex-slaves' ability to subcontract supplemental tracts was eroded, and the arrangement at times gained for plantation labor the services of elderly workers whose age had excused them from regular field labor as slaves. Heyward appreciated the supplement to field labor that he had gained through adaptations of labor rents by 1869:

102. E. W. Everson to R. K. Scott, 3 May 1866, M 869, r 9.
103. [Hammond], *South Carolina*, p. 29.
104. E. W. Everson to Bvt. Maj. Edw. L. Deane, 18 Jan. 1867, enclosed in Everson to Deane, 17 Jan. 1867, M 869, r 12; summary of report from subdistrict of Charleston, R. K. Scott to O. O. Howard, 25 Sept. 1867, M 752, r 51, 0055–68; Constantine Bailey to R. K. Scott, 4 May 1868, M 869, r 16.
105. James W. Grace to R. K. Scott, 4 May 1868, M 869, r 16.

I have at certain times every body in the field, even old people who
have done nothing for twenty years, and the Drivers smile when they
hear Jimmie read out the lists, and order each old one out by name.
This is accomplished by their being forced to contribute their labour
as pay for the patches of land which they all plant.[106]

Former slaves gained but a semblance of tenant status on lands which
they acquired through labor rents. Formal constraints on subsistence production accomplished by the allocation of fixed acreage, and by advances
of provisions only in return for plantation labor, left many workers especially vulnerable to fluctuations in the local food supply. In the scarce season before garden crops ripened, households could not be self-supporting
for seven days of the week on rations gained by two or three days of contract labor. Many resorted to seeking work on neighboring plantations in
order to obtain food. A planter on the coast in Beaufort district offered
only land in return for "one third" of the labor of his contract workers in
1868. For the use of "two good mules to cultivate their crop," the workers agreed to offer an additional "slight consideration."[107] As the antebellum task system became a form of piecework after the war, where daily
tasks were assigned on the basis of "work done by the best man," workers' tasks included larger amounts of cotton land. In peak seasons or when
the crop was overrun with grass, more intensive work in these larger cotton tasks consumed the time that freedpeople had contractually withheld
from general plantation work. They frequently abandoned their supplemental crops altogether.[108] Hence, ex-slaves who received fixed cash
wages in return for two or three days' labor often complained that compensation remained the same, whereas fluctuating intensities in field cultivation often obligated them to neglect their own plots and give more
time to their contracted tasks during peak seasons.[109]

So little could life be nourished from the produce of "their" time that
some former slaves found themselves seeking to increase the time they
gave to plantation labor. In 1866, because of her indebtedness to the com-
missary on the plantation operated by the Wadmalaw Island planting
firm of S. H. and E. M. Jenkins, a freed woman who had contracted to
work three days requested permission from the plantation storekeeper to
work a fourth day in order to liquidate her debt for supplies. Charged

106. Edward Barnwell Heyward to Tat, 18 Apr. 1869, Edward Barnwell Heyward Pa-
      pers, SCL.
107. J. E. Lewis to [Horace] Neide, 16 April 1868, M 869, r 17, 0664; Geo. W. Gile to
      Horace Neide, 25 July 1868, M 752, r 60, 0365–67; summary of report from sub-
      district of Charleston, in R. K. Scott to O. O. Howard, 20 March 1867, M 752,
      r 44, 0468–80; [agreement], E. E. Ellis and Freedmen, 1 March 1868, Ellis Family
      Papers, SCL. Cf. Morgan, "Work and Culture," pp. 585–86.
108. *Nation,* 7 Sept. 1865, p. 295.
109. J. C. Cornelius to H. W. Smith, 1 July 1866, M 752, r 31, 0109–15.

with theft when the landowner discovered her picking cotton after the stipulated quitting time of 3 P.M., she rebuffed the planter's accusation by claiming her right to work on the plantation as long as she pleased. After all, she insisted, "the cotton belonged to the colored folks."[110] In language that reiterated ex-slaves' demand for control of the crop, she phrased a defense against the consequences of wage labor by claiming not her own time, but overtime.

Constraints on subsistence production, larger tasks in cotton work, and the need to trade labor services for the use of work animals and farm implements eroded the independence that freedpeople had sought to anchor in contractual guarantees of time. By the end of the 1860s, labor rents were proving no impediment to planters' ability to gain more than two or three days of plantation labor under the nominally two- or three-day "system." A woman hired to work several days weekly for a planter on John's Island before the First World War later recalled the uncertainty that had surrounded the domestic production she and her husband attempted to sustain:

> We used to work for our rent and our food. You got to work like the Devil! Plant your cotton. Plant your corn. You have to work five task for that land and that house. Take oxen and plow. You have to work that 'fore you work your crop. That's you house. That's the rent. If he [the landowner] calls every week, you'll have to go.[111]

Labor rents proved less an alternative to wage labor than a local adjunct of the wage relationship.

Uncertain Harvests: Seasonalization of Agricultural Employment

Freedpeople managed to establish neither share arrangements nor labor rents as forms of tenancy. The typical outcome of share workers' attempts to acquire a harvest separate from landowners' control was described by a freed man in Marion district in December 1867: "[W]hen we make our crops they takes it away from us. . . . we labor from one end of a year to another one & we then goes of[f] with nothing."[112] Low-country renters witnessed the erosion of the time that they had sought to safeguard for household production. When an Edisto Island landowner ordered a ten-

110. *United States* v. *Peggy Frazier*, 7 Nov. 1866, Case No. 15, Proceedings of Provost Courts, Military Tribunals, and Post Court-Martial Cases Tried in North and South Carolina, ser. 4257, Department of the South, RG 393 Pt 1 [C1526].
111. Carawan, *Ain't You Got a Right*, p. 40.
112. Charles W. Mc[illeg], 13 Dec. 1867, enclosed in Roland Rhett to R. K. Scott, 13 Dec. 1867, M 869, r 14.

ant to pick his peas, the man boldly announced his independence from such management. "I's free & go when I pleas[e]," he responded. To a neighbor, however, he admitted that "he could not pick his peas as he had to pick his [own] cotton."[113] Without independent access to the harvested crop or time in which to produce household support, share workers and part-time renters worked to produce daily necessities, not to enhance them. That task became even harder as periods of seasonal unemployment came to characterize the conditions of wage labor.

Seasonal labor arrangements reflected postwar changes in the availability of dietary staples. Cyclical grain shortages, which had caused slaves to describe April, May, and June as "the hungry months," stretched beyond accustomed seasonal bounds in the first years after emancipation.[114] Traditional sources of relief seemed as dry as the crops parched by localized summer droughts in 1866 and 1867. Landowners, many of whom had commenced planting only by obtaining supplies at unprecedented rates of interest secured by mortgages on land, crops and farming stock, hesitated to procure provisions to relieve grain shortages once intensive field cultivation ended and crops had been laid by.[115] In the season of slackened cultivation that now derived its character as much from market tempos as from rhythms of agricultural production, landowners roughly projected the value of growing crops. The lay-by became a season timed to employers' desire to free themselves from the necessity of purchasing staples that workers required for daily support.

Once the heaviest labor of tillage had passed, landowners pronounced workers free to consume household production or to create their own support. In attempts to substitute the produce of employees' household gardens for purchased rations, employers cut back or altogether eliminated advances of corn, or substituted vegetables for grain in weekly rations, but did not grant workers the right to seek alternative employment.[116] In the summer of 1866, an Orangeburg employer discovered that the share of the

113. *Primus Bragall v. Jenkins Mikell*, 27 Nov. 1866, Case No. 30, Proceedings of Provost Courts, Military Tribunals, and Post Court-Martial Cases Tried in North and South Carolina, ser. 4257, Department of the South, RG 393 Pt 1 [C-1529].

114. Summary of report from subdistrict of Charleston, R. K. Scott to O. O. Howard, 23 May 1867, M 752, r 44, 0731-47.

115. Summary of report from subdistrict of Edisto, R. K. Scott to O. O. Howard, 26 Oct. 1867, M 752, r 51, 0185-96; W. G. Stewart to Ed. R. S. Canby, 29 Feb. 1868, Letters Received, ser. 4111, 2d Military District, RG 393 Pt 1 [SS-108]; J. P. S. Gobin to [Quincy A.] Gillmore, 17 Aug. 1865, M 752, r 17, 0603-10; Endorsement of Geo. W. Gile, 3 Aug. 1866, on R. J. Brown to O. O. Howard, 20 July 1866, M 869, r 9; James L. Orr to R. K. Scott, 10 May 1867, M 869, r 17; Jno. N. Frierson et al. to James L. Orr, 26 April 1867, Governors' Papers, SCDAH. Repeal of the usury law smoothed the creditors' path. See *SC Statutes*, 1866, p. 463.

116. T. H. Legare to Wm. H. H. Holden, 8 May 1868, Letters Received, ser. 3156, Columbia, Subordinate Field Office Records, RG 105; Bvt. Lt. Col. L. R. Bliss to Bvt. Lt. Col. H. W. Smith, 1 Aug. 1866, Letters Received, ser. 4112, Department of the

crop that would fall to the contract worker Ned would not pay for grain already advanced, and stopped selling him corn. Ned did not propose to fill the void by drawing upon supplies raised by his family of eight. Instead, in mid-August, he urged the Freedmen's Bureau agent at Orangeburg to insist that his employer permit him "to work elsewhere for food for his family."[117]

Where household production was slight, because workers were single or because their families contained large numbers of young children, landowners seem to have been more inclined to employ dismissals to escape midsummer indebtedness. The Richland district farmer Abner Turnipseed recounted to the post commander at Columbia the advice with which he dismissed the share worker Alick Martin in early August 1866:

> I told him as the crop was a failure he would better go and work and try and make something to help out a short crop and that I would Loos my part of the time and to return back [in] January and receive his portion up to the time he left.[118]

The end of the growing season thus marked the beginning of a search for new employment by many workers who had been hired on yearly share contracts. Like Alick Martin, many freedpeople sought temporary work to ward off summer hunger. Others, like Ned, took to the roads rather than expend products of family labor to conserve employers' working capital.

Planters at times employed midsummer dismissals with an eye on the harvest rather than on the immediate problem of indebtedness for summer supplies. Mass evictions then surfaced after crops had been laid by, even in areas where household production was substantial. An army surgeon who traveled on the mainland of lower Beaufort district in late July 1866 encountered "several troops" of freedpeople "who had just been discharged from plantations and were looking for work they knew not where."[119] Peak demand for harvest labor was satisfied in part from reserves of laborers dismissed during the lay-by. From his headquarters on

South, RG 393 Pt 1 [C-1430]; summary of report from subdistrict of Kingstree, J. R. Edie to O. O. Howard, 14 Aug. 1868, M 752, r 60, 0378–92; Endorsement of A. P. Caraher, 17 Oct. 1867, on Wm. H. Gist to E. R. S. Canby, 3 Oct. 1867, Letters Received, ser. 4111, 2d Military District, RG 393 Pt 1 [SS-32].

117. Vol. 254, 17 Oct. 1866, p. 46, Register of Complaints, ser. 3309, Orangeburg, Subordinate Field Office Records, RG 105 [A-7272]. The household production of the freedmen Ned has been inferred from the large size of his family but was not stated directly by the agent. Bureau agents did not always grant permission to seek additional work. See, for example, p. 51, 20 Aug. 1866, p. 73, 31 Aug. 1866 in the same register.

118. Abner Turnipseed to Gen. Green, 22 Sept. 1866, Letters Received, ser. 3156, Columbia, Subordinate Field Office Records, RG 105.

119. Summary of report from southern portion of subdistrict of Lawtonville, H. W. Smith to O. O. Howard, 6 Aug. 1866, M 752, r 39, 0329–45. See also G. Franklin et al. to Daniel Sickles, 8 Aug. 1866, enclosed in Wm. J. Harkisheimer to [Caraher], 27 July 1866, M 752, r 36, 0118–20; A. P. Caraher to H. W. Smith, 12 July 1866, r 36, 0122–23; both in M 752.

Hilton Head Island, Freedmen's Bureau agent Martin R. Delany complained that cotton planters dismissed families after crops had been laid by and then hired people during the harvest who were paid by the pound of cotton picked.[120] By such tactics, planters gained immediate possession of harvested crops and defeated freedpeople's claims to process, store, and market their shares.

In a region where a resident slave labor force had been the mainstay of specialization in the production of agricultural commodities, itinerant freedpeople who set out to "make extra work" crossed a historical divide.[121] The unprecedented phenomenon drew comment, if not comprehension, from an up-country planter who reported the countryside of Chester district "inundated with idle darkies wandering about without home or employment" in August 1866.[122] A share worker in Spartanburg district linked the purpose of such wanderings to intermittent food shortages: "When I get out of corn and out of meat both, and anybody has got corn and meat, I jump out and work for a bushel of corn and a piece of meat, and work until I get it."[123] Supplementary short-term labor was necessary to piece together yearly household support.

Regional opportunities for local seasonal employment varied. Ex-slaves often turned to nonagricultural employment when credit dried up during slumps in cultivation. Supplementary employment was most needed during lay-by and in the postharvest season between December and the commencement of planting arrangements in late February or March. Principal low-country industries, such as phosphate mining and turpentine collection, grew up in the 1870s with the blessing of the old planter class.[124] Coastal planters sold their lands or lent the weight of influence, if not capital, to the new enterprises. Before the concentration of ownership in phosphate mining and turpentine camps in the 1880s, coastal industries relied extensively on seasonal labor stints from local agricultural workers and the area's black smallholders. Full-time employees in turpentine collection came primarily from outside the state.

In the up-country, by contrast, postwar nonagricultural employment was more a competitor than an auxiliary to plantation labor. Relations

120. M. R. Delany to R. K. Scott, 30 Dec. 1867, enclosed in wrapper labeled Headquarters Assistant Commissioner, South Carolina, Officers and agents who have made reports in response to circular of Hon. T. D. Elliott, M 869, r 18, 0032.
121. The quoted phrase appeared in vol. 254, 20 Aug. 1866, p. 51, Register of Complaints, ser. 3309, Orangeburg, Subordinate Field Office Records, RG 105 [A-7272], where the bureau denied the freedman's request and referred him to his employer.
122. Quoted in Ford, "Labor and Ideology," p. 31.
123. *KKK Testimony,* vol. 1, p. 436.
124. Shick and Doyle, "South Carolina Phosphate Boom"; Foner, *Nothing But Freedom,* p. 85.

between railroad and mining employers and local landholders were often brittle. When a local resident tried to hire workers from the road crew repairing tracks along the roadway between Columbia and Hamburg in 1866, he provoked a dispute with the superintendent of roadwork, who informed him that "*they are free* & you may hire them but you cannot do it during work hours while I am responsible for what is going on." The superintendent shot the man when he "cursed him & applied every abusive epithet he could to him shaking his fist in his face & swearing all the time he *would* whip him." [125] Up-country railroad laborers informed federal investigators of Ku Klux Klan activity in 1871 that they had been harassed and whipped by disguised bands who ordered them to return to farm work. [126] The region's principal industrial employment, cotton textile mills, did not develop until the 1880s, and then assumed the character of segregated company towns established for full-time residents. [127] Mob action, then, impeded the extent to which former slaves could combine seasonal nonagricultural labor with crop work. [128] Obstacles to local seasonal employment frequently sent them into towns or out of the state in order to gain a family living.

Among agricultural employers, large planters stood to reap the fullest benefits of the seasonal displacements that freedpeople experienced at the hands of large and small landowners alike. The commander of the military post at Lawtonville in Beaufort district thought that planters gained additional summer labor for a trifle when laborers temporarily quit smaller places to seek "an opportunity of earning the means of subsistence." Such workers were "compelled to work, perhaps a week for their food and a bushel of corn," he reported to his commanding officer in late July 1866. Though he objected to the nominal compensation, "I am powerless to give aid in such cases," the officer confessed, "as I am told that employment was given through charity, labor not being actually required." [129]

Work performed by seasonal laborers created added uncertainties for resident workers, who often objected when widespread unemployment

125. James G. Gibbes to James L. Orr, 16 Mar. [1866], Governors' Papers, SCDAH.
126. *KKK Testimony*, vol. 2, pp. 27, 538–40.
127. Carlton, *Mill and Town*.
128. Julius J. Fleming to Judge Aldrich, 3 Nov. 1866, enclosed in Julius J. Fleming to R. K. Scott, 8 Feb. 1867, M 752, r 44, 0222–23; Samuel Place to Wm. Harkisheimer, 21 Oct. 1866, Letters Received, ser. 3156, Columbia, Subordinate Field Office Records, RG 105. Although regional differences in patterns of migration out of the state are difficult to reconstruct, many bureau agents in the upper districts early called attention to the migration of young freed men from the up-country.
129. Summary of reports from subdistricts of Lawtonville, Beaufort, and Aiken, H. W. Smith to O. O. Howard, 6 Aug. 1866, M 752, r 39, 0324–45. See also summary of report from eastern and northern subdistricts of Charleston, R. K. Scott to O. O. Howard, 20 Sept. 1866, M 752, r 39, 0493–51; summary of report from subdistrict

provided opportunities for landowners to introduce temporary workers on terms that compromised the interests of residents. A Richland district farmer reported the response of share worker Alick Martin when the latter returned to the farm from which he had been dismissed at lay-by and discovered "an old woman & her daughter" picking the ripening cotton:

> [He] told her that she was a dammed old bich and if she did not leave he would make her do it dam quick. . . . he Left the field went to my yard [and] in the preasants of My wife & Daughters [said] that all the white people was mean and that he wished theay wer all dead and in Hell and that he could see them Burning[130]

The destitution of temporary workers at times affected the response of plantation residents who saw brigandage in the arrival of the newcomers. In early September 1866, for example, residents of James Shoolbred's plantation on the Santee River drove away two women whom Shoolbred had hired to hoe a crop of potatoes. "Red Ned" Small, who led residents in driving the day workers away, justified the act by explaining that "their crops of corn, peas &c were in close proximity to the potatoes and that these strangers might, if an opportunity offered, steal a portion of their crops."[131]

The introduction of temporary workers during work stoppages, or the stipulation that hired workers he paid from resident workers' shares, often insured the newcomers a strikebreakers' reception. An employer of contract workers on a plantation in lower Colleton district appealed for military assistance when his attempt to employ day laborers to break the undisclosed "insubordination" of his regular work force failed. "Day laborers, sent to work on the plantation, are abused by the negroes living there," the planter complained to Freedmen's Bureau assistant commissioner Robert K. Scott in June 1866, "& it is now impossible, to get a day laborer, to come to work on this plantation."[132]

of Columbia, R. K. Scott to O. O. Howard, 24 Aug. 1867, M 752, r 48, 0590–604; summary of reports for parishes of St. James Goose Creek, St. Johns Berkeley, and St. Stephens, and subdistrict of Columbia, in R. K. Scott to O. O. Howard, 9 July 1866, M 752, r 36, 0085–100; David Golightly Harris Farm Journals, 11 July 1866, UNC. A Northern storekeeper who had lived in Clarendon district since 1867 explained to a congressional committee, "A great deal of labor could be procured there, and was procured for a trifle, in the summer time, when the negroes are generally improvident." See *KKK Testimony*, vol. 2, p. 285.

130.   Abner Turnipseed to Gen. Green, 22 Sept. 1866, Letters Received, ser. 3156, Columbia, Subordinate Field Office Records, RG 105.

131.   Testimony of James Shoolbred, enclosed in John C. Chance to E. W. H. Read, 21 Nov. 1866; Testimony of Charles Kollh[o]ff, enclosed in John C. Chance to E. W. Read, 21 Nov. 1866; Edward F. O'Brien to Bvt. Maj. A. McL. Crawford, 11 Oct. 1866; all in M 869, r 9.

132.   [Contract], J. L. Coker and Ripon Terry et al. [1867], enclosed in *J. L. Coker v. George Terry et al.* [28 Oct. 1867], M 869, r 12; C. Witsell to R. K. Scott, 19 June 1866, M 869, r 34, 0557–59.

Some planters managed to retain control of plantation routines by periodically hiring noncontract laborers, needing only small amounts of cash or small surpluses of meat and grain to procure temporary workers. In areas where household economies were buffered from the shocks of irregular employment by a combination of seasonal work in nonagricultural enterprises and family cultivation of tracts excluded from plantation production, contract workers and nonresidents most effectively regulated planters' use of short-term labor. North of Charleston, rice workers and the area's black smallholders and squatters gradually shaped the source of much temporary help and restricted part-time hiring during the growing season. By the end of the decade, Georgetown's rice planters had been forced to seek winter ditching gangs well beyond the immediate neighborhood. In the late 1860s, they hired largely Irish labor crews in Charleston after no local workers could be hired to repair the extensive networks of irrigation canals and trunks on which freed men had initially refused to work during a popular campaign to thwart restoration in the winter of 1865–66.[133] The solidarity over seasonal work arrangements that Georgetown rice workers achieved manifested the local outcome of more general postwar movements to stem the chaos of postwar reconstructions of agricultural employment.

The struggles that convulsed postwar planting in the aftermath of emancipation reveal a contestation obscured by the deceptively static pronouncements of written contractual agreements. Every season, every field, and every crop carried a reminder that landowners' power was not self-generating.

133.   J. H. Read to Edward N. Thurston, 9 Feb. 1868, Read–Lance Family Papers, SCL; Ben Allston to Charles Petigru Allston, 21 Jan. 1869, Allston Family Papers, SCL; Ben Allston et al. to Colonel, 20 Oct. 1865, Letters Received, ser. 2392, Department of the South, RG 393 Pt 2 No 142 [C-1602]; Lt. Col. A. J. Willard to Capt. Geo. W. Hooker, 20 Oct. 1865, M 869, r 8, 0650–54; Lieut. Col. A. J. Willard to Capt. Geo. W. Hooker, 7 Nov. 1865, Letters and Reports Received Relating to Freedmen and Civil Affairs, ser. 4112, Department of the South, RG 393 Pt 1 [C-1503]; Lt. Col. A. J. Willard to Geo. W. Hooker, 19 Nov. 1865, Letters and Reports Received Relating to Freedmen and Civil Affairs, ser. 4112, Department of the South, RG 393 Pt 1; Doar, *Rice and Rice Planting*, pp. 45–46; Strickland, " 'No More Mud Work.' "

Laborers returning from cotton fields near Mount Pleasant, SC, c. 1874–75, photograph by George N. Barnard. Courtesy of the New-York Historical Society, New York, NY.

5

The Work of Reconstruction

The Reconstruction Acts of 1867, which created about a million new voters in ten of the eleven former Confederate states, marked a singular moment in national political life. By congressional fiat, men of no property and scant standing immediately became lawful voters. Because the overwhelming majority of the new voters were ex-slaves, this sweeping extension of the franchise colored politics in distinctive hues. In 1867, landless rural workers and common laborers in towns and cities became an unprecedented proportion of regional electorates. With the enfranchisement of former slave men, emergent wage earners in the former Confederate states gained broader access to the ballot than their increasingly foreign-born or female counterparts in other areas of the country then enjoyed. In the Reconstruction South, wage laborers' struggles would enter the arena of formal politics during "the Negro's hour."[1]

Sudden expansion of the electorate brought the arm of government within reach of an incipient social movement burgeoning in the Southern countryside. The congressional measures derived their distinctive social force from freed men and women eager to forge a political solution to conflicts opened by emancipation. Acts conceived in Congress came to life as Republican radicals' rank-and-file constituency took up its Reconstruction work.

Light in August

The sky had barely begun to lighten on the last Friday in August 1866, when a former slave began to call on a few landowners in his neighborhood in Orangeburg district. That late in the first full planting year since abolition, he might have designed his morning differently. At the end of the lull before harvest, no one – whether worker or employer – was likely to have noticed had he slept past sunrise or stretched out his morning meal, even on a workday. But in extraordinary times even more ordinary moments had their pressures. By the dawn's early light in August, he resolved to steady himself on the cleaving ground between slave past and unfold-

---

1. Wendell Phillips, quoted in Foner, *Reconstruction*, p. 255. DuBois, *Feminism and Suffrage,* slights class dimensions of obligatory male suffrage in the former Confederate states.

ing freedom. Furtively, and probably with troubled mind, the freedman approached several landowners in his neighborhood, confiding news that he intended to take to his former owner in Barnwell district as well.

Summoned to an unexpected counsel, the planter John D. Palmer listened closely, for the ex-slave was a man "in whose truthfulness he ha[d] reasons for confidence." For more than a week now, Palmer learned, freedpeople had been discussing visits to the quarters by a man whom they called Johnson. "Johnson," whom Palmer surmised to have been a veteran of the Fifty-fifth Massachusetts Volunteer Infantry then residing in the village of Orangeburg, had been urging freed men to form "companies" to aid the "military companies" that ex-slaves further east on the Santee River were then organizing. Many volunteers had come forward; the former slave identified three men on Palmer's plantation alone who were now "officers" in the new organization. In haste, Palmer summoned a neighbor, to whom the former slave had also paid a dawn visit. By day's end, both landowners had sworn statements respectful of their confidante's pleas for anonymity but detailed in precise description of the imminent danger to which they had been alerted:

> [T]he military Companies formed on the Santee, would, on the night of Sunday the 2d September next, march under the lead of the said Johnson, for Barnwell Court House, cross the Edisto River at Orangeburg C[ourt] H[ouse], and then devide the force into two bodies, one taking the Cannon's Bridge, and the other the Bennakers Bridge Road, and unite again in Barnwell District – the Volunteers from each section, joining them at various points on the march: . . . [I]t was intended to kill every white man they could find, and take what they wanted.[2]

Former slaves on the Santee mounted no such attack that fall, or, indeed, elsewhere in the state at any other moment during Reconstruction. Was it the unnamed freedman or alarmed landowners who first construed the military rubric by which male plantation laborers attempted regional consolidation as mobilization for a second war? John Palmer grounded his convictions on personal confidence in an alleged ex-slave informant and in his firm opinion, sanctioned often enough by President Andrew Johnson, that "it is the object of the Radical party at the north to bring about collisions between the negroes and whites."[3] Authoritative accounts of the ex-slave's exact communication are wanting. It is nevertheless clear that by 1866 some former slaves had begun to use quasi-military "companies" to shape collective behavior.

2. Affidavit of J. D. Palmer, 25 Aug. 1866, enclosed in vol. 254, Register of Complaints, ser. 3309, Orangeburg, Subordinate Field Office Records, RG 105 [A-7272].
3. Ibid.

Their own eyes rather than quiet counsel from a trusted former slave confirmed for a few proprietors the popularization of military rituals among freedpeople on the mainland. As early as the 1865 harvest, ex-slaves living near federal garrisons manned by black soldiers began to dress work routines and frolics with a military air. In the fall and summer of 1865, small work groups experimented with precision marches in several areas of Barnwell district, where units of the Thirty-fifth U.S. Colored Infantry and the Fifty-fourth Massachusetts Colored Volunteer Infantry were stationed. For example, four men concluded a day's work breaking corn on a farm in the vicinity of Barnwell Court House by waving aloft a corn stalk as they "kept step" along the "main road" at sundown.[4]

Drilling in the manner of soldiers enlivened social life on larger plantations as well. The jovial mood of one nighttime gathering sometime in the late fall or winter of 1865–66 impressed Ralph Ely, federal commander of the state's Western Military District. Spurred by conversation among fellow passengers traveling by coach between Newberry and Columbia, Ely rode out from his headquarters in Columbia to investigate their "stories about negroes drilling." Standing "where he could see and not be seen," Ely watched evening festivities among residents of one plantation's quarters:

> Negroes to the number of thirty or forty men, women, and children had gathered themselves together near their cabins and were drawn up in line. Some shouldered sticks, some had gun-stocks, some gun-barrels, some guns, and some were empty-handed. They marched and countermarched and halted, and marched again in straight lines and curves for nearly half an hour, their evolutions being interspersed with dancing and rough play, and accompanied by much laughter and noise.[5]

Such evident delight in a novel form of recreation, that was as much dance as drill, reiterated the significance of an emancipation gained by armed victory. A kind of folk drama came to life in the quarters as marchers repeatedly trod over Confederate ambitions.

Emulation of a military style, first evident in scattered parts of the mainland in the wake of federal occupation in 1865, spread during 1866, as groups of black Union veterans made their ways home. Under their in-

4. Col. E. A. Kozlay to Capt. L. B. Perry, 30 Aug. 1865, Letters and Reports Received Relating to Freedmen and Civil Affairs, ser. 4112, Department of the South, RG 393 Pt 1 [c-1443]; James C. Beecher to Maj. Kinsman, 7 Oct. 1865, M 869, r 7; drilling on the mainland of Beaufort district in the neighborhood of Grahamville is described in Wm. F. Robert to General [Nov. 1865], enclosed in Gen. Thomas H. Ruger to Col. Theo S. Bowers, 1 March 1866, Letters Relating to Military Discipline and Control, ser. 22, 2d Military District, RG 108 [s-15].

5. *Nation*, 4 Jan. 1866 p. 15.

fluences, entertaining elements of drills and marches acquired more instrumental social purposes, and men quickly assumed the most prominent roles in emerging company organizations.

Freed men adapted military rituals to make their presence as organized bodies visible. No doubt rural ceremonies paled in comparison with a more elaborate procession in Charleston, where, in October 1866, some seventy black men marched to the Citadel "in full Zouave uniform, red cap, blue jacket, red breeches, white legging and low quarter shoes" to receive a "beautiful banner" from "some of their colored female friends."[6] In the countryside, the display of arms – most often makeshift surrogates fashioned from remnants of hunting weapons, or raised standards of wooden clubs and corn stalks – was the more typical ceremonial rite. Intense execution of coordinated drills perhaps compensated for whatever spectacle the rural clubs lacked in costume. Some drills were the deliberate handiwork of black veterans returning to plantation labor, like the former slave James Bowen of Fawn Hill plantation, who instructed thirty men "going through the manual of arms" near that North Santee plantation in December 1866. To beats drummed on an occasional tin pan, male marching companies paraded in scattered plantation neighborhoods from the coast to the lower Piedmont by the winter of 1866–67.[7]

In their loosely structured offices, marching companies helped to connect areas of social existence fragmented under slavery. Adapting the command hierarchy of the regimental company, freed men devised networks of communication that circumvented the localism of slave life. A flexible chain of authority linked company members on individual farms and plantations to one or more resident "captains" and their aides in the neighborhood. In the village of Gadsden, in Richland district, for example, a society captain being questioned by a U.S. Army post commander identified his "first lieutenant" and also supplied the names of other designated officers on four neighborhood plantations and at a local "meetinghouse." Confederate mobilization occasionally echoed in a society's titles, as when the foreman on a Georgetown district rice plantation re-

6. Charleston *Daily Courier*, 18 Oct. 1866, p. 2, col.2.
7. In addition to the sources cited in notes 2 and 4, see Maj. [James P. Roy] to Lt. Col. W. L. M. Burger, 9 Dec. 1865, Unregistered Letters Received, ser. 4109, Department of the South, RG 393 Pt 1 [C-1385]; Citizens of Gadsden, SC to Col. Green, 2 Aug. 1866 and Wm. H. H. Holton to W. J. Harkisheimer, 23 Aug. 1866, both in Letters Received, ser. 3156 Columbia, Subordinate Field Office Records, RG 105; W. J. B. Cooper to dear Jim, 11 Dec.1866, Governors' Papers, SCDAH; James M. Johnston to A. J. L. Crawford, 17 Dec. 1866, M 869, r 10; E. W. H. Read to E. L. Deane, 3 Jan. 1867 [C-1619] and Lt. W. M. Wallace to Bvt. Maj. E. W. H. Reed, 8 Jan. 1867 [C-1619], both in Letters Received, ser. 2273, Department of the South, RG 393 Pt 2 No 132; Endorsement of John C. Chance, 4 Jan. 1867, on Bvt. Maj. E. W. H. Read to Lt. John C. Chance, 3 Jan. 1867, vol. 154 DS, pp. 128–29, Letters Sent, ser. 2389, Department of the South, RG 393 Pt 2 No 142 [C-1619].

ferred to "minute-men" who had been appointed on each plantation in the parish to summon men to assemble.[8] Routinizing and perhaps expediting the dissemination of news long carried along slavery's mysterious grapevine, company officers coordinated communication among neighborhood plantations and, if need be, with personnel in federal military and civil agencies. The effectiveness of communication among plantations was appreciated by an army officer stationed in Georgetown district in January 1866 during work stoppages to shape the terms of yearly contracts. "It is really wonderful how unanimous they are," the officer marveled, "communicating like magic."[9]

In the federal army ex-slaves discovered not only local activists but a framework for self-organization. Companies visibly reshaped public space to accommodate a working-class male structure of social authority independent of the old regime's obligations. Symbolically, at any rate, orders from captains introduced a mediating authority in areas where the claims of masters had once been sovereign. Budding commissions endowed their bearers with titles equivalent to the ranks of local antebellum authorities who had once commanded patrol beats, and to federal officers who now headed investigations of local affairs. The rank of sergeant enjoyed less favor than variations on commissioned officers' ranks. Company "captains" generally affiliated with first, second, and occasionally even third "lieutenants." Whether slave patrol, antebellum militia, Confederate mobilization, or the federal army suggested the precedent, there was more social criticism than imitation underlying popular adaptations of military forms.

Drills and marches were the most ceremonial, public face of laborers' attempts to establish a basis for more collective decision making in rural areas. Ex-slave John Washington, who had been among the thirty to forty men attending a company meeting on the North Santee in early December 1866, explained that "they had only met together to consult about making contracts for the next year." Around that same time, further to the east in Williamsburg district, investigation of freed men's threatening military organizations uncovered a series of meetings "for the purpose of regulating their mode of living" whose deliberations had drawn more than two hundred people. Discussion of the June 1866 congressional homestead act, which opened public lands in five Southern states to actual set-

8. Citizens of Gadsden, SC to Col. Green, 2 Aug. 1866; Wm. H. H. Holton to W. J. Harkisheimer, 23 Aug. 1866; both in Letters Received, ser. 3156, Columbia, Subordinate Field Office Records, RG 105; E. W. Everson to Bvt. Maj. Edw. L. Deane, 18 Jan. 1867, enclosed in E. W. Everson to Bvt. Maj. Edw. L. Deane, 17 Jan. 1867, M 869, r 12. See Rogers, *Georgetown County*, p. 372, regarding the formation of the "Winyah Minute Men."

9. B. F. Smith to Lieut., 21 Jan. 1866, Letters and Reports Received Relating to Freedmen and Civil Affairs, ser. 4112, 2d Military District, RG 393 Pt 1.

tlers, drew some of the largest gatherings that year. The large December meetings in Williamsburg had considered resettlement on public lands in Florida "if they cannot get such terms as they think reasonable and just from the planters." Similarly, "a large number of freedmen Nambering about 1000" in St. Matthew's Parish had decided that October to settle in Florida under the leadership of former sergeant William M. Viney of the Fifty-fourth Massachusetts Volunteers. Internal discipline, as much as relations with landowners, claimed the attention of some rural clubs. John Adams, captain of a society near Gadsden, reported in August that bodies "in one or two instances have punished members of their own companies for stealing" in keeping with their goal of the "suppression of vagrancy and lawlessness among the Freedpeople." The inactivity of civil authorities prompted a group of freed men in Orangeburg district to arm themselves "as best they could" in December. The armed men successfully apprehended and turned over to military authorities three members of a gang who claimed to have beaten and robbed recently ordained Methodist minister Tom Phillips because Phillips, a former slave, "was a leading negro and belonged to the d--d Abolition church."[10] By the end of the first full planting year since emancipation, rural clubs had taken up a range of activities, all geared to reshape the social and economic content of emancipation.

Federal commanders, typically sharing the view of the Western Military District commander in Columbia that "[S]tories about negroes drilling are not worthy of serious consideration," confiscated companies' military regalia and advised members that armed assemblies were prohibited.[11] Nevertheless, to most ex-masters and ex-slaves, acting like soldiers was something other than sport.

Southern alarmists readily interpreted these unprecedented gatherings as dreaded manifestations of the conspiratorial violence that proslavery ideology had long decried in the North's abolitionism, secret fraternal orders, and trade unions.[12] To military headquarters in Georgetown in November 1865 came reports that freed men "exhibiting signs of dissatisfaction and insubordination" had been "holding secret meetings and arming themselves with knives and what other weapons they can lay

10. Endorsement of John C. Chance, 4 Jan. 1867, on Bvt. Maj. E. W. H. Read to Lt. John C. Chance, 3 Jan. 1867, vol. 154 DS, pp. 128–29, Letters Sent, ser. 2389, Department of the South, RG393 Pt 2 No 142 [c-1619]; James M. Johnston to A. M. L. Crawford, 17 Dec. 1866, M 869, r 10; Wm. M. Viney to Bvt. Mag. Gen. R. K. Scott, 10 Oct. 1866, M 869 r 21, 0808 and published as Doc. 365 in Berlin, Reidy, and Rowland, eds., *Black Military Experience*, pp. 819–21; Alonzo Webster to O. O. Howard, 20 Dec. 1866, M 752, r 45, 0359–67. A contemporary biographical sketch of Viney appears in Abbott, ed., "Yankee Views." Sketch of Rev. Thomas Phillips in Williamson, p. 186.
11. *Nation*, 4 Jan. 1866, p. 15.
12. Davis, *Slave Power Conspiracy*, pp. 41–42.

their hands upon, preparatory to a general revolt on or about the first of January."[13] From Sumter district, a resident reported in alarm that "Negro meetings plotting insurrection murder & conflagration generally excepting none but young women, who are reserved for a worse fate" portended a "war of races."[14] Freedmen's drills and meetings fed conspiratorial thinking that was ready to sketch insurrection in lurid detail.

Freed men's quasi-military associations fueled nightmarish prophecy because their members marched over real contradictions in a social order that had wed the master's absolute authority to nominally democratic forms of government.[15] Ex-slaves' simple expectation that they had become like other free people was deeply rooted in democratic ideologies of the Age of Revolution.[16] On emancipation, they tended to anticipate no social rank to designate men who were free but who were somehow left outside the scope of public institutions. Members of a company organized in the vicinity of Santee River rice plantations under the acknowledged leadership of fellow plantation laborer "Colonel" Sam Pyall illustrate this trend. Questioned by the local Freedmen's Bureau officer in late December 1866 about a marching company whose members were drawn from at least three neighboring plantations, they frankly declared a broadly political goal. "They avow," the agent reported, "their purpose to be the protection of their rights." Believing themselves free subjects of government in full right, they assembled to defend more particular claims. Company members informed the federal commander who investigated "armed organizations" on these plantations a few days later "that they have concluded to work (per week) two days for the planter, three days for themselves, and that on Saturdays and Sundays no work should be done."[17] Ex-slaves' implicit judgments that public institutions were accessible to working people did not nourish conspiratorial intent.

13. George H. Nye to Charles R. Fillebrown, 5 Nov. 1865, Letters and Reports Received Relating to Freedmen and Civil Affairs, ser. 4112, 2d Military District, RG 393 Pt 1.
14. R. W. Habersham to O. O. Howard, 6 Dec. 1865, M 869, r 7.
15. Genovese, *Roll, Jordan, Roll*.
16. This discussion has been influenced by Genovese, *From Rebellion to Revolution*; Gaspar, *Bondmen and Rebels*; Foner, *Reconstruction*, p. 75; and the contrast with the weakening of the medieval state in France and Burgundy described in Bloch, *Feudal Society*, vol. 1, p. 261. Geggus, "Haitian Revolution," p. 30, regards the 1791 insurrection on St. Domingue's north plain as "one of the first of a new type of slave revolt soon to become typical, in which the insurgents claimed to be already officially emancipated."
17. Quoted passages appear respectively in Bvt. Maj. Edw. L. Deane to Bvt. Maj. E. W. H. Read, 31 Dec. 1866, vol. 82/161 DS, p. 75, Letters Sent, ser. 2269, RG 393 Pt 2 No 132 [C-1619] and Lt. W. M. Wallace to Bvt. Maj. E. W. H. Read 8 Jan. 1867, Letters Received, ser. 2273, RG 393 Pt 2 No 132 [C-1619]. See also E. W. Everson to Bvt. Maj. Edw. L. Deane, 18 Jan. 1867, enclosed in idem to Bvt. Maj. Edw. L. Deane,

However much they premised their collective actions on a rightful public role, as former slaves company members also had firsthand acquaintance with direct subjection to personal power. Once themselves the lawful objects of direct coercion, they understood social authority to encompass measures of forceful intimidation. Under such circumstances, their drills, marches, and assumptions of military titles were not altogether figurative challenges. When a young boy at play waved a sword while he marched around a farm in Beaufort district, only days after some workers had fallen on the owner and "tried to give a beating," the youth made, so the farmer well knew, a gesture that "bids defiance."[18] Exposure to actual assaults heightened the symbolic appeal of organizations formed somewhat along military lines in parts of Barnwell district, where a regulator band of vigilantes looted, whipped at least four women farm laborers, and repeatedly fired on workers in the fields during the fall of 1865. Armed bands deployed live shot against freed men who marched with corn stalks.[19] Under no illusions about their relative weakness, companies on the North Santee assessed members ten cents each in order to buy ammunition in the week before the Christmas holidays in 1866.[20]

Assuming the posture of an all-male institution authorized to wield disciplined force, marching companies symbolically recast local power relations at a time when no civil institutions guaranteed their right to exist. Marching and drilling ritualized ongoing if unsanctioned attempts to forge a disciplined solidarity across plantation boundaries. Drills demonstrated to the plantations' other working people ceremonial resolve to "stand by each other."[21] By such measures, ex-slaves were fashioning a corporate identity advanced in comparison with other American agricultural workers of the time. Company spokesmen typically disavowed insurrectionary intent; but holding unprecedented assemblies, making attempts to collectively regulate working conditions, drawing on national legislation to shape neighborhood plans, and acting in place of local officeholders inevitably shoved against local structures of power. As Congress shaped the terms of the first Reconstruction Acts during the planting

18 Jan. 1867, M 869, r 12. The company leader's name variously appears as Pyall, Tyall, and Pyatt.

18. [J. Y.?] Bostick to Capt. [Sept.? 1865], Letters Received ser. 2384, Department of the South, RG 393 Pt 2 No 141 [C-1588].

19. James C. Beecher to Maj. Kinsman, 7 Oct. 1865, James C. Beecher to Maj. O. D. Kinsman, 15 Oct. 1865, both in M 869, r 7; Col. E. A. Kozlay to Capt. L. B. Perry, 30 Aug. 1865, Letters and Reports Received Relating to Freedmen and Civil Affairs, ser. 4112, Department of the South, RG 393 Pt 1 [C-1443].

20. E. W. Everson to Bvt. Maj. Edw. L. Deane, 18 Jan. 1867, enclosed in Everson to Deane, 17 Jan. 1867, M 869, r 12.

21. The quotation appears in James C. Beecher to T. D. Hodges, 1 Dec. 1865, Letters and Reports Received Relating to Freedmen and Civil Affairs, ser. 4112, 2d Military District, RG 393 Pt 1.

season of 1867, neighborhood bodies of freed men loosely patterned on the model of the regimental company began to assume responsibility for organized regulation of public affairs. Suffrage rights forged in Congress would encounter a rural activism that had germinated without authorization, in the shade of political life.

Marching companies sprouted on unstable social terrain. Public demonstrations and assemblies remained inseparable from organizational secrecy and direct coercion where there was no legitimate political sphere. An understandable uncertainty about the intent or the consequences of local organizing might well have unsteadied the unnamed freedman who had reportedly sought refuge in some favored landowners' personal protection early that August morning in 1866.

Why Can't We Be Friends?

Ex-slaves' unauthorized efforts to hew out political space gained support when the sudden jolt of the Reconstruction Acts cracked local foundations of political power.[22] By congressional order, slavery's "mudsill" became a political constituency. From Charleston, at the end of March, a correspondent of the *New York Times* pronounced the measures' earliest effects "scarcely less striking than the results of Emancipation itself."[23]

Between March and July 1867, two distinctive party organizations proffered appeals to ex-slave voters. Within days of the passage of the first Reconstruction Act on 2 March, a fourteen-member committee in Charleston spearheaded the formation of a state Republican Party. Chaired by the publisher of the short-lived Charleston *Advocate*, the committee was composed of twelve black members drawn from Charleston's freeborn elite and Northern professional backgrounds, and the U.S. federal marshal.[24] An opposition party that embraced a scattering of the state's existing political leadership also proposed a style of political affil-

22. On 2 March 1867, congressional Republicans enacted the first of a series of measures that directly restructured government in ex-Confederate states, which, with the exception of Tennessee, had rejected the Fourteenth Amendment. Between March and July, four congressional acts instructed commanders of five newly designated military districts about the terms of special elections required of states placed under military jurisdiction. All male citizens who were at least twenty-one years old and who were not disfranchised under the Fourteenth Amendment were declared eligible to register to vote in federally mandated state elections. In these special elections, registered voters would first cast ballots for or against conventions authorized to rewrite state constitutions. Voters were then also to elect delegates to serve in the constitutional conventions in the event that results of the first referendum should call for their assembly.
23. *New York Times*, 3 April 1867, p. 1, cols. 3–4.
24. Charleston *Daily Courier*, 22 March 1867, p. 1, cols. 2–4; *Nation*, 14 March 1867, p. 203; Holt, *Black Over White*, pp. 27–28, 122.

iation with former slaves. Columbia's Union Brotherhood Society, in whose name appeared a published call for a meeting on 14 March "to devise some expression of the rejoicing at the passage of the recent Military Universal Suffrage Bill," did not share the Republican allegiances of the Charleston group. Drawing on social networks of Columbia's slaveborn urbanites and several other black benevolent societies, the Union Brotherhood sponsored a public ceremony on 18 March in which now-disfranchised members of the state's former political leadership assumed a prominent – to some, overshadowing – role. Confederate hero and scion of the cotton-planting aristocracy Wade Hampton, Columbia's ex-mayor James G. Gibbes, State Representative William H. Talley, and former U.S. senator William F. DeSaussure joined slaveborn minister David Pickett and ex-slave hotel servant William Beverly Nash on a platform whose "principal motto" promised "Unity and Friendship to all Men."[25] Small wonder that the Columbia coalition's public "rejoicing" did not take the name of the Republican Party.

Advocates and opponents of the Reconstruction Acts both approached the state's newest voters with the public meetings, parades, and musical entertainment that were staples of nineteenth-century popular politics. On 21 March, the Charleston committee presented its fifteen-point "Platform of the Union Republican Party of South Carolina" to a "densely packed" public meeting in Military Hall. After a series of addresses by committee members, including black New Jersey Congregational minister E. J. Adams and freeborn Kentucky Presbyterian minister and ex–army chaplain Benjamin Franklin Randolph, the meeting "unanimously adopted" the committee's resolutions "amidst great cheers."[26] A few days later, the committee again presented its platform for discussion and adoption at an afternoon rally of some two thousand men and women assembled at the Citadel green. In Columbia, a procession of "various societies" of the city's black residents, headed by a "band of music," made its way from the African Methodist Episcopal Church through the "principal streets" to hear scheduled speakers in a vacant lot just outside the city. An evening torchlight procession that paid its respects to "prominent citizens," who obliged with "impromptu addresses," concluded the 18 March ceremony in the state capital.[27]

25.   Meeting's published call quoted from *New York Times*, 23 March 1867, p. 2 col. 1; principal motto quoted in Charleston *Daily Courier*, 23 March 1867; see also *New York Times*, 16 March 1867, p. 2, col. 2, and 19 March 1867, p. 5, col. 4; Williamson, *After Slavery*, p. 350; Holt, *Black Over White*, p. 29, Table 5; Rable, *But There Was No Peace*, pp. 67–68. A *New York Times* correspondent objected to the New York *Tribune*'s characterization of the Columbia meeting as a "farce of the most disgraceful character." See *New York Times*, 2 April 1867, p. 2, col. 1–2.
26.   Biographical information of Adams and Randolph appears in Holt, *Black Over White*, p. 89, Table 5, and *Official Army Register*, p. 197.
27.   Charleston *Daily Courier*, 20 March 1867, p. 1, col. 4.

There was, however, something in a name. The handful of South Carolina's onetime political leaders who pursued a selective alignment with "old issue" and "new issue" free men proposed a restricted franchise when the state's emerging Republican organization had no place for the measure. Conservatives like Governor James L. Orr and planter Wade Hampton, who led the move, appealed to a fundamentally hierarchical social order in which mass political organizations had no meaning.[28] In Charleston, before a predominantly black meeting of more than two thousand people in Richard Harvey Cain's African Methodist Episcopal church, Orr consolidated slavery's series of unequal social ranks into "the difference between those who have capital and those who have none." Firmly, if obligingly, he excluded the latter group from the postwar political community. "Do not trouble yourselves upon the subject of politics," Orr advised. "Do not stand at street corners idling away a half hour talking politics, but go to work."[29] The governor resurrected – for audiences still visited by the ghost – the body of contempt for propertyless laborers that had been substantive in antebellum political ideology. On behalf of a still unnamed alliance, he improvised unfamiliar airs of political cooperation with selected black men in the harmonies of a familiar key.

Whereas Orr located the sources of social order in divine commands "which neither you or any one else have a right to dispute," Wade Hampton appealed to more earthly but similarly nonhuman standards.[30] Hampton urged a political coalition among "Southern men" made "friends" by the effects of physical environment on an abstract human life cycle. "Is this not your home as well as ours?" he asked the predominantly black audience gathered in Columbia to celebrate the Reconstruction Acts. In affirmation, he urged, "Does not that glorious Southern sun above us shine alike for both of us? Did not this soil give birth to all of us? And will we not all alike, when our troubles and trials are over, sleep in that same soil, in which we first drew breath?" William H. Talley similarly explained that "the interests of the white man and the colored man of the South were one and the same," because "[t]hey are parts of the same society, inhabiting the same land, under the same sun, breathing the same atmosphere."[31] These conservatives rendered southern social ties almost literally organic, with heavy infusions of helium.

28. Ford, *Origins of Southern Radicalism*, attributes the absence of enduring parties in the state on the eve of the Civil War to social harmony; Klein, *Unification of a Slave State*, explores social realignments that underlay the seeming harmony of patron–client relations. See also Cooper, *South and Politics*, and Greenberg, *Masters and Statesmen*.
29. An extensive first-person account of Orr's speech appears in Charleston *Daily Courier*, 15 Feb. 1867, p. 2, cols. 2–3.
30. A "full report" of Hampton's address at the Columbia gathering occasioned by the Reconstruction Acts appears in ibid., 23 March 1867, p. 1, cols. 3–4.
31. Quotation appears in ibid., 20 March 1867, p. 1, col. 4; similar accounts of Talley's

Drawing a political circle of "best friends" left ample room to disparage those outside the ring. Orr dismissed Union military service as a sufficient claim for suffrage rights by suggesting that, until 1808, the state constitution's fifty-acre freehold requirement has wisely "excluded from the ballot-box" many "soldiers who fought through the Revolutionary war, who aided in achieving the independence of the country." "[T]he wise men of that day, the legislators themselves," he maintained, "waited until a new generation grew up and had some advantages of education before even the white race was permitted to vote." Orr failed to specify how he stood on the issue of suffrage for "hundreds of thousands of whites standing in the same relative condition" as freedmen, "thrown upon your own resources, without capital and without lands." Although he exaggerated the disfranchisement of free white men between 1783 and 1808 and also overstated the extent of landlessness among white South Carolinians, his allusions to the unequal standing of white men was nevertheless an unusual theme in public speech making.

Wade Hampton, early disposed to show the kinder, gentler face of an authoritarian state, was not inclined to enforce retroactively the educational and property requirements for voting that he now endorsed. The future was altogether another matter. "I agree," he pledged, "that all, white as well as black, who do not possess these qualifications shall be excluded" once the measures were enacted.[32] Much as antebellum thinkers had long argued the illusory nature of human equality, so Hampton now explained, "There was no such thing as universal suffrage" among free men. A hierarchy of particularized suffrage rights linked the "Englishman knowing all about our laws and our system of Government, and having great wealth," who still had to satisfy naturalization and residence requirements, the free man who would come to satisfy educational and property requirements sometime during his life, and the free man who might pass his days without ever meeting them. Postwar defenses of limited suffrage were played in the register of proslavery ideology.

Conservatives' brief flirtation with ex-slaves' and freeborn black people's "best men" produced no durable union in 1867. The scattering of ex-slave spokesmen did not return in full their suitors' ardor for the limited franchise. A more individualist rendering of free-market morality, no doubt cemented by pre-existing ties of patronage, brought them to the conservatives' forum.

remarks in *New York Times*, 21 March 1867, p. 1, col. 7 and 23 March 1867, p. 2, cols. 1–2.

32. All quotations taken from account of Hampton's speech in Charleston *Daily Courier*, 23 March 1867, p. 1, cols. 3–4.

Only ex-slave minister David Pickett joined conservatives in endorsing restricted suffrage rights at the Columbia celebration of the Reconstruction Acts.[33] Affirming that "[t]he good of his people was his first consideration," Pickett offered a formulation of citizenship premised on access to the skill and property on which he believed informed political participation rightfully rested. "He was opposed to universal suffrage for two reasons," Pickett announced, "the want of education and property qualification." His optimistic assessment that education was now "readily attainable," and his moral conviction that with "industry and economy" a smallholder's competence "would surely come," were not rooted in ordained social divisions. Rather, Pickett portrayed the restrictive franchise as a necessary but permeable boundary to political participation.

Notwithstanding his spirited devotion to full male suffrage, ("I want to see everybody vote, except the women," he thundered), Virginia-born ex-slave William Beverly Nash was the South Carolina conservatives' best-known black spokesman in the spring of 1867.[34] Distrustful and somewhat contemptuous of poor whites, bruised by recent discriminatory treatment in the nation's capital, sobered by defeats of referenda to extend suffrage to black men outside the former Confederate states, and deeply moved by overtures from disfranchised "gentlemen in whom we have more confidence than any body else," Nash rallied to the conservatives' appeals. With fervor he urged political alliance with those "Southern white men" whom he viewed to be "the best friend of the black man." Southern wartime unionists were excluded from the friendship. "I would rather trust General Hampton riding at the head of his [Confederate] column, and shouting to his men to follow," Nash insisted, "than any man who has stayed at home." It was, however, in the Republican Party that, by midsummer, Nash found fullest accommodation for his insistent appeals for "absolutely universal suffrage without distinction of property or education."[35]

The rhetoric of South Carolina's emerging Republican Party drew broadly from Northern free labor ideologies. In consequence, its organizing initiatives proceeded without the coherence of southern conser-

33. Quoted passages from the third-person summary of Pickett's remarks appear in ibid., 20 March 1867, p. 1, col. 4; another summary of the same speech appears in *New York Times*, 23 March 1867, p. 2, cols. 1–2. A summary of Pickett's remarks at the Union Brotherhood's planning meeting appears in *New York Times*, 23 March 1867, p. 2, col. 1. See also *Christian Recorder*, 2 Feb. 1867, p. 1, col. 2, 16 Jan. 1873, p. 1, col. 5.
34. With the exception of the excerpt cited in note 35, quotations come from Nash's speech as published in the Charleston *Daily Courier*, 21 March 1867, p. 2, col. 3. It was transcribed "*verbatim,*" the reporter advised, "merely smothering off the rough edge, and dropping the peculiarities of accent and pronunciation."
35. Quoted in *New York Times*, 23 March 1867, p. 2, col. 1.

vatives' more unified social vision. All Republican Party spokesmen, however, endorsed mandatory male suffrage as vigorously as their opposition discountenanced it. A wide range of beliefs bolstered initiatives to rally ex-slave laborers to the new party's standard.

Some Republican spokesmen cast the work of party organization in millennial proportions. From a belief in human perfectionism and an absorption with accounts of the erosion of servile labor in other times and places, they fashioned an interpretation of the American Civil War's historic significance. Black Congregational minister Enals J. Adams, for example, fired his spirit for political work after the passage of the Reconstruction Acts, hopeful that struggles on earth drew their fullest possibilities from the transforming powers of divine mercy.[36] The path to the ballot box began, by Adams's view, with divinely sanctioned free will:

> I am in favor of universal suffrage, upon the ground that every man
> is endowed with a certain degree of volition, having the right to
> choose or refuse that which is good or evil; that he has a right to
> choose the God whom he will serve, and if a man may choose the God
> he wishes to serve, has he not an equal right to choose the ruler that
> shall rule over him?

Ongoing global upheavals made Reconstruction, for Adams, part of the ferment of "revolutionary times." Like serf emancipation in Russia, national unification movements in Italy and Germany, and movements for political independence in Ireland and Canada, Reconstruction seemed to him a decisive turning point in an age-old "contest, terrible in its nature, . . . between despotism and republican principles, between freedom and slavery." The minister saw in these international events the "genius of republican liberty, bearing its escutcheon upon the capital of every nation, waving its banner in triumph over every continent, sea, and ocean." Nation-states unfolded with the glory of scriptural prophecy. Spokesmen like Adams loved organizing on behalf of the party of national reunification as they loved their powerful but compassionate god. Like black Pennsylvania-born lawyer and teacher Jonathan Jasper Wright, some Republicans believed that they took up party work "standing upon the Lord's side."[37]

Mass political parties also boded well to larger numbers of early Republican spokesmen who fixed their gaze most closely on concerns with earthly authority. In a state where social alternatives to ex-slave Repub-

36. All quotations appear as Adams's speech was reported in Charleston *Daily News*, 22 March 1867, p. 1, cols. 2–4. For a biographical sketch of Adams, see Ripley, ed., *Black Abolitionist Papers*, vol. 4, pp. 320–21.

37. Charleston *Daily Courier*, 27 July 1867, p. 1, cols. 2–5. Biographical sketches of Wright are offered in Holt, *Black Over White*, p. 42, and in Logan and Winston, eds., *Dictionary of American Negro Biography*.

licans were few, political affiliation among men of unequal social standing seemed to even the most moderate Republicans a style of party organization essential to social harmony. The Massachusetts-born collector of
internal revenue, Frederick A. Sawyer, who had moved to South Carolina
before the war and broken with the Democratic party in 1860, questioned
the theory "popular . . . with many [local] gentlemen of intelligence and
refinement, that only a few men are fit to vote." Sawyer thought the
broader franchise a valuable opportunity to extend the influence of social
elites. "We all know," he advised delegates to the convention that inaugurated the statewide organization of the Republican Party in July 1867,
"that intelligence, refinement, and wealth have a great influence on all
men, and this is as true in politics as in anything else."[38]

Where the Republicans' conservative opposition had seen in unrestricted suffrage a catastrophic leveling of social rank, Republican mod-
erates expected universal suffrage to blunt the antagonism of subordinate
social groups. By making common men "stockholders in the Government," another party organizer proposed, equal voting rights offered an
antidote to threats of revolutionary upheaval.[39] Such spokesmen found
political parties of broad class composition well-suited to link men who
shared few other direct ties.

The lowest common denominator of Republican Party rhetoric portrayed a political space large enough for socially unequal men to share.
As a theory of citizenship, Northern free labor ideology celebrated self-
government by the working man of independent means. General Daniel E.
Sickles, newly installed in Charleston as commander of the Second Military District, interpreted the broadened franchise as further vindication
of a distinctively American political history.[40] He greeted some three hundred freedmen, who had concluded a large Republican rally in Charleston
with a torchlight serenade at his residence, as "citizens of the Republic,"
and then explained, "So far, in this country, experience has shown that

38. Quotations from first-person account of Sawyer's speech that appears in Charleston
Daily Courier, 31 July 1867, p. 1, cols. 2–4. See also Holt, *Black Over White*, p. 122;
Williamson, *After Slavery*, p. 376.

39. Christopher Columbus Bowen well expressed the view that elections transcended
social conflict. During the presidential contest of 1868, he reflected on how elections
under unrestricted male suffrage "settled beyond all possibility of a doubt, the question of a war of races. They gave them something to protect themselves and stand up
and fight for as American citizens. The colored men have now no cause to inaugurate
a war of races. They are citizens of the U.S., stockholders in the Government, and
it is their duty to stand by and support it." Charleston *Daily Courier*, 19 Oct. 1868,
p. 1, cols. 3–5.

40. Quotations from the text of Sickles's speech as published in *New York Times*, 3 April
1867, p. 1, col. 4; see also the report of his speech reported in Charleston *Daily
Courier*, 29 March 1867, p. 2, col. 3, and the paper's corrected report on 30 March
1867, p. 2, col. 3.

union, liberty, and power are safe in the hands of those who earn their bread by the sweat of their brows." As an ideology of patriotism, Sickles continued, free labor was the warrant of the citizen-soldier. "None love the land of their birth more fondly," he declaimed, "none will defend it with more constancy and valor than those whose labor make up the sum of a nation's wealth."

Socially broad and militarily secure, the Republicans' common political ground was nevertheless fragile terrain. Laboring men shed few obligations of social deference – even to political opponents – when they mounted the Republican platform. Military officers and Freedmen's Bureau officials were especially likely to emphasize social deference as a component of the newest voters' responsibilities. The commander of the Second Military District early itemized components of the decorous behavior expected of the newest voters. Speaking "as a friend," General Daniel Sickles admonished freed men "to preserve at all times the utmost moderation of language, temper, and conduct," to "avoid everything like violence, impatience, or indecorum." Deference sustained social harmony and was therefore, he explained, also a political obligation. Essential to "the prosperity of the South [and] the welfare of the country" were "the harmony and good-feeling which should exist between people of both races and the South." Free labor ideology's muted but clear insistence that it was the burden of labor to maintain such harmony received the general's full endorsement.[41] Even the freedmen's "adversaries," Sickles counseled, should have no "just occasion" to complain that they had been shown the "least disrespect" in freedmen's "discussions, private or public."

Endorsing suffrage rights of ex-slave workingmen who were predominantly agricultural laborers exposed ambiguities fundamental to free labor ideology. Laborers' relative standing in the political community seemed less certain than when, at the onset of the Civil War, President Abraham Lincoln had asserted, "Labor is the superior of capital, and deserves much the higher consideration."[42] A relationship that to Lincoln had seemed exceptional because he viewed working for wages as a transient feature of working life now struck some postwar party organizers as more pervasive in its southern context. William Beverly Nash, for example, applied these social categories when he reasoned, "The white man has land, the black man has labor." He reversed Lincoln's formula, however, to conclude, "and labor is worth nothing without capital."[43] Although

41. For skilled workers' formulations of republicanism, see Salvatore, *Eugene V. Debs*, pp. 22–32, 48, 50.

42. Abraham Lincoln to Fellow Citizens of the Senate and House of Representatives, 3 Dec. 1861, in *OR*, ser. 3, vol. 1, pp. 709–21; the quotation appears at 720.

43. Charleston *Daily Courier*, 21 March 1867, p. 2, col. 3.

Nash offered these reflections before he became an ardent Republican organizer, his formulation was scarcely a brief for equality in political partnerships. Lincoln's formulation also bedeviled General Sickles when the latter tried to construct social harmony from elements of social inequality. Modifying Lincoln's equation, Sickles advised former slaves, "Intelligence, culture, capital, land, are not less essential than labor, and yet without a prosperous, contented and happy laboring class, society lacks an essential element of strength and repose."[44] Inscribing equal political rights among socially unequal men was not a straightforward matter.

Rare were those Republicans whose faith in the ballot linked electoral politics to larger views of social order. Certainly all defended the ballot as free laborers' right. Freeborn ex-army chaplain Benjamin Franklin Randolph elaborated a popular Republican view when he emphasized the ease with which men could master electoral politics. "I believe we can learn to vote," he advised a predominantly black Republican gathering in Charleston. "I see no difficulty in a man's investigating and discovering as to who are his friends and voting for them, and also who are his enemies and refusing to vote for them. It is a learning easily acquired."[45] William Beverly Nash similarly insisted that skill in political affairs was as accessible as skill in any craft. "Give a man tools," Nash explained, "and let him commence to use them, and, in time, he will learn a trade. So it is with voting."[46] At the same time, however, however, some Republican spokesmen clearly anticipated that the most fundamental restructuring of political institutions in the nation's history would have no effect on existing social relationships. The commander of the Second Military District advised South Carolina's new voters, "It will not be necessary . . . for you to neglect your regular employment and associations to attend to political affairs."[47] The *New York Times*'s Charleston correspondent felt confident that ex-slave voters would not strengthen the radical wing of the party because they were overwhelmingly employed by southern landowners. Freedpeople "would take heed how they put their livlihood [*sic*] in jeopardy, for the sake of . . . a mere political abstrac-

44. Quoted from Sickles's speech as reported in *New York Times*, 3 April 1867, p. 1, col. 4. That text corresponds to the corrected version that appeared in Charleston *Daily Courier*, 30 March 1867, p. 2, col. 3. An earlier account of the same speech in Charleston *Daily Courier*, 29 March 1867, p. 2, col. 3 had reported the general saying "Intelligence, culture, capital, land, are not less essential than labor, and yet without labor, these can have no solid and enduring foundation." The *Courier* corrected the passage in the later issue, blaming "typographical errors" that had "materially impaired [the] sense" of Sickles's speech.
45. Charleston *Daily Courier*, 22 March 1867, p. 1, cols. 2–4.
46. Ibid., 21 March 1867, p. 2, col. 3.
47. *New York Times*, 3 April 1867, p. 1, col. 4.

tion," the reporter approvingly predicted.[48] There was often a curious tendency in much Republican political rhetoric to isolate politics from other aspects of social life. The quest for harmony among unequal men made electoral politics a narrow strait.

Southern opponents of congressional Reconstruction admitted no such inconsistencies. A contempt for laborers fundamental to proslavery ideology had shaped even the limited attempts made by those small numbers of conservatives who made a case for limited suffrage in the wake of the Reconstruction Acts. That movement was dead by the fall of 1867, when, in a published address, South Carolina conservatives assessed the significance of the Reconstruction Acts' having claimed a place for labor in the body politic. "The war that has always existed between capital and labor," the conservative convention judged, "is decided in the favor of the latter, and the wealth of the country is prostrated at the feet of those who have nothing at stake but their daily wages and their daily dread." Far from making a distinction between political and social affairs, the convention concluded, "this wild and reckless experiment comes home to the hearth-stone of every citizen, and involves family and property, society, liberty, and even life itself."[49]

For better and for worse, ex-slaves rejected the patronage proffered by southern conservatives and moderate Republicans alike when they came to the aid of the Republican Party.

There's a Meeting Here Tonight

"[W]hat in h—— are the negroes doing[?]" The question exploded in July 1867 from the mouth of an irate white resident of Macon, Georgia. "[H]ave they found Thad Stevens[?]" he demanded of a man whom he saw leaving an exuberant meeting at an African Methodist Episcopal church well past midnight. "No," came the quick reply, "[w]e are raising John Brown from the dead."[50]

The resident of Macon was probably not alone in his stupefaction during that miraculous "registration summer" of 1867. By midsummer, countless emissaries were broadcasting the new terms of suffrage. Their reports extended news about enfranchisement beyond major cities like Charleston and Columbia, and outside the federal enclaves of wartime federal occupation like Beaufort, or market towns like Orangeburg and

48. Ibid., cols. 3–4.
49. Charleston *Daily Courier*, 9 Nov. 1867, p. 1, cols. 3–5.
50. Extract of Rev. Henry M. Turner to [Thomas L. Tullock?], 9 July [1867], Robert C. Schenck Papers, r 6. Michael Fitzgerald kindly brought this collection of papers to my attention.

Lexington, where public discussions had begun earlier that spring. Grass-roots organizing gained momentum during the summer and fall as messengers followed the paths of railroad lines; hitched rides or walked along country roads; mounted the hustings in wooded arbors and open fields; and secured churches, schools, country stores, plantation quarters or lone cabins, and, occasionally, even county courthouses, where registration and its portents could be aired. The turmoil and routines of small worlds broke their bounds to increasingly common rhythms under the pressure of canvassing for the Reconstruction measures. More than a political party, a social movement was in the making.

The building movement required self-conscious activists, people informed and ready to explain voting and registration, and to tackle larger aspects of political education. At the outset, conditions for making the congressional measures widely known favored literate canvassers sympathetic to the Republican program. Even the most solidly trained found their talents expanded by their organizing efforts. Rev. John V. Given, who left Washington, DC, to take up intensive grass-roots organizing in Virginia, was somewhat impressed by reports of his popularity. "[P]lease do not think me egotistical," he advised his Republican supporters in Washington, but "the white men [in Virginia] tell me . . . that I am the equal of Fred. Douglass."[51] Unlike Given, most early political organizers among freedpeople in South Carolina were already state residents.

Inclination to undertake local organizing was strong among many civilians attached to (though rarely direct employees of) federal agencies in South Carolina. Benjamin Franklin Whittemore, a white Methodist minister and ex–army chaplain of Mauldin, Massachusetts, had been supervising twenty-eight common schools under sponsorship of the American Missionary Association and the Freedmen's Bureau, in the neighborhood of Darlington district on the eve of the Reconstruction Acts. Members of his Lincoln Debating Society, which Whittemore had organized early in 1867 with the motto "Progress Our Aim/Success Our Right," were no doubt among the first to hear from Whittemore himself about the early Republican Party activities in which he was a participant.[52] Freeborn black men like Jonathan Jasper Wright of Pennsylvania, who with support from the American Missionary Association had begun a school for noncommissioned officers of the 128th United States Colored Infantry near Beaufort in the summer of 1865, and who advised freedpeople in matters of law, had been readying his students for some formal political

---

51. Excerpts from Rev. John V. Given to Mr. Tullock, 15 July [1867], Robert C. Schenck Papers, r 6.
52. B. F. Whittemore to Rev. Geo. Whipple, 25 Feb. 1867, AMA, South Carolina, Letters Received; Williamson, *After Slavery*, pp. 205–06.

role for nearly two years. Wright, a former delegate to the November 1865 state convention of "colored people" in Charleston, had taught with the goal of "getting ready for the educational clause" that he had wrongly anticipated in the 1865 state constitution.[53] Such literate men who first spread the news of the congressional measures were usually veterans of other organizational efforts among freedpeople.[54]

To the ranks of men of broad formal training should be added men of more than rudimentary literacy whose leadership talents had been developed during tenures as noncommissioned officers of black regiments of the federal army. Young men like the twenty-five-year-old former sergeant of the Fifty-fourth Massachusetts Colored Volunteer Infantry, William M. Viney, at times remained in the region after being mustered out of federal service. After his discharge, Viney had purchased land in Colleton district, where his authority became great among freedpeople while he "labert her a mong them . . . maken speeches to them an tring to lern them habits of In dustry and to live a truthful and Verchus an anest life."[55] The congressional measures seem to have halted Viney's role in assisting families in his neighborhood to arrange to settle on public lands in Florida under the Homestead Act. By the time of the founding convention of the Republican Party in late July, Viney had traveled "all through his District holding meetings," "taking no notice" of threats made on his life "over and over again."[56]

Congressional Republicans lent assistance to the young movement when the executive committee of the Union Republican Party's congressional delegation made party funds available to Union League organizers in the Southern states. The Union League, which had emerged as a popular body to support the federal war effort, probably had as many origins as there were groups in Northeastern, Midwestern, and border states who rallied to the Union cause.[57] In the spring of 1867, the league's national officers decided to aid the deliberate organization of local Republican clubs, acknowledging that speakers were more effective than printed

53. Jonathan J. Wright to Rev. S. Hunt, 4 Dec. 1865, AMA, South Carolina, Letters Received; Williamson, *After Slavery*, p. 330; Holt, *Black Over White*, pp. 17, 81–83; Logan, and Winston, eds., *Dictionary of American Negro Biography*.
54. Holt, *Black Over White*, pp. 27, 73–74.
55. Quotations appear in E. G. Dudley to Hon. John A. Andrew, 31 July 1867, in Abbott, ed., "Yankee Views," p. 248; Wm. M. Viney to Bvt. Mag. Gen. R. K. Scott, 10 Oct. 1866, M 869, r 21, 0808 and published as Doc. 365 in Berlin, Reidy, and Rowland, eds., *Black Military Experience*, pp. 819–21. See also Holt, *Black Over White*, pp. 79, 115.
56. E. G. Dudley to Hon. John A. Andrew, 31 July 1867, in Abbott, ed., "Yankee Views," p. 248.
57. Fitzgerald, *Union League Movement*, p. 10. Various origins of the Union League are offered in Foner, *Reconstruction*, p. 283; Owens, "Union League of America" abridgment, p. 3; Drumm, "Union League in the Carolinas," 1955, pp. iv–v; Silvestro, "None But Patriots," pp. 10–19.

tracts in appealing to largely illiterate, rural electorates.[58] At least 11 of the 118 organizers and speakers who by late summer were receiving assistance from Republican Party funds canvassed in South Carolina.[59] Small amounts of critical financial assistance came from Washington. The doctrines themselves evolved closer to home.

Wherever they traveled, Union League organizers sought out likely political constituencies. They especially wanted to reach freedpeople on plantations and farms beyond easy access of rail, steamer, or coach. Such places, thought Philadelphian James Lynch, were home to a social isolation and ease of intimidation that gave shelter to "the rebel hope."[60] At times, speakers judged areas too dangerous for immediate organization, but seldom for long. When Rev. John V. Given learned that a "colored speaker" had been killed weeks earlier in Lunenburg, Virginia, he altered his itinerary at once. "I shall go there, and speak where they have cowed the black man so that they dare not even register," Given declared, "and, by the help of God, give them a dose of my radical Republican pills and neutralize the corrosive ascidity [*sic*] of their negro hate."[61] With an eye to remaking southern political alliances under Republican auspices, itinerant organizers such as Henry Jerome Brown, as well as state activists like William M. Viney and Robert Brown Elliott in South Carolina, took special pains to reach white tenants, petty landowners, and factory hands as well as ex-slave laborers. Viney was confident that because of his efforts in South Carolina's Colleton district, "as many as five hundred of the poor whites . . . have joined him and would vote the Republican ticket."[62]

Politics vibrated with the urgency of spiritual salvation and the mass appeal of the frontier camp meeting. At times, crowds too large for any local meetinghouse to accommodate awaited an arriving lecturer. Rev. John V. Given exulted when, during a mid-July speaking tour in southeastern Virginia, he addressed "a multitude beyond the capacity of any

58. Abbott, *Republican Party and the South*, pp. 87–91; see also Fitzgerald, *Union League Movement*, pp. 37–66.
59. "Names of Speakers & Organizers Employed or aided by the Union Republican Congressional Committee" [c. Sept. 1867 to early 1868], Robert C. Schenck Papers, Hayes Presidential Center Library, r 6. Michael Fitzgerald considerably brought this manuscript collection to my attention. In addition to the seven men identified on this list as South Carolina organizers, Henry J. Brown, John F. Costin, Henry M. Turner, and James M. Simms are also known to have spoken in the state during the 1867 canvassing.
60. Excerpt from James Lynch to My dear Sir, 9 July [1867], Robert C. Schenck Papers, r 6.
61. John V. Given to Mr. Tullock, 15 July [1867], Robert C. Schenck Papers, r 6.
62. E. G. Dudley to Hon. John A. Andrew, 31 July 1867, in Abbott, ed., "Yankee Views," p. 248; extract from Dr. H. J. Brown to Dear Sir, 23 July [1867], Robert C. Schenck Papers, r 6; Charleston *Daily Courier*, 24 Aug. 1867, p. 2, col. 2.

church in the United States to hold."[63] Messengers spreading the league's political gospel in South Carolina annoyed one Ridgeway physician who complained, in September 1867, about the effects on freedpeople of "emisaries [*sic*] who are traveling the country over most of them in the style of *preachers* to turn them fool."[64] While clergymen were widely represented, not every itinerant league partisan was a parson. Of the eight black and three white organizers active in South Carolina, only two men – South Carolina's freeborn African Methodist Episcopal minister Henry NcNeal Turner, and Savannah's Baptist minister James M. Simms – are known to have been practicing clerics.[65] The spirit of registration campaigns, as much as the ministerial backgrounds of the organizers themselves, marked the onset of public meetings that recalled the large crowds and emotional intensity of camp meetings.

Some Union League organizers deliberately embraced aspects of evangelical religion's widespread social idiom. James Lynch believed that his clerical duties enabled him to venture off more well-beaten paths in Hinds County, Mississippi, in relative safety, assuring congressional Republicans' executive committee that as a minister, he could "work back in the counties without difficulty." His speeches, Lynch noted, intentionally fused counsels about life everlasting with injunctions directed at more immediate episodes on this side of eternity. "*Where visions of the 'halter' rise up before me*," Lynch explained, "I *commence as a preacher and end as a political speaker!*"[66]

Mechanisms of lay religious instruction proved valuable in disseminating word-of-mouth notices about upcoming meetings. It was from a class leader and fellow church member that Armstead Terry, an ex-slave laborer in Horry district, South Carolina, received notice to attend a meeting called by slaveborn Methodist minister and convention candidate Isaac Brockenton. When Terry's employer, one Major Coker, took steps to dismiss several men for unauthorized absences, the class leader George Terry measured Coker's threat of immediate eviction by the standard of laborers' and employers' transcendent obligations under a common

63. Extracts from [John V. Given] to Mr. Tullock, 15 July [1867], Robert C. Schenck Papers, r 6.
64. John R. Cook to Major Genl. Canby, 27 Sept. 1867, 2d Military District, Provost Marshal, Letters Received, ser. 4280, RG 393 Pt 1; Testimony of Simpson Bobo, *KKK Testimony*, vol. 2, p. 806, in which Bobo credits black itinerant "carpetbag" ministers with organizing churches that were actually the first Union Leagues in his upcountry district.
65. "Names of Speakers & Organizers Employed or aided by the Union Republican Congressional Committee" [c. Sept. 1867 to early 1868], Robert C. Schenck Papers, r 6.
66. Quotations from extracts of James Lynch to My dear Sir, 9 July [1867], Robert C. Schenck Papers, r 6. Punctuation varies slightly in the two different copies of the letter that appear in this collection.

Gospel. "I wish to try to get along in peace with the Major [Coker]," the class leader explained, "but I do not wish that he (Major) should hinder a man from attending a meeting to save his soul, and I did not know that he would prevent any man from goin[g] to church."[67] Intermingled as forms of social expression, religion and politics increasingly articulated heightening social divisions.

Shaping religious institutions to the work of political education could provoke social antagonisms within existing black congregations. The simultaneous organization of African Methodist Episcopal churches and local Republican clubs is illustrative. On the one hand, the denomination's institutionalization supported the emergence of an indigenous leadership.[68] Henry McNeal Turner, for example, reported in July 1867, "Every preacher in the African Methodist Episcopal Church in [Georgia] is working well in the Republican cause except two." At the same time, however, dissension flared in some established congregations when laborers, small landowners, urban artisans, and remnants of antebellum freeborn and slaveborn elites gathered together in His name. "There is some grumbling with a few of our fastidious church members," Turner reported. Discontented church members had complained, he noted, because they found that "of late, my sermons were dry and cold and they thought I had better desist a while from political declamations."[69] In South Carolina, no denomination surpassed the African Methodist Episcopal church in mobilizing voters for the Republican cause.[70] Nevertheless, the underlying social cohesiveness of the denomination's rural congregations probably was more effective than religious doctrines and practices alone in consolidating a remarkable unity of action.[71] Indeed, some grass-roots organizers assumed (optimistically, to be sure) that a kind of universalism infused Republican gospels that Protestantism's more specifically theological appeals could not match. Court-martialed ex-Confederate soldier Christopher Columbus Bowen, who canvassed widely in low-country plantation districts of South Carolina on behalf of

67. *J. L. Coker v. George Terry et al.*, [28 Oct. 1867], M 869, r 12.
68. Holt, *Black Over White*, p. 90.
69. Excerpts from Henry McNeal Turner to Hon. Thomas L. Tullock, 23 July [1867], Robert C. Schenck Papers, r 6.
70. The success with which the A.M.E. church registered Republican voters, early noted by Williamson, *After Slavery*, p. 369, is not illuminated by Walker, *Rock in a Weary Land*.
71. Late in 1868, the church's district bishop agreed to change the date of the meeting of the South Carolina conference from March to early January, explaining, "Most of our Ministers, save those stationed in cities, are compelled to depend upon the cultivation of their *little gardens*, and as it is impossible for them to get settled, and have their gardens in working order, as well after March as they would, had they the time preceding it, to locate themselves. . . . [T]his busy and numerous class far outnumber our city brethren." See *Christian Recorder*, 18 Nov. 1868.

the Republican Party, reported that in his travels he had "found bodies organized by persons who were mixing religion with politics," and that he had to "bridge between the different denominations."[72]

Whether they emphasized their missions' secular or religious aspects, political circuit riders rarely presumed a welcoming reception. Some relied on local bureau agents and army officers to arrange their meetings. Rev. James Lynch, addressing an "immense meeting" in Jackson, Mississippi, adopted an unusual practice of appearing on a platform with the mayor and several state officials and "prominent citizens." Some organizers called attention to an explicitly nonpolitical theme when publicizing their lectures. Dr. Henry Jerome Brown, who had previously been organizing in Virginia and North Carolina, announced his arrival in the village of Darlington, South Carolina, in January 1868, with printed announcements of his upcoming lecture, "Physiology and Phrenology." Denounced by the local post commander as a "Mulatto Charlaton," Brown was forced to end his speaking engagements in the village when the officer found him "in front of the ruins of the Old Court House," delivering a "political Speech to a crowd of some 200 Negroes, who had apparently been notified of his intention."[73] Few subjects were arcane in these heady days.

With an assurance variously remarkable or distressing to their contemporaries, ex-slaves rallied to political life. Registration tallies compiled in the Second Military District's office of civil affairs in Charleston suggest the successes of the unprecedented canvassing. By mid-November 1867, nearly ninety percent of the state's eligible black electorate had registered to vote in the referendum on the constitutional convention.[74] At the district level, there were no exceptions to the tendency for substantial majorities of newly eligible black voters to register. Using data from the 1870 census to construct rough estimates of the number of potential black voters, it seems that when 77 percent to 79 percent of the eligible black

72. Charleston *Daily Courier*, 27 July 1867, p. 1, cols. 2–5. Accounts of Bowen's speaking tours appear in R. K. Scott to O. O. Howard, 22 June 1867, report summary, subdistrict of Charleston, r 48, 0162–76, and R. K. Scott to O. O. Howard, 20 July 1867, report summary, subdistrict of Charleston, r 48, 0449–66, both in M 752.

73. Thomas L. Tullock to Edw. R. S. Canby, 30 Jan. 1868, Bvt. Lieut. Col. Henry E. Maynadier to Lieut. L. V. Caziarc, 2 Feb. 1868, both in 2d Military District, Letters Received, ser. 4111, RG 393 Pt 1 [SS 112]. See also extract from Dr. H. J. Brown to [Thomas L. Tullock?], 23 July [1867], Robert C. Schenck Papers. Brown's name appears on the undated list, "Names of Speakers & Organizers Employed or aided by the Union Republican Congressional Committee" [c. Sept. 1867 to early 1868], Robert C. Schenck Papers, r 6. Approximate dates of this list are offered in Foner, *Reconstruction*, p. 286n and Abbott, *Republican Party and the South*, p. 256n.

74. The absence of precinct-level election returns for South Carolina in the records of the Second Military District prevents close assessment of regional variations in registration and voter turnout. District-level figures for the number of black voters registered

voters registered in Anderson, Lancaster, Newberry, and Richland districts, they became the smallest proportions of potential black voters to gain access to their district's polls. In many districts – Greenville, Laurens, Lexington, Kershaw, Orangeburg, Charleston, and Colleton – it seems that virtually every black man eligible to vote had registered by the eve of the special election. Signs of political indifference publicized in some areas proved misleading. In late July, a newspaper correspondent in York district had judged, "The freedmen are taking but little interest in political matters."[75] But black men in York district, like their counterparts in the upper Piedmont districts of Pickens, Greenville, and Spartanburg, registered in numbers comparable to registration rates in the state as a whole. Better than eight of every ten eligible black voters in York had registered by the eve of the special elections on 19 and 20 November.

Tantalizing puzzles surround ex-slaves' broad political participation. People largely bereft of animal transport showed up at meetings, and at registration and election sites. Men, most of whom could neither read nor write, and the few who could decipher print but not script, cast written ballots in large numbers. Moreover, these rank-and-file Republicans met and registered and voted in explicit opposition to a more mobile, literate electorate composed in bulk of their employers. Disparities of power did not determine the disposition of ex-slaves' political behavior. The forging of their political courage began outside the arena of formal politics.

The social fabric of popular Republican clubs wove together threads of association that originated outside party organizations. Women and men, young and old poured into public meetings called in the wake of the Reconstruction Acts. Between fifteen hundred and two thousand men, women, and children attended a mid-April 1867 Republican rally in Beaufort called to "ratify" the platform adopted in Charleston the previous month. Most probably arrived aboard the steamers provided by the meeting's organizers. When word reached outlying plantations that people were being summoned to Beaufort "by the order of the Government to vote for Mr. Lincoln's son," rare was the man or woman willing to be left behind. Skiffs, carts, and "every mode of transportation which the wit

by 19 November were reported in "Recapitulation of Registration and Elections on Convention," in Secretary of War, Annual Report, 1867, 40th Congress, 3d sess., 1868, U.S. ser. 1367, 521–22. Rough estimates of the potential number of black voters in each district were calculated from the number of male citizens in each district reported in *Ninth Census, Population*, pp. 60, 635. Because federal census data published in 1870 did not distinguish the number of male citizens in each district by race, the proportion of the black population in each district was used to estimate the proportion of black male citizens. The method yielded a state average registration rate of 89.6 percent, which is in keeping with the average turnout of black voters of 85 percent in the November 1867 elections as calculated in Williamson, *After Slavery*, p. 343.

75. Charleston *Daily Courier*, 30 July 1867, p. 1, cols. 2–3.

of man could devise" were pressed into service. Even those for whom the process was still hazy found it worthwhile to seize the closest of human, animal, and waterborne resources within reach in order to vote. Keen popular interest expanded the transportation arrangements that carried people to the first public meeting whose size approached earlier gatherings in Charleston.[76]

Curiosity knew no bounds of age or sex when speakers or convention candidates made an appearance. Neighborhood meetings smaller in size but similarly broad in social representation assembled whenever a speaker's appearance was announced to "wide awake" workers on the mainland that summer and fall. Rallies on behalf of candidates for the constitutional convention kindled anew freedpeople's expectations that rights withheld since the conclusion of the war would soon be gained. Work halted when the arrival of "any person known to be in sympathy with the Republican party and the North" suggested that hoped for changes might be at hand. Planter Augustus Shoolbred complained during campaigning for the constitutional convention on the Santee in November 1867, that the region's rice workers "are easily led astray & imposed upon by any one (especially of their own color) encouraging this hope [of rights to be gained] & they eagerly run off to any call for a public meeting however unauthorized in total disregard of their contracts, keeping the labor uncontrolable [*sic*] at best; constantly disorganized."[77]

Freedpeople's widely shared sense that emancipation was incomplete, compromised, or perhaps betrayed outright ensured spokesmen for a new order an eager and attentive audience. Caricature could not conceal the mass character of even smaller indoor meetings. When convention candidate and former army chaplin Benjamin Franklin Randolph addressed a "large" audience of freedpeople in Chester, South Carolina, in late July, those in attendance proceeded to elect delegates to attend the upcoming convention in Columbia that would form a state Republican Party. Age was widely represented even in a reporter's ridicule of the "old countryman" who moved a "secunt," and the "little negro sitting in the window in the rear of the hall" who had reportedly shrieked "No!" when the chairman announced the name of the first elected delegate.[78] Popular Republican clubs emerged surrounded with a passion for politics that infused the fibers of neighborhood life.

76. Ibid., 24 April 1867, p. 2, cols. 2–3; a brief account of the same meeting appeared in the *Christian Recorder*, 4 May 1867, p. 70, col. 3.
77. Extract from "Colored Speaker and Organizer in South Carolina," 2 Aug. [1867], Robert C. Schenck Papers, r 6; Augustus Shoolbred to Maj. Gen. E. R. Canby, 30 Nov. 1867, 2d Military District, Letters Received, ser. 4111, RG 393 Pt 1 [SS-77].
78. Charleston *Daily Courier*, 30 July 1867, p. 1, cols. 2–3.

Multiple social identities intertwined in the neighborhood clubs that flowered during "registration summer," where compounded social ties made for strong alliances. Members regarded their associations as perpetual, more like lineages than leagues. In July 1867, Wesley Staggers, an ex-slave soldier who had organized a military company on Fenwick's Island, "positively refused" a provost marshal's order to disband an organization that, a planter had charged, promoted "[c]onduct tending to disorganize labor." According to the officer, Staggers insisted that members "were sworn into service for life," and that he "would stick by them until compelled to break up, by force of arms." A fellow society captain, Monroe McDowell, reportedly reinforced Staggers's stand, insisting that the company "was formed for life" and that he "*would* stick by it."[79] Neighborhood radical clubs linked captains, brothers, cousins, friends, church members, "fellow servants," and neighbors for lifetime projects.

Club members shared overlapping social attachments, woven from ties of marriage, kinship, common workplace, and close residence. A rich realm of informal political power therefore shaped the elaboration of formally political roles. Gossip, ridicule, nonlethal assault, and regulated vandalism were among the means by which a laboring community kept its voters faithful to Union League principles.

To enforce political loyalty, neighborhoods drove their hardest bargains with the currency of social support. Social isolation and humiliation had a value greater than money dues in sustaining large league memberships among people for whom cash was ever short. Church members refused to help bury a man who had voted the Democratic ticket; neighbors abducted and subjected to "all manner of indignities" short of lasting physical injury a fellow society member who quit attending Loyal League meetings.

Voting was too important a matter to be entrusted only to the enfranchised. Women guarded muskets brought to defend public meetings against attack. Wives and lovers wielded sanctions of bed and board on behalf of political action.[80] News about a "speaking" drew the "single" freedwoman Lucy McMillan, whose husband had been sold away before the war, to attend a political meeting in the town of Spartanburg.[81] Women and men alike rallied to Henry McNeal Turner's appeal to "save their Congressional districts from the wicked designs of men who are

79. Charges and Specifications against Monroe McDowell et al. [June–Oct. 1867]; Affidavit of John Jenkins, 25 July 1867; Affidavit of Lt. J. M. Johnston, 25 July 1867; all in Charges and Specifications against Monroe McDowell et al. [June–Oct. 1867], Letters Received, ser. 4111, RG 393 Pt 1 [SS-8].
80. Charleston *Daily Courier,* 21 July, 25 Sept., 19 Oct. 1868; Holt, *Black Over White,* pp. 34–35; Williamson, *After Slavery,* pp. 343–44.
81. *KKK Testimony,* vol.2, p. 605.

trying to prevent our people from registering." In the summer of 1867, employing a pattern of parallel gender organization widespread among freedpeople, freed women and men in central Georgia formed separate associations of "fifty subscribers" each and assessed each member ten cents weekly in order "to pay a lecturer to travel through their Congressional district."[82] Male adolescents not yet of legal voting age often brought previous military experience to ardent league activities on behalf of legal voters.[83]

Monday, foreman of a Santee River rice estate, vividly described popular mechanisms for enforcing political loyalty. His employer recalled how Monday explained why he would again vote the Republican ticket in the first state elections after the 1876 campaign that marked the political end of Reconstruction:

> I got tuh vote de 'Publican ticket, suh. We all has. Las' 'lection I voted de Democrack ticket an' dee killed my cow. Abum, he vote de Democrack ticket; dee killed his colt. Monday counted off the negroes who had voted the "Democrack" ticket, and every one had been punished. One had been bombarded in his cabin; another's rice crop had been taken – even the ground swept up and every grain carried off, leaving him utterly destitute.

Extending a working-class variant of patronage, Monday explained that he actually safeguarded the interests of his Democratic employer and his own effectiveness as a plantation foreman by voting the Republican ticket. "I tell you, suh," said Monday, "I got tuh do it on my 'count, an'on yo' 'count. You make me fo'man an' ef I didn' vote de 'Publican ticket, I couldn' make dese niggers wuk. I couldn' do nothin' 'tall wid 'em."[84]

Political discipline was a community affair.

A Perfect System?

The twenty-five member "Tiger Zouaves No. 12" came into being late in November 1867 in an unusual way. Its membership, composed of veterans of black regiments recruited in North Carolina, South Carolina, and Florida, was drawn from a wider geographic area than most popular Republican clubs; but in a sense, the "Tiger Zouaves" was also a kind of neighborhood association. It formed in the Charleston jail and was organized by black veterans, most of whom had run afoul of prosecution for petty crimes against property. The prisoners had failed at extralegal and illegal attempts to claim hogs, "a pair of boots," an "old harness," cloth-

82. Extract from Rev. Henry M. Turner to nn, 9 July [1867], Robert C. Schenck Papers, r 6. See also Charleston *Daily Courier,* 10 July 1867, p. 1, cols. 2–3.
83. Silvestro, "None But Patriots," p. 329.
84. Avary, *Dixie After the War,* pp. 346–47.

Proconvention ballot, Darlington district, SC, November 1867. Courtesy of the Amistad Research Center, New Orleans.

ing, cotton, and a "monkey Wrench" (these they identified as articles whose alleged thefts had led to their convictions). Such were the risks of poaching and embezzlement. By November, elections for the constitutional convention were less than two weeks away, and some members had "our Crops in the ground to gather." Under their captain, London Simons, the Tiger Zouaves organized in the city jail "under the Same Rules as the Union League" and petitioned the commanding general to pardon them "because there is so many of us that is in here for nothing." "We have Joined the league Society," Simons explained, "and intend if we can get out of Jail to try to be as men."[85]

85. London Simons to Cmdg. Genl., 10 Nov. 1867, Provost Marshal, Letters Received, ser. 4280, Dept. of the South, RG 393 Pt 1. In the same series, see also London Simons to Genl. Comdg., 14 Nov. 1867, which indicated that "about half of the members has been Released from Jail While the rest remains here."

Although political discipline was embedded in networks of community life, the act of voting remained, for the most part, man's work.[86] In the councils of their radical societies, union clubs, and Loyal Leagues, freed men invented new forms of mass behavior to safeguard recent rights of suffrage. The political practices that they created made them effective partisans at the polls. E. W. Seibels, leader of an 1870 opposition party, bestowed grudging praise. Popular organization of Republican voting was "so perfect a system," Seibels informed a congressional committee, "that it is impossible to break through it." Seibels believed that his conservative coalition had managed to gain some black men's votes "by [the voters'] mistake" in 1870 state elections. "But," he reflected, "it was the hardest matter I ever undertook to do."[87]

Ex-slaves' political practices bore the imprint of the popularized military company, a means of organizing male crowd behavior that revived independent of the Union League's official organizers to strengthen the hand of largely nonliterate members at the polls. Preparations for voting began before the two-day balloting that was most typical of elections in 1867 and 1868. Neighborhood voters assembled at some previously designated spot a few days before the polls opened. The secretary of an early November 1867 meeting of freed men in St. Helena Parish issued ex-slave Wally Smith "a piece of paper, written on" that authorized Smith "to warn all the people in my neighborhood to 'attend the election'" ordered by the first Reconstruction Act. Smith's commission "endowed [him] with authority from the Chief Committee to go round to all the peoples in this parish" to advise them to assemble at the Eustis plantation four days before the polls opened on 19 November.[88] Such pre-election assemblies became occasion for ceremonial drills and volleys that made rank-and-file Republicans visible and audible in their neighborhoods.

Underlying the noisy demonstrations in which company members celebrated their political partisanship was an organization determined to conquer distance. Even in neighborhoods where farm workers were less densely concentrated than St. Helena Parish, marching companies gradu-

86. An officeholder in the state reform party insisted that ex-slave women had voted in 1870 elections. In 1871, E. W. Seibels informed the congressional committee investigating KKK activities: [W]omen and children voted. Women gave votes for their husbands, or their brothers, who they said were sick." See *KKK Testimony*, vol. 1, p. 123.
87. Quoted in Testimony of E. W. Seibels, *KKK Testimony*, vol. 1, pp. 122, 135 respectively.
88. [Notice of meeting], Paul Chisolm, J. P. De Vaux, 6 Nov. 1867, filed with B. W. Martin, 6 Nov. 1867, in Letters Received, ser. 4111, 2d Military District, RG 393 Pt 1 [SS-72]. Smith's complete authorization read: "We have hereby endowed Mr Smith with authority from the Chief Committee to go round to all the peoples in this parish to in form all of them to meet at Mr Eustices on the 15th of this month. If any refuse to report them and they shall be put in jail by law."

ally expanded the scale of public assembly. By 1868, freed men coordinated some of their largest public gatherings. That summer, drill societies
mounted demonstrations whose participants numbered in the thousands
in Union county, and made sizable countywide and even broader regional appearances in Sumter and Fairfield.[89] Ex-mistress Lalla Pelot identified the neighborhoods represented by a contingent of black-, red-, and
gold-costumed marchers who made "quite a show" in Laurensville one
Saturday in late July 1870: "[O]ur darkies [from Laurensville] were
dressed in black coats & white pantalons those from Cross Hill in Red
Coats & white pants – Clinton men in Yellow Coats & White pants."[90]
Drill companies broadened the geographic mobility and scale of assembly of their foot-bound rural membership.

There was both ceremony and political method in this quasi-military
coordination of travel. Where voters were scattered and local power relations placed a premium on secrecy, would-be voters attempted no comparable redefinitions of social space. The exertions of lone voters, who at
times swam rivers, waded streams, and hiked byroads to reach the polls,
were indeed great.[91] Nevertheless, ritualized drills and mass assembly lent
dignity to Republican partisans who generally walked to polls that the opposition reached on horseback. Rank-and-file Republicans often marched
to the polls in squads, seeking enhanced physical safety in collective election forays.[92] Facing an armed and largely mounted political opposition,
virtually all of whom had long known the use of arms and most of whom

89. Charleston *Daily Courier*,31 July 1868, p. 4, col. 2, 26 Aug. 1868, p. 4, col. 3; Testi-
     mony of James B. Steadman, *KKK Testimony*, vol. 2, pp. 1011, 1025.
90. Your affectionate mother to My dear Robert, 2 Aug. 1870, Lalla Pelot Papers, Duke
     University. Pelot may be correct in her belief that the demonstration was a parade of
     state militia organized by Governor Robert K. Scott. Whether or not the men were au-
     thorized militia members, the parade and uniforms were certainly a local innovation.
     The "laxity of uniform regulations [that] allowed considerable freedom in the matter
     of military dress," reflects the influence of the close neighborhood loyalties and strong
     personal attachments on which a nominal state force was organized. See Singletary,
     Negro Militia and Reconstruction p. 101.
91. Testimony of Henry Lipscomb, *KKK Testimony*, vol. 2, p. 683. Some voters claimed
     that fear of the consequences of not casting ballots had driven them to the polls. An
     ex-slave thought to be in his eighties reported that, after hearing a speech by Jonathan
     Jasper Wright near Port Royal Ferry during canvassing for the constitutional conven-
     tion, he understood "that they must all put in their Vote even if they had to limp to
     the polls, and anyone that did not Vote he [Wright] would put in Jail." The first day
     of the elections found the former slave crying on the roadside, lamenting that "[h]e
     had already walked 4 miles & had 7 miles more to go." Notwithstanding his alarm,
     he rejected counsel from white residents who advised him that "he need not go with-
     out he wished to." See W. H. Griffin to Bvt. Brig. Genl. E. W. Hinks, 27 Nov. 1867,
     and Statement of Tony Squier; both in Provost Marshal General, Letters Received,
     ser. 4280, 2d Military District, RG 393 Pt 1.
92. Testimony of E. K. Everson, *KKK Testimony*, vol. 1, p. 344; Testimony of Daniel
     Lipscomb, ibid., p. 435.

had recent experience of the battlefield, ex-slave Republicans organized voting on the expectation that elections would reflect rather than transcend disparities of social power. Their collective structuring of voting practices undermined ex-governor James L. Orr's confident prophecy before a congressional committee that "when you put what would practically be an organized mass against an unorganized mob you will at once perceive what the result would be."[93] Neighborhood political clubs organized the casting of votes, achieving more of a contest than Orr anticipated.

Of necessity, clubs kept a sharp watch over ballots. Illiterate Republican voters could scarcely comply with the expectations of the Second Military District's chief civil officer, Ammiel J. Willard, that voters themselves would supply ballots for or against a constitutional convention "in Conformity with the usual custom."[94] Even so, voters who could not read letters well knew how to read men. Club members therefore pledged to accept a ticket at the polls or other prearranged sites from the hands of only one designated person, who would have received his tickets under the same strictures in a chain that linked small numbers of literate voters to the nonliterate majority of club "captains."[95] Had conservatives been more adept in taking Republican tickets, perhaps their political challenges would not have included taking lives. When Republican tickets could not be distributed, as was reportedly the case in several precincts in Newberry county in 1868, "of course [freed men] could not write them, and they had no vote the next day."[96] Most men who handed out Republican tickets in 1867 and 1868, however, probably fulfilled their duties to standards achieved by ex-slave Willis Johnson, who judged that he had "done right smart" when he "took the tickets around among the black people."[97]

Before voting proceeded against a grim backdrop of terror, it went forward as rough sport. Agents who distributed tickets were fair game, as when, during state elections in 1870, groups of freed men watching various polling places in the low country seized the opposing Union Reform

93. Testimony of James L. Orr, ibid., p. 15.
94. A. J. Willard to Commanding Officer, 12 Nov. 1867, 2d Military district, ser. 4357, pp. 20–21 (rear of volume).
95. Testimony of E. W. Seibels, *KKK Testimony,* vol. 1, p. 122; Testimony of Willis Johnson, ibid., p. 327; Testimony of Henry Johnson, ibid., p. 326. See also Tho. M. Williamson to Hon. Sir, 28 April 1868, ser. 4111, RG 393 Pt 1 [SS-118] in which "a true League man" who was "[s]ent from the Republican mass meeting" in Abbeville to give out tickets at Ninety Six recounts threats and harassments that led to his incarceration. An account of a black voter's difficulty in securing the Republican ticket that he desired at a Laurens County poll appears in *KKK Testimony,* vol. 2, p. 1168.
96. Testimony of James L. Orr, ibid., vol. 1, pp. 13–14; see also Testimony of James H. Goss, ibid., p. 67.
97. Testimony of Willis Johnson, ibid., p. 327.

Party's ballots and drove their distributors from the polls.[98] To approach the ballot box was sometimes to begin a strenuous athletic match. A crowd surrounded the bearer of an unfavored ticket, who then had to run a gauntlet of blocks and shoves in order to deposit his ballot. The object often was to occupy the polls early and thereby impede the opposition's access to the ballot box. The four hundred freed men – some wearing their old army uniforms – who "took possession" of the Grey's Hill polls in Beaufort, or the eight hundred men who similarly occupied the polling place on St. Helena Island during November 1867 elections, had clearly mastered the strategy.[99] Voters deposited their tickets to raucous cheering. However, charges that former slave Robert Smalls, during elections for the constitutional convention in which he was a candidate, had urged freed men at a polling place in Beaufort district "to shoot, knock the brains out, or kill any man who attempted to vote any other ticket than the so called red ticket" seem exaggerated.[100] A former Union Reform candidate, bested (in part) by rough tactics at the hands of "a rabble of colored men, sometimes by white republicans," better conveyed the rules of the game. "A crowd can push a man off," Robert Aldrich explained, "without laying hands on him."[101] Athletic confrontations helped male voters size up the competition at many polls on election days.

Printed ballots kept few secrets; on the contrary, local ballots were emblems whose distinctive designs and colors broadcast a voter's allegiance to all who watched.[102] And many watched. Authorized men from both parties tallied ballots as they were cast. Staged dramas of intimidation followed the voter to the ballot box. Tench Blackwell, a white Republican manager of elections in Spartanburg County, recalled, "When a republican would go up to vote," Democratic watchers "would jerk their repeater strap, and look as if they were whipping somebody, looking at the man who was voting."[103]

98. Testimony of Richard B. Carpenter, ibid., pp. 229, 251.
99. Charleston *Daily Courier,* 25 Nov. 1867, p. 2. col. 4.
100. Charge and Specification against Robert Small [Nov. 1867], enclosed in Bvt. Brig. Gen. E. W. Hinks [Nov. 1867], Letters Received, ser. 4111, 2d Military District, RG 393 Pt 1 [SS-135]. Similar charges, of which he was subsequently acquitted, were raised against Pompey Coaxem, member of a Union League in the vicinity of St. Helena Island. See *United States* v. *Pompey Coaxem, Colored,* 29 April 1868, and Special Order 114, 2d Military District, 16 May 1868, Proceedings of Provost Courts, Military Tribunals, and Post Court-Martial Cases Tried in North and South Carolina, ser. 4257, Judge Advocate, 2d Military District, RG 393 Pt 1.
101. Testimony of Robert Aldrich, *KKK Testimony,* vol. 1, p. 176.
102. Republicans' silhouettes of Lincoln, or blue eagles or red ink on a red background, were as recognizable as the black border that trimmed some reform ballots in 1870 in tribute to the death of Robert E. Lee. Charleston *Daily Courier,* 25 Nov. 1867, p. 2, col. 4 (red and black tickets); A. S. Wallace to R. W. Wallace, 29 Oct. 1868, Robert K. Scott Papers; Testimony of John Genobles, *KKK Testimony,* vol. 1, p. 361.
103. Testimony of Tench Blackwell, *KKK Testimony,* vol. 1, p. 555.

The public nature of voting provoked more secretive adherence to party tickets among white Republican voters, whereas ex-slave Republicans tended more toward strategies relying on amassing large numbers. Literacy enabled some Republican voters, usually yeoman partisans, to camouflage how they had voted. Pasting a newly written Republican slate inside a visibly Democratic covering was one favored stratagem. Black rank-and-file Republicans opted for monopolizing particular polls and voting en masse. C. H. Suber, a Democratic lawyer, irritatedly recounted how black Republicans voted at the courthouse in Newberry village in 1870: "[T]he colored people were invited to come from all parts of the county to the court-house and vote. They came from the remotest parts of the county to vote. . . . They congregated around the boxes at 4 o'clock in the morning, before they were opened, and monopolized all the precincts until about 10 or 11 o'clock in the day."[104]

Force more or less restrained and stylized hovered in the very act of voting. Rank-and-file Republicans accepted certain forms of physical assault as being within bounds when political enemies confronted each other at the polls. Election "riots" that erupted at polls in St. John's, Berkeley and outside Charleston during elections of local officeholders in June 1868 suggest the limits of popular political coercion. At Black Oak precinct in St. John's, Berkeley, a freeborn black voter no sooner requested the ticket of one Sigwald, the Democratic candidate for sheriff, than he was pummeled with "sticks, stones, and whatever else" an "infuriated mob" of Republicans could lay hands on. Sigwald's candidacy also became occasion for direct action at the Club House poll in St. Andrew's Parish outside Charleston. On arriving at Club House, a squad of men from Buleau plantation, led by ex-slave minister and schoolteacher Ishmael Moultrie, discovered that some ex-slave voters had placed tickets for Sigwald in the election box. Questioning the propriety of permitting tickets for several candidates for sheriff to be available at the polls, Moultrie charged the election managers "that by allowing the Freedmen to vote the Sigwald Ticket, which was a Rebel Ticket, they were trying to bring them into slavery." On hearing Moultrie's claim, the crowd rallied and "demanded that the Sigwald Tickets be taken out, and they be allowed to vote over." When the managers refused, large numbers of men, brandishing sticks, clubs, or firearms, seized the election box, removed 190 Sigwald tickets, and replaced them with an equal number of tickets for the Republican candidate.[105]

104. Testimony of C. H. Suber, ibid., p. 150.
105. Charleston *Daily Courier,* 3 June 1868, p. 2, col. 4; C. J. F. Caldwell to Col. Judd, 24 June 1868, 2d Military district, Provost Marshal, ser. 4280, Letters Received, RG 393 Pt 1; Petition of Ishmael Moultrie, James Russell, Hastings Ford, Benjamin Glover, and Peter Polite to Judge Advocate, 7 July 1868, 2d Military District, ser.

For better and for worse, ex-slave voters wielded coercion rooted in the nonlethal force of neighborhood sanctions for strictly political ends. Roughing up a wayward voter of their own relative social position, or forcibly replacing ballots in order to "vote over," gained victory for Republican candidates. Party regulars of local influence tolerated what were at most overly zealous indiscretions when the most severe consequences stayed within class bounds. Arriving at the Club House polls later that same day, Charleston party stalwart Samuel Dickerson remarked that the men from Buleau plantation had "acted right." The Republican candidate for sheriff gained victory. Five of the "rioters" including Ishmael Moultrie (regarded as "manager of the spiritual, political, and business affairs of his people" at Buleau plantation) gained one month at hard labor in military custody.[106] Moreover, conservatives loath to concede legitimacy of Reconstruction governments gained propaganda for the view that such clashes left "lives imperiled."[107]

"On Duty" in the League

On the morning after New Year's Day, 1868, Jefferson Reece donned his uniform for the second time in as many days. The former slave was an officer in a company that had "paraded" and "discharged their fire-arms by platoons and companies" in Orangeburg district's village of Lewisville the day before. Time probably had seldom seemed to be as much on his side as when Reece strode toward the residence of his employer, Dietrich J. Hames, on 2 January. Planters seemed reconciled to New Year observances of the Emancipation Proclamation, like the one in which Reece had just marched; a major Democratic organ pronounced such events "[a] celebration which we think very proper, and considerably more appropriate than [freedpeople's] celebration of the 4th of July."[108] The commemoration in Lewisville had featured an address by Charleston's African Methodist Episcopal minister and delegate-elect to the constitutional convention, Richard Harvey Cain. Within two weeks, the constitutional convention, for whose assembly a local leader like Reece had surely voted, would convene in Charleston. The Union League in Reece's neighborhood had begun to organize wage actions among the many fam-

4111, Letters Received, RG 393 Pt 1 [SS-133]; Henry B. Judd to Lieut. Louis V. Caziarc, 8 July 1868, enclosed in Petition of Ishmael Moultrie [and others] to Judge Advocate, 7 July 1868, ibid.

106. In addition to the sources cited above, see General Orders No. 134, 9 July 1868, vol. 2, pp. 321–23, 2d Military District, ser. 4126, General Orders, RG 393 pt 1.

107. Charleston *Daily Courier*, 3 June 1868, p. 2, col. 4. Fields, "Ideology and Race," especially p. 167; Powell, "Southern Republicanism"; and Foner, *Reconstruction*, pp. 346–79, more fully consider the sources and impact of a broader crisis of legitimation of southern Republican governments during Reconstruction.

108. Charleston *Daily Courier*, 3 Jan. 1870, p. 1, col. 4.

ilies who worked on shares, urging them to refuse work that offered less than the half share of the crop that the league was demanding. Emancipation figured in leagues' judgments that one-third the crop was unworthy of free people. In demanding one-half the crop, league opinion could cite employers' reputed judgments that "it took a third to keep hands when they held slaves."[109]

It was the year that had ended rather than the year ahead to which Reece's thoughts most surely turned as he approached the Big House. For at least six weeks, maybe longer, the planter Hames had been holding corn that Reece's household had cultivated along with cotton on Hames's land in 1867. There was no getting the cotton from Hames, who was having it ginned and waiting to settle accounts with his shareworkers with proceeds from the sale; but Reece probably considered the immediate uses his family could make of the corn – eat it themselves, feed it to hogs, or perhaps use it in a bit of local trading.

"Give me my cor[n]," Reece demanded, when Hames came outside.

"You owe me already," Hames responded. "I'll settle with you after the cotton is ginned. Now get off my place."

Voices rose as Hames, repeatedly ordering Reece to leave, insisted, "I do not want to be bothered with you [I]f you do not go away I will hurt you."

Unmoved by threats, conscious of the figure he cut in uniform, Reece insisted, "I'll leave when you give me my corn, and when the cotton is gin[n]ed, I will pay you Like A Gentleman."

In less gentlemanly manner, Hames shot Reece in the back at some point during their dispute.[110]

To the dismay of planters and federal officials alike, former slaves did not readily segregate daily routine from the agenda of Reconstruction politics.[111] As surely as Reece's uniformed foray associated social dignity with how and when he was paid, ex-slaves more generally linked local grievances to the restructuring of political institutions. The assembly of the constitutional convention in Charleston in mid-January 1868 instantly

109.   League affiliation of the unidentified rural delegate from Chester County to the 1869 Laborers' Convention in Columbia has been inferred. His remarks are quoted in Foner and Lewis, eds., *Black Worker*, p. 26.

110.   The episode has been reconstructed in dialogue form from J. W. Prickett et al. to Gen., 2 Jan. 1868; Capt. Jas. W. Piper to Bvt. Capt. J. A. Fessenden, 5 Jan. 1868; Statement of F. M. Wannamaker, 6 Feb. 1868; John B. Hubbard to G. A. Williams, 7 Feb. 1868; Statement of Joseph Yong, n.d.; Statement of Jefferson Reas, 7 Feb. 1868; Statement of Arron Williams, 6 Jan. 1868; all in 2d Military District, ser. 4111, Letters Received, RG 393 Pt 1 [SS-83]. Some quotations have been invented by the author but correspond with testimony offered in the file. Reas's name also appears as Reece.

111.   Holt, *Black Over White*, p. 170, and Foner, *Nothing But Freedom*, especially pp. 3, 45–47. Cf. Joyner, *Down By the Riverside*, p. 235.

became a component of negotiations over work arrangements on the Cooper River rice plantation of S. Emelius Irving. Workers received Irving's yearly contract, drawn in conformance with Freedmen's Bureau guidelines, with a "flat refusal." "They went on to say," Irving reported to a bureau officer, "that they would work the lands, but until something was decided in their favor by the sitting of the Convention, they would not sign any agreement or make any terms with me whatsoever."[112]

Irving's employees were not unusual. In 1868, neighborhood leagues and similar organizations took up issues of employment as part of their political work. Rural clubs spearheaded movements to standardize yearly tenure agreements in Orangeburg, Edgefield, and York districts and were principal coordinators of strikes for wages of $1.75 per day during the rice harvest on the Combahee River.[113] A range of popular actions in the countryside gave the lie to a Charleston newspaper's endorsement of the view that "labor is not a question of principle, it is a mere question of necessity."[114] Emancipated workers honed their political principles on the whetstone of daily affairs.

Obligatory manhood suffrage gave an explicitly political form to social divisions between employer and employee. As the direct employers of their political opponents, planters wielded labor discipline as an immediate means of stemming political mobilization in the countryside. Fines for unexcused absences and threats of eviction became resources for prescribing political behavior no less than they were tools of plantation management.[115] Registering voters and issuing registration certificates,

112. S. Emelius Irving to Captain F. W. Leidtke, 14 Jan. 1868, published in *Constitutional Convention of South Carolina*, pp. 111–12. Quotations appear on p. 111.
113. Regarding the league contracts, see John B. Hubbard to G. A. Williams, 7 Feb. 1868; Capt. H. M. Lazelle to Lieut. L. V. Caziarc, 20 Jan. 1868; C. A. Graeser, F[rancis] M. Wannamaker to Brig. Genl. H. S. Burton, 6 Jan. 1868; Capt. P. H. Remington to Lieut. H. B. Reed, 10 Jan. 1868; all in 2d Military District, ser. 4111, Letters Received, RG 393 Pt 1 [SS-83]; Stagg, "Problem of Klan Violence," p. 310; Williamson, *After Slavery*, p. 114. For harvest strikes on the Combahee, see Charleston *Mercury*, 27 Aug., 5, 10 Sept. 1868; Albert R. Heyward to R. K. Scott, 11 Aug. 1868; Alfred Rhett to R. K. Scott, 14 Aug. 1868; all in Governors' Papers, SCDAH; Affidavit, Nathaniel Heyward, 20 Aug. 1868, ser. 4116, Letters Received, 2d Military District, RG 393 Pt 1. Foner, *Nothing But Freedom*, pp. 90–110, offers an important interpretive analysis of the strikes among Combahee rice workers in 1876, when a combination of payment in chits and reduction of daily wages from fifty to forty cents provoked strikes that "epitomized in microcosm a host of issues central to the legacy of emancipation in the United States."
114. Charleston *Daily Courier*, 29 Feb. 1868, p. 2, col. 2, endorsing an editorial in the New Orleans *Picayune*.
115. Testimony of Henry Johnson, *KKK Testimony*, vol. 1, p.323; Testimony of Robert W. Shand, ibid., vol. 2, p. 973; Lt. A. P. Caraher to Bvt. Lieut. Col. John N. Andrews, 21 Aug. 1867, ser. 1295, RG 393 Pt 4; R. James Donaldson to Maj. Gen. Canby, 4 Nov. 1867, Letters Received, ser. 4280, Provost Marshal, 2d Military District, RG 393 Pt 1.

arrogating the right to "not only inform [freedpeople] ourselves when any
. . . [authorized meetings] are to take place but [to] make no deductions
for such absences, in order that they may hear all that will instruct them
in thier rights and priveleges" – such were the rearguard efforts by which
some planters first proposed to legitimate their social authority in the political space that the Reconstruction Acts opened to their employees.[116] As
political assassination and paramilitary actions inscribed electoral politics
by the fall 1868 federal elections,[117] direct domination of employees' political behavior became an instrument of landlordship. A Clarendon
County planter made no bones in September 1868 about political tests for
workers on his lands:

> I have given those on my places to understand if they vote the Radi-
> cal ticket again that [I] will not keep them on my places. So they have
> quit going to the Negro meetings and say they do not intend voting
> again. the only way to manage them is to drive them into measures.[118]

Neighborhood movements to award "certificates of democracy" to
black men who voted the Democratic ticket so that "they could get
employment from any one, and could rent houses and lands" inspired
Spartanburg County Democratic clubs in 1870.[119] Livelihood, physical
security, and even life itself were regularly candidates at Reconstruction polls.

Grass-roots Republican clubs staved off social domination with vigi-
lant and combative political partisanship. By 1868, a rural laborers'
movement (which had emerged under the auspices of ex-slaves' military
societies) sought to consolidate its existence in neighborhood leagues. Institutionalization rested on deeply local initiatives whose timing varied
from neighborhood to neighborhood. Ripening in the hotbed of "registration summer," the movement sprouted in waves of local organization
visible into the early 1870s.

Whenever they surfaced, neighborhood leagues imposed an organized
and public working-class presence. Direct assertions of standards of popular justice were unmistakable signs by which a league society announced
its existence. A Freedmen's Bureau agent in Colleton district investigating
charges "that white citizens of Ridgeville are honestly in fear of the Union

---

116. Opinion # 24 [17 Sept. 1867], p. 21, vol. 45, 2MD, Opinions of the Chief of
      the Bureau of Civil Affairs Relating to the Administration of Civil Affairs, ser.
      4368, 2d Military District, RG 393 Pt 1; Augustus Shoolbred to Maj. Gen. E. R.
      Canby, 30 Nov. 1867, 2d Military District, Letters Received, ser. 4111, RG 393
      Pt 1 [SS-77].
117. Foner, *Reconstruction,* pp. 342–43, 425–44; Trelease, *White Terror;* Powell, "Cor-
      recting for Fraud."
118. John I. Ragins to John H. King, 9 Sept. 1868, King Family Papers, SCL.
119. Testimony of Gabriel Cannon, *KKK Testimony,* vol. 2, p. 781.

League of the place," anticipated signs of a league's consolidation. "I find the colored people outside of the League as a rule Quiet, Courteous, and well disposed," the agent observed. His encounter with members of the Ridgeville league confirmed the unfortunate symptoms of league influence that he expected. Union League president Wade Hampton arrived for questioning escorted by "some twenty, or twenty five of his men"; vice-president Louis T. Wilson "made himself very conspicuous" in presuming to explain the organization's powers under law in a "very defiant and insulting" manner; only two men volunteered statements about their organization; the others left the interview "[s]coffing and geering whooping and yelping like incarnate Demons." The agent had seen such symptoms before. "[T]he Same Evil virus Exists among the Freedpeople here who belong to the League that I found on the Sea Islands w[h]ere I formerly acted as Agent," he concluded.[120]

Distinctive standards of political obligation underlay the loud cheering and stylized militancy that characterized some forms of league demonstrations. Societies ritualized solidarity by clear if rude insignia; wooden sticks "all about the same length," blue rosettes, small flags, or (quickly prohibited) officers' epaulets were among locally derived emblems indicating that a league member was "on duty."[121] The visible if fragile symbols in which ex-slaves ritualized their political partisanship had no counterpart among yeoman Republicans. Whereas ex-slave men vigorously wielded badges of political identification, yeoman Republicans strained to fulfill party loyalty without fracturing larger patron–client obligations. Yeoman republicans often continued to fulfill reciprocal obligations of neighborliness to ardent Democrats in their locale. Hugh A. Glover of Spartanburg County, for example, was whipped by his Democratic neighbors when he joined them at a local corn shucking. White Republican farmer John Genobles worried when, in his role as manager of polls located at his residence, a local black Republican magistrate required him to ask two Democratic poll watchers for whom he had great regard, to leave his house and monitor the balloting from the

120. H. M. Henry to General H. B. Clitz, 8 Jan. 1868, 2d Military District, Letters Received, ser. 4111, RG 393 Pt 1 [SS-84]. Similar changes were attributed to the appearance of a Union League in Conwayboro; see Charleston *Daily Courier*, 19 Sept. 1867, p. 1 cols. 3–4.

121. Affidavit of Wade Hampton in the Case of *Patrick Feilds* v. *Theodore Cordes* [Jan.? 1868], 2d Military District, Letters Received, ser. 4111, RG 393 Pt 1 [SS-84]; Affidavit of J. J. Murray, 27 July 1867, enclosed in Charges and Specifications against Monroe McDowell and others, Letters Received, ser. 4111, 2d Military District, RG 393 Pt 2 [SS-8]; Wm. Griffin to Bvt. Lt. Col. Geo. A Williams, 25 Jan.1868, Provost Marshal, ser.4280, Letters Received, RG393 Pt 1; M. L. Bonham to Robert K. Scott, 19 Aug. 1868; Jno. B. Hubbard, Report of an investigation at Santuc Depot, Union County, 3 Sept. 1868; both in Scott Papers, SCDAH.

yard outside. Encountering one of the men sometime after he had been the object of a Ku Klux Klan "thrashing," Genobles sought reassurance that this request had not provoked his whipping. "Says I," he informed a federal subcommittee, "Mr. Smith, were your feelings interrupted with me for making you and Mr. West go out of my house on such a time of the election?"[122] Genobles thus attempted to maintain a social deference that ex-slaves' frequently more aggressive displays of collectivity purged from political space.

Concrete struggles of daily existence flowed into the social projects undertaken by neighborhood Republican clubs. Political mobilization exacerbated existing labor struggles and suggested new purposes for collective action. If elections became the "school" on which some early Republican organizers had rested their faith in universal male suffrage, its lessons began long before campaigns opened.

Echoes of a slowdown rumbled in the background of elections. Given the size of the groups that ex-slave men assembled in order to travel to polling sites, and the premium that they placed on advance assembly, a pending election shrank the immediate work force. The mass appeal of neighborhood political meetings beyond the ranks of the enfranchised further appropriated "working time" from landowners' jurisdiction.

Time for political education remained inseparable from time at work. Some of the thousand former slave men who assembled with armed escort on a Wednesday in late August 1867 at a registration site in St. Thomas Parish expressed grave concerns about disciplinary fines to the three-member board of registrars. Lawrence P. Smith, a northern planter who chaired the board, answered their question about "the rights of planters with whom they had contracted for labor to deduct from their wages for the time during which they were absent from work for the purpose of being registered" with what a conservative journal deemed "the proper response." Less satisfied with Smith's reply, the ex-slave registrar Aaron Logan told the men "that they had a right to come every day to the polls if they pleased, and their employer could not deduct from their wages for such absence." When Smith objected to Logan's portrayal, the former slave vehemently elaborated "[t]hat now was the time when the freedmen should show that they possessed rights which they meant to maintain." Logan addressed the right to bear arms and then explained why ex-slaves should vote only for "white Radicals" or "men of their own color." Ensuing disputes halted local registration for several days. Not until a federal detachment of thirty men and Freedmen's Bureau officer Robert K. Scott visited the area did would-be voters relinquish their de-

122.   Testimony of Landon M. Gentry, *KKK Testimony*, vol. 1, p. 185; Testimony of John Genobles, ibid., p. 361. See also ibid., pp. 362–63 and vol. 2, p. 898.

mand to "exercise such rights as Logan had declared they were entitled to enjoy" and their insistence that the arrested Logan be released from military custody.[123] Electoral politics was a component of, not an alternative to social struggles.

Freedpeople devised mechanisms, particularly after the first waves of political agitation in the summer of 1867, to distinguish political assembly from a walkout. Plantation "captains" or a specially delegated neighborhood resident often served as the eyes and ears of a larger body. Jack Johnson, a black stonemason in Laurens County, used his mule – whose purchase after emancipation had helped Johnson to secure cash rental of a small tract of land – as a resource for local black Republicans. Explaining how he came to take "a great propriety in counseling the people which way to vote," Johnson noted: "I had been riding about a good deal. I was the only colored man that had a mule anywheres nigh my house, and I would go 'way off to speeches, and come back and tell the news how the speeches were."[124] Leagues helped stabilize absences by holding larger events on Saturdays, although most landowners still claimed Saturday labor.[125] In the end, of course, it was the substance of the gatherings, not their timing alone, that provoked opposition. Saturday picnics, church meetings, weekend dances – all could precipitate political threats.[126]

The course of political mobilization produced local league organizations whose aims reached beyond the specific goals of organizing and delivering votes for Republican candidates. Where leagues sustained a fairly continuous and open existence, averting threats such as those that led Pleasant Grove's league in Anderson County to disband and destroy its books and papers in October 1868,[127] they aspired to coordinate a remarkable range of community initiatives. The coherence of Horry County's five-year-old Union League in Conwayboro was probably rare in 1872, when President John R. Ransom informed Governor Robert K.

123. Charleston *Daily Courier,* 29 Aug. 1867, p. 2, col. 2, 30 Aug. 1867, p. 2 col. 4; General Order No. 126, 21 Nov. 1867, pp. 362–65, ser. 4126, 2d Military District, RG 393 Pt 1. See also Charleston *Daily Courier,* 6 Sept. 1869, p. 1, col. 4, for an account of subsequent difficulties between the planter Smith and the then-trial justice Aaron Logan. Logan by 1877 speculated in St. Thomas Parish lands. See Holt, *Black Over White,* p. 164.
124. Testimony of Jack Johnson, *KKK Testimony,* vol. 2, p. 1168.
125. Capt. J. McCleary to Leiut. [sic] Louis V. Caziarc, 27 Nov. 1867, ser. 920, pp. 167–69, RG 393 Pt 4; Affidavit of Wade Hampton in the Case of *Patrick Feilds* v. *Theodore Cordes* [Jan. 1868], 2d Military District, Letters Received, ser. 4111, RG 393 Pt 1 [SS-84].
126. Joseph Walsh to Maj. E. W. H. Read, 5 Sept. 1867, ser. 482, RG 393 Pt 4; Clinton Ward to [Robert K.] Scott, 19 Nov. 1869, Robert K. Scott Papers; *Christian Recorder,* 5 Dec. 1868, p. 142, col. 4; Office of Regulators to nn, 12[?] Oct. 1872, enclosed in Charles Wright to Scott, 13 Feb. 1872, Robert K. Scott Papers.
127. Charleston *Daily Courier,* 10 Oct. 1868, p. 1, col. 4.

Scott of the many projects that radiated from Conwayboro's "grand union Council." Most urgent was the council's desire to "rais our union republican Stor to preserv our vonts [votes]." In addition, the Conwayboro league was sponsoring construction of a new church building, coordinating the ongoing formation of countywide laborers' councils, requesting a charter and official recognition for a unit of the state militia, and seeking remedies for unsatisfactory public schools, regressive tax policies, and the nonrepresentative character of local juries. The association had been born during grass-roots activism of "registration summer," and had rallied and expanded while its president was receiving "many letters" from Scott during the first Republican election campaigns. By March 1872 the council was troubled by the governor's silences. "I want to No what is the Mater that I cant get no ancer from you," Ransom bluntly asked Scott. "[W]e don all we Cold to onlect you in offic," he reminded the state party's chief officeholder. "So you orto do Somthing for ous."[128] Conwayboro's "grand Union council" had acquired purposes not central to the party head.

Like Conwayboro's council, other popular Republican clubs addressed general matters of social welfare. Under local league auspices, a number of different organizations emerged to expand the social centers of rural life. Although it is not possible to delineate how Republican clubs, Union or Loyal Leagues, laborers' councils, companies, and union societies distinguished their social functions, it is clear that club projects embraced broad concerns of rank-and-file members. Cooperative marketing of articles of local consumption, searches for a physician who would not require payment before end-of-the year settlements, internal matters of plantation discipline, review of punitive legal judgments against small landowners who rented lands to freedpeople, and acquainting Republican voters with legal means to resist threats of eviction were among the myriad projects that neighborhood leagues tackled during the first years of Republican state government.[129]

Social realignments specific to Reconstruction underpinned the diversity of projects undertaken by local leagues. Rural neighborhood leagues formally (if unevenly and sporadically) affiliated Republican elected officials, men and women of varying professional training and recognition – particularly ministers, lawyers, and teachers, as well as artisans of wider social experience – with a preponderant majority of illiterate ex-slave common laborers. Some league work placed the literacy, familiarity with

128. John R. Ransom to Mr. guvener Sott, 22 Jan. 1872, John R. Ranson to Ser, 28 Jan. 1872, J. R. Ranson to [Scott], 18 March 1872, Robert K. Scott Papers.
129. In addition to sources cited in notes 128, 131, 134, and 137 , see Charleston *Daily Courier*, 28 Aug. 1869, p. 2, col. 2; [Affidavit of Douglas Fox], 17 Oct. 1867, Miscellaneous Letters and Reports Received, ser. 4366, Civil Affairs, 2d Military District, RG 393 Pt 1.

written law – and on occasion, the real property and credit – of the league's somewhat more socially secure members at the disposal of its ex-slave core. For example, ex-slave state senator Lucius W. Wimbush, elected from Chester County, also served as secretary of a Chester Union League, and provided books and pamphlets to a Sabbath school that he organized sometime after his first election victory in 1868.[130] Similarly, William M. Champion, a white farmer and miller of Spartanburg County, admitted that he "read the law to the negroes" in league meetings.[131] Like other nineteenth-century working-class mobilizations, the Union League's social movement incorporated some momentary alliances among small property owners, clerical and lay professionals, skilled tradesmen, and wage earners.[132] Cooperative stores, religious instruction, rudimentary training in literacy, and dissemination of written law required and received the support of emerging middle-class groups not yet antagonistic to a laboring majority.[133]

At the same time, Republican club's non–wage-earning membership did not endorse or participate in all league activities. Republican small-holders were usually keen to safeguard the interests of renters and their sympathetic landlords. On behalf of his Chester league members, for example, Lucius Wimbush secured a governor's pardon for white small landowner, Mrs. Nancy Hudson, that kept her from serving a year at hard labor in the state penitentiary. Wimbush and the league president attributed Hudson's conviction for theft both to her having had "upon her Farm Quite a number of Colored people" and also to her appearance before a jury composed of "a Set of Men who would regardless of oath find a True Bill against any parties who did not affiliate with them politically."[134] At the same time, Wimbush strongly objected to an 1869 laborers' initiative urging regulation of land rents and agricultural wages by state government.[135]

130. L. Wimbush to Rev. George Whipple, 29 May 1869, AMA; Holt, *Black Over White*, Table 5.
131. Testimony of William M. Champion, *KKK Testimony*, vol. 1, p. 371; Testimony of Alberry Bonner, ibid., pp. 443, 445; Testimony of Clem Bowden, ibid., p. 382.
132. Sources of tensions and fragmentation of such alliances are explored in Montgomery, *Beyond Equality*, pp. 387–424; Wilentz, *Chants Democratic*, pp. 176–83, 210–11, 335–43, 350; and Stansell, *City of Women*, pp. 144–49, 153.
133. A formulation influenced by the late Walter Rodney's account of postemancipation Guyana. Rodney, *History of the Guyanese Working People*, pp. 139–50.
134. [Nancy Hutson, Petition for Pardon], 19 April 1870, Robert K. Scott Papers. The landowner's name appears variously as Hudson and Hutson. Similarly, an organizing Union League in Abbeville County appended to a description of the need of "poor republican Blak people" for provisions, an appeal on behalf of a white widow, "for She has Six Children to Support no friends because her husband was a republican and Died in the [war] of that side." Charles Logan to Gov. [Scott], 13 June 1870, Robert K. Scott Papers.
135. Foner, *Reconstruction*, p. 377. A Chester delegate to the 1869 Laborers' Convention

Direct action against plantation owners and managers, neighborhood drills unrelated to party campaigns, internal plantation discipline, and strikes did not originate among the league's small-property–owning members or its elected state officers. It was plantation workers of the Loyal League of Africa who in January 1869 issued an overseer of a plantation on the Savannah River a written order to leave the plantation. When Georgetown's Union League decided to give "'three groans' and to play the dead march" at the home of the editor of the Georgetown *Times*, to protest his "slanderous articles," the American Missionary Association's schoolteacher, whom they had invited to attend the league meeting at the schoolhouse, declined to participate.[136] The popular character of Union League membership rendered neighborhood associations hybrid organizations, part political machine, part labor union, part popular tribunal, part moral or intellectual improvement body, part renters' association, part retail cooperative. There were occasions when, under a league banner, rural workers acted by their own lights or marched more or less alone.

Popular tribunals, variously called courts or committees when contemporaries saw occasion to name them at all, were agricultural laborers' most direct contribution to league business. Their extent remains uncertain, although isolated signs of their existence are widespread. Neighborhood councils often acted at the behest of resident plantation workers. Sometime in April 1867, for example, members of the Dimery family in Darlington district approached ex-slave Ebby Johnson to complain about abuses at the hands of their employer, W. Z. Wingate. Taking to heart Wingate's threat that "he would kill him" if he approached civil authorities, John Dimery instead sought assistance from Johnson's committee regarding a disputed plantation account and the landowner's assault of Dimery's daughter. Ebby Johnson, claiming authority from local Freedmen's Bureau agent and Republican Party organizer B. F. Whittemore, summoned a group of some fifteen men to "arrest" Wingate. After inspecting the men's weapons, Johnson, accompanied by his guard, overtook the planter in his buggy in order to present the Dimery family's complaints. Returning to the planter's house, in amicable negotiations Wingate and Johnson reached a written agreement in which Wingate

had insisted that "except laborers get some relief it seems impossible to live." See Foner and Lewis, eds., *Black Worker*, p. 26.

136. Charleston *Daily Courier*, 8 Jan. 1869, p. 1, col. 2; J. H. Simonson to E. P. Smith, 23 Aug. 1869, AMA Papers. The teacher noted, " I did tell the colored people to warn [the editor] through a committee to be appointed by them that unless a stop was put to the publication of such articles that they might (in the event that they continued to ridicule them) that they should then express their indignation in whatever manner they might see proper."

"agreed to cross out an account against the members of the Dimery family." With a cordiality perhaps shaped by the recent military occupation, Wingate then "invited Johnson into another room & treated him to liquor."[137]

At their fullest development, popular committees of justice joined regulation of day-to-day routine with special oversight of local sheriffs, magistrates, and county juries.[138] League members exercised the powers of a posse comitatus, claiming authority to "arrest" suspected violators of the public peace. In military fashion, league posses guarded premises to detain alleged offenders while a designated squad went in search of a local magistrate to procure an arrest warrant. In late December 1867, for example, members of Ridgeville's Union League hurriedly quit their Saturday meeting when a former slave rushed in to tell them that a companion had been seriously wounded by a slingshot fired by a young gentleman of the neighborhood. A guard stationed itself outside the assailant's residence while another group, led by president Wade Hampton, carried the injured man before a local magistrate, whom they awakened with the demand that "they were entitled to the warrant." The league's guards not only relieved each other through the night until they were satisfied that a warrant had been served, but also "furnished their President Wade Hampton with funds to go to Charleston." In Charleston, Hampton brought the case to the attention of a Republican lawyer recently elected to the constitutional convention. League members were adamant that neighborhood law officials acknowledge accountability to a superior authority, guards insisting their "power to protect this place" derived "a long way" from Ridgeville or that "they had their authority from Washington."[139] Leagues challenged the discretion of sheriffs and local magistrates to exclude club members from local civil procedures.

137. General Orders No. 41, 12 June 1867, pp. 101–04, ser. 4126, 2d Military District, RG 393 Pt 1. In subsequent investigations, military authorities sentenced Ebby Johnson to two months confinement and W. Z. Wingate to thirty days' hard labor at a federal garrison, and ordered him to pay Dimery's daughter twenty-five dollars for his unnamed assault.

138. With the appearance of federal garrisons and Freedmen's Bureau posts, freedpeople typically sought redress outside the civil authorities during presidential reconstruction. They coordinated and expanded such activities during the political mobilization that followed the Reconstruction Acts. An earlier raid by a neighborhood posse of ex-slave men led to the arrest of some of the alleged murderers of the minister Tom Black, as already discussed.

139. Affidavit of Wade Hampton in *Patrick Feilds* v. *Theodore Cordes* [Jan.–Feb.? 1867] and the enclosed Affidavit of James M. Cantwell, H. M. Henry to General H. B. Clitz, 8 Jan. 1868, Affidavit of Thomas H. Goodwin, Affidavit of Thomas Gadsden, George Lee to C. C. Bowen, 29 Dec. 1867, Affidavit of P. M. C. Earnest, 31 Dec. 1867, all in 2d Military District, Letters Received, ser. 4111, RG 393 Pt 1 [SS-84].

League members' determination to engage civil institutions in their popular arrests and detentions distinguishes ex-slaves' forms of popular justice from the summary acts of Ku Klux Klan–style vigilante bands. They supervised local officeholders with a vigilance that martial law had actually placed at the disposal of an occupying army. They served warrants on parties local authorities were slow to apprehend. They investigated Klan raids about which local officers claimed ignorance. They formed themselves into constabulary forces, ignoring the disinclination of local officers of the court to appoint them. They rallied to defend elected officers from forceful expulsion from office. Neighborhood league president Clarke Cleveland, Sr., identified this monitoring of law enforcement as central to league mobilizations. Asked whether the Union League at Walhalla was a military organization, Cleveland proposed that league societies were "a kind of semblance of such a thing," but insisted that "the main point now is to abide by the laws, and to learn us how to know about the law."[140]

"We the Laboring Men out of Doors"

Unlike the birds of the air, ex-slave members of neighborhood clubs had no ready nests.[141] As ardent Republicans, they were unsuitable clients of Democratic employers. As propertyless citizens, their circumstances defied nineteenth-century liberal notions of self-government. It was fitting that the president of the state's Union League should express this historically peculiar dimension of ex-slaves' combination of politically active citizenship and economic dependency. In language that reiterated the wage earner's anomalous standing in a political tradition that premised capacity for self-government on economic independence, Gilbert Pillsbury demanded of the constitutional convention that assembled in Charleston in January 1868, "What can a people do out of doors, who cannot advance one yard on earth without asking permission of some lord of the soil?"[142] For ex-slave rural workers, landed employers, and political officeholders alike, competing visions of social power converged on issues of land reform.

It is sometimes hard to understand why popular opinion attributed an imminent seizure and redistribution of plantation lands to the state's emerging Republican Party.[143] Thaddeus Stevens had certainly forced the

140. Cleveland quoted in Secretary of War, *Annual Report,* 1868, p. 403.
141. Patricia Heard Saville and Alphonso F. Saville, III, helped identify the New Testament allusions derived from Matthew 8:20 or Luke 9:53.
142. Constitutional Convention, *Proceedings,* p. 384.
143. Holt, *Black Over White,* pp. 18, 68–69; Foner, "Thaddeus Stevens," in Foner, *Politics and Ideology,* pp. 128–149; idem, "Black Reconstruction Leaders," in Litwack

subject into congressional debates in the spring of 1867; but neither the organizing convention of the state Republican Party nor the 1868 constitutional convention endorsed his appeal. On both occasions, Republican delegates took special pains to repudiate confiscation. At the party's founding convention in July 1867, a freeborn delegate from Charleston, Robert C. DeLarge, was reluctant to use "radical" in the state party's name because "Radicalism meant by some confiscation."[144] At the constitutional convention, Republicans summarized a broad range of efforts intended to banish the ghost of confiscation from their political enterprise. Delegates offered "the whole power of this [federal] Government," the interventions of national and state officials of the Freedmen's Bureau, and their own personal labors as testimony against confiscation. At the prompting of state Freedmen's Bureau director Robert K. Scott, the convention on 3 February 1868 cast yet another spell against the troublesome specter. A resolution prepared by Georgetown's freeborn delegate Joseph H. Rainey declared "to the people of South Carolina, and to the world" that the convention had "no land or lands at their disposal," reiterated "that no act of confiscation has been passed by the Congress of the United States," and opined "that there never will be." The resolution passed without debate, Berkeley delegate Daniel H. Chamberlain affirming that he "would vote for it every day in the week."[145]

However well Republican delegates knew what they had meant, they failed to appreciate how what they had actually said contributed to what listeners believed that they had heard. Ownership of land was hardly irrelevant to symbols of political right expounded on Republican hustings. Would ex-slaves have understood that rapturous paeans to the landowning farmer excluded those who had not bought acreage with money? An inveterate opponent of confiscation *and* state regulation of the price of forced land sales, Barnwell's representative Charles P. Leslie nevertheless affirmed that "the colored people may be provided with homes" because of his belief that, within six months of the convention, lands in the state would sell at ten to twenty-five cents per acre.[146] Did ex-slaves heed more closely Richard Harvey Cain's insistence that "I do not desire to have a foot of land in this State confiscated," or his proposal that the convention petition Congress for $1 million to be earmarked for buying land for for-

and Meier, eds., *Black Leaders*, pp. 227–29 consider the significance of popular responses to confiscation.

144. Charleston *Daily Courier*, 27 July 1867, p. 1, cols 2–5. DeLarge averred that "he claimed to be a Radical, if radicalism meant truthfulness towards principles."

145. Constitutional Convention, *Proceedings*, pp. 213, 416. See also Robert K. Scott to Hon. A. G. Mackey, 23 Jan. 1868 [misdated 1863], ibid., p. 111.

146. Constitutional Convention, *Proceedings*, pp. 164, 391.

mer slaves?[147] Would freedpeople appreciate that theirs was not the legal form of homestead that Lexington's representative Simeon Corley defended when he declared "The freedom of the people cannot be long preserved unless they obtain an interest in the soil"?[148] Landowners in the vicinity of Lawtonville themselves understood Jonathan Jasper Wright's appeals to freedpeople – to rent land rather than "contract with the landowners" – as "harangues" on behalf of confiscation.[149] Ideologies that vested political capacity in the ownership of productive property were unpredictable as an arsenal against confiscation. Sent on a mission to put out rumors of confiscation, they could as readily ignite a spark of fear or hope.

Confiscation found its most favorable haunts outside Republican political meetings. Northern peddlers traded on beliefs in the likelihood of confiscation – and no doubt heightened expectations – as they made their way through Fairfield district selling fraudulent "land warrants" to former slaves at two dollars per hope. Planters heard its ominous portents in many a slowdown and sensed its workings when farm laborers negotiated tenure arrangements. Ex-slave Lucy McMillan, for example, had her house razed when, after having attended a Republican "speaking" in Spartanburg, she remarked, "I wanted to rent land enough . . . for me and my daughter to tend on this side of the river." Her statement galvanized a Ku Klux Klan band that "said all they had against me was that I was bragging and boasting that I wanted the land."[150] Indictments of the Freedmen's Bureau as an agent of violent confiscation found their way into hiring arrangements of some Abbeville district landowners in 1868. Landowner James McCaslin, for example, extracted from his employee Wade Kennedy a signed statement that a local bureau officer not only had insisted that "the Colored people must have both land and mules," but also had advised that "if they cannot get them any other way, they mean to do so by means of the torch." Ex-slave voters reportedly linked suffrage rights to an imminent redistribution of land at the polls near Adam's Run, when, according to a twentieth-century reminiscence, they "came to the polls bringing halters for mules which they expected to carry home."

147. Constitutional Convention, *Proceedings*, p. 381; for discussion of the petition for a congressional loan, see ibid., pp. 376–86, 389–406, 409–439.
148. Constitutional Convention, *Proceedings*, p. 492.
149. Joseph M. Lawton et al. to Brevet Major Gen. Ed. R. S. Canby, 19 Nov. 1867, 2d Military District, Letters Received, ser. 4111, RG 393 Pt 1 [SS-57]; Affidavit of E. L. Ducom, 7 Dec. 1867, enclosed in Wm. Griffin to E. W. Hinks, 15 Dec. 1867, 2d Military District, Letters Received, ser. 4111, RG 393 Pt 1 [SS-65]. Wright's appeals were described as urging freedpeople to secure rental agreements in Wm. Griffin to E. W. Hinks, 15 Dec. 1867, 2d Military District, Letters Received, ser. 4111, RG 393 Pt 1 [SS-65].
150. Testimony of Lucy McMillan, *KKK Testimony*, vol. 2, p. 605.

What figured as jest in the Redemption climate of Adam's Run had portended dire peril in Beaufort district after elections to the constitutional convention. In December 1867, landowners in the vicinity of Lawtonville appealed for federal troops because an ex-slave military company was reportedly "drilling with the avowed intentions of having lands or blood."[151]

Combinations of old hopes, ambiguous accommodations of wage earners in republican political theories, quick scheming, and ex-masters' unwitting complicity fed popular beliefs that confiscation was plausible as a component of congressional Reconstruction. More than planters' chimera, less than freedpeople's aim, confiscation resided in 1867 in a murky realm dimly charted by rumor, grim fear, or faint prospect.

At bottom, it was redistribution of social power that landowners and former slaves contested when they spoke of redistribution of land. In July 1867, a sea-island planter directly opposed the rights of popular assemblies to his property rights in plantation lands. Confronted with a newly constituted marching company that included many of his employees, planter John Jenkins advised the provost marshal that society members "could not have the sanction of the proprietors of the soil on which they were drilling [and] marching."[152] Public elections provoked some proprietors to define specific features of their rights in property other than land. On behalf of wardens of All Saints Church on the Waccamaw, for example, two rice planters demanded that election managers leave the "parsonage" that they were using as polls in the April 1868 elections. "This is private property, not Public," the planter trustees of the unoccupied minister's residence urged, insisting that the "place has *never* been so used by any [persons?] since the foundation of the Government."[153] New claims

151. S. Emelius Irving to Captain F. W. Leidtke, 14 Jan. 1868, in Constitutional Convention, *Proceedings*, p. 111; Wm. Griffin to Major Jas. P. Roy, 11 Oct. 1867, enclosed in Lieut. J. W. DeForrest to Bvt. Maj. Edw. L. Deane, 18 Oct. 1867, in wrapper labeled Robert, W. F., 3 Oct. 1867, ser. 4366, RG 393 Pt 1; Avery, *Dixie After the War*, p. 346; Lt. S[?] Almy to Bvt. Maj. L. Walker, 21 Dec. 1867, 2d Military District, Letters Received, ser. 4111, RG 393 Pt 1 [SS-40]; W. F. DeKnight to James McCaslin, 16 Sept. 1868; W. F. DeKnight to Lt. Wm. Stone, 20 Sept. 1868; both in vol. 99, Press Copies of Letters Sent, pp. 19[4], 196, ser. 3025, Abbeville, Subordinate Field Office Records, RG 105.

152. Affidavit of Lt. J. M. Johnston, 27 July 1867, enclosed in Charges and Specifications against Monroe McDowell et al., Letters Received, ser. 4111, 2d Military District, RG 393 Pt 1 [SS-8].

153. Charles Alston for himself and D[?]D[?] Rosa . . . to the Managers of the Election at Troop Muster shed, 14 April 1868, ser. 482, Georgetown, SC, Letters Received, Returns of Prisoners, and Reports of Arrests, RG 393 Pt 4. In reply, election managers advised Alston that the commanding officer at Georgetown had authorized them to make use of "any vacant house for the purpose of holding the Polls" and assured him that "the greatest care will be taken of the same – and everything replaced properly." See Manager of Elections to Mr. Alston [April 1868], ibid.

sprouted on familiar places, if with less speed than the *Daily Courier*'s ultimatum, "Every foot of ground has its legitimate owner."[154]

Freedpeople's ardent longing for land did not breed lasting belief in the likelihood of confiscation.[155] It coexisted with growing movements in local Republican clubs premised on acknowledgment that emancipation would be landless. To give up on confiscation was not to give up on justice.

Concrete experiences gave former slaves new reasons to stake a claim on fast-eroding social terrain. Stephen Brown's attempts to organize local councils in the Cooper River rice region in the spring of 1870 persuaded him that "there is no place on the River that we can do them in Safety." "[Y]ou know Sir Jest as well as I do," Brown reiterated to governor Scott, "that it can not be done on those Planter lands." Brown turned to the uncertain prospects of collective purchase of land from the state's ineffective Land Commission with the appeal, "[L]et us get Head quarter" safe from political risk.[156]

The fragility of landless laborers' claims on substances of social existence – tools, animals, shelter, and food – hounded neighborhood leagues like no other problem. The narrow terms by which share workers secured year-round dietary staples preoccupied many Union County laborers who rallied to local "Major of Battalion" John Bates, as he gained influence as a league organizer in 1868. One man, who had been severely wounded while on duty cutting the league's emblematic wooden sticks after a rendezvous called by Bates, recalled the terms in which Bates had pledged the newly elected Republican governor's social faith to his earliest and most numerous constituents. Bates had steeled political will with his assurance that Robert K. Scott "was to furnish him with Ten thousand pounds [of bacon] to feed the Union League."[157] Seasonal shortages of subsistence, the wants of "old men & woman which is not able to help them Selves," or precise judgments that 236 bushels of corn "will help us to cecure [sic] our Crops" drove forward rural clubs' efforts to beat back a crisis that hovered over daily life.[158]

154. Charleston *Daily Courier,* 29 July 1867, p. 2, col. 1.
155. Significantly, a Freedmen's Bureau official on Edisto Island found ex-slaves – in that center of earlier agitation for lands under the terms of Sherman's wartime field order – generally skeptical, on the eve of elections to the constitutional convention, of claims that "the Govt will place them in possession of land." J. M. Johnston to Edw. L. Deane, 15 Nov. 1867, M 752, r 51, 0302–12. Johnston observed from his headquarters on Edisto Island, "An effort has been made by renegade (white) northerners and Southerners to make the freedmen think the Govt will place them in possession of lands: but this idea is *not* generally received by the freedmen."
156. Stephen Brown to his Exel Govrner Scott, 15 April 1870, Robert K. Scott Papers.
157. Charleston *Daily Courier,* 31 July 1868, p. 4, col. 2, 29 Aug. 1868, p. 1, col. 1, 9 Sept 1868, p. 1, cols. 3–4; 14 Sept 1868, p. 2, col. 3; Jno. B. Hubbard, Report of an investigation at Santuc Depot, 3 Sept. 1868, Robert K. Scott Papers.
158. Chas. Logan to Gov. [Scott], 13 June 1870; [petition], E. D. Williams and twenty-two others to [Daniel A. Chamberlain], 5 June 1876, Daniel A. Chamberlain Papers.

Ordinary because recurrent uncertainties informed but did not inspire leagues' most determined collective efforts. It was vulnerability to eviction that sparked some of the largest collective actions mounted by neighborhood clubs. Dismissal from work, which was also ejection from residence for the vast majority of farm workers who also rented houses on their employers' lands, had had no place in contests between masters and slaves. War-end issue of struggles between private employers and plantation laborers in Port Royal, evictions or the threat of them came of age with postwar disputes between agricultural laborers and landlords.[159]

As an instrument of landlordship, evictions were no respecter of terms of employment, judging by two notable episodes of early Reconstruction.[160] Large numbers of Edisto laborers, who worked under a "two-day" agreement with island planters, received ejectment orders in July 1869. They had refused for nearly two weeks to make restitution to their landlords for a Monday that the laborers had taken for their own time in a year when the Fourth of July fell on Sunday. By contrast, the "captain" whom an overseer stabbed and drove off a Newberry County plantation the following year probably worked on shares on lands owned by the overseer's father-in-law.[161]

In both instances, the evictions provoked demonstrations second in size only to the political rallies of the era. Some three hundred plantation workers on Edisto Island turned out at the house of a local magistrate to demand release of a male plantation worker who had been arrested under the magistrate's order for returning to a cabin from which he had earlier been evicted. In September 1870, an "armed band" of some sixty to eighty men converged in the neighborhood of Belmont, "swearing to burn out and kill" the offending overseer. The demonstration in Belmont rippled through at least two other counties, as armed forces of six hundred to eight hundred white residents of Laurens and Union joined their Newberry counterparts at the plantation outside Belmont, expecting to confront bands of ex-slave men and Republican officeholders rumored to be mobilizing in Laurens, Union, Edgefield, and Newberry counties.[162]

159. Landlords' selective employment of seasonal dismissals and laborers' equally seasonal resort to walk-offs during lay-by and postharvest seasons are considered in Chapter 4.

160. Accounts of the evictions on Edisto appear in Charleston *Daily Courier*, 17 July 1869, p. 1, col. 3, 21 July 1869, p. 1, col. 3, 3 Aug. 1869, p. 1, col. 3. Events near Belmont are recounted in ibid., 23 Sept. 1870, p. 2, col. 3, 26 Sept. 1870, p. 1, col. 3; Testimony of C. H. Suber, *KKK Testimony*, vol. 1, p. 143.

161. It is ambiguous whether the evicted share worker was "captain" of a neighborhood league organization, of a detachment of the state militia, or of both. For testimony to the last of these, see *KKK Testimony*, vol. 1, p. 143.

162. In addition to sources cited in this chapter, note 160, see Capt. J. A. Walker to [Scott], 20 Sept. 1870, Robert K. Scott Papers. For accounts of violence that impeded league mobilizations in Laurens County, see Your affectionate mother to My dear

Confrontations triggered by evictions on these Edisto and Newberry plantations strained political loyalties and local civil authority. The demonstrations on Edisto pitted Republican voters against Republican planters, a local magistrate, and a Republican sheriff and his deputies from Charleston. Political opponents more clearly confronted each other in the two armed encampments that assumed positions overnight outside Belmont. Newberry's Republican sheriff spent the night in the overwhelmingly larger camp of Democratic landowners. The state-appointed constabulary, whom the sheriff had ignored, arrived the next morning in company of "colored men from the town" of Newberry, its authority acknowledged only in the camp of outnumbered Republican demonstrators. Five men were arrested as "ringleaders" of the demonstration on Edisto, while the overseer and twenty-three of the protesters in Newberry were also arrested. What contemporary newspapers described as nearly "war" in Newberry and as "riot" on Edisto eventually made its way to local courts.

Evictions also galvanized the most regular educational energies of local league officers, many of whom were determined to arm sharecropping members with knowledge of written law that would help defend leagues' ongoing attempts to bargain for half the crop. League councillors countered threats of eviction by insisting that farm workers enjoyed legal right to reside on a landlord's premises that ended with the calendar year, not the harvest.[163] League members thus understood eviction as a political threat to Republican mobilization during Reconstruction, and as a new social catastrophe born on emancipation's changed terrain of labor.

Terms of national unification defined in Congress provided occasion for emancipated rural laborers to address political and economic concerns in neighborhood league associations. Terms of emancipation hammered out from field to field, from day to day, and from season to season flowed into league affairs. No single strategy guided rural societies as they sought someplace secure enough, time long enough, or wages high enough to

Bob, 21 Sept. 1870, Lalla Pelot Papers, Duke University. Pelot also reported that the eviction in Newberry had aroused "[s]ome [radicals? rascals?], white & black" and that four black men and one white man were killed during the confrontations. H. H. Witson to Capt. Jno. B. Hubbard, 21 Sept. 1870, Robert K. Scott Papers, reports his observations of a "complete military organization, armed and equiped [*sic*] for the purpose of defying the Laws and menacing the Authorities of the State" in the towns of Clinton and Laurens Court House, but makes no mention of their relationship to events in Newberry.

163.   Testimony of William M. Champion, *KKK Testimony*, vol. 1, p. 371; for testimony from black members of the Spartanburg league in which Champion offered legal advice, see Testimony of Clem Bowden, ibid., pp. 382–85 and Testimony of Alberry Bonner, ibid., especially p. 445.

ground claims born with the dawning of freedom. Whatever the instrument, people whose urgencies were evoked by nineteen male petitioners near Beech Island in Edgefield district, when the men signed as "We the laboring men out of doors," had made their ways across a historical divide, looking to wrest new possibilities from new problems.[164]

164. Milledge Cooper [and eighteen others] to [Scott?], 15 Dec. 1870, Robert K. Scott Papers.

Afterword

A web of contradictions surrounded the clubs that marched and drilled the hopes of an emerging social movement onto the terrain of Reconstruction politics. Reconstruction agrarian policies proved a narrow channel for emancipated workers' aspirations to gain recognition of their interests in the crop apart from wages. Reconstruction elections, in symbol and in practice, remained inseparable from physical struggle.[1] Consequently, league members' commitment to lawful procedures and political action did not preclude either illicit means or coercive force. Skillful poaching could gain seed cotton or fodder that law placed out of reach. Direct coercion, ruffianism, and intimidation sustained the exercise of suffrage rights. However readily ex-slaves took to public display of political solidarities, clandestine action remained indispensible to their political survival.

Insurrectionary moments therefore hovered in a burgeoning social movement's bid to defend its claims within the bounds of law. Recruited to form the most local units of the Republican Party, rural Republican clubs nevertheless embraced social purposes that made them something other than the narrowly political organizations that their would-be sponsors envisioned. Scarcely distinguishable from outlaws in the view of a conservative opposition, local companies remained in some respects illicit bands even in the eyes of many Republican officeholders.

The dualities that clung to popular Republican societies would intensify after the General Assembly attempted to re-establish the state's police power in the spring of 1870. The act that reconstituted the state militia also threatened fine and imprisonment against military associations that organized, drilled, or paraded without authorization. The legislature's threat of sanction attached to Republican drill societies no less than to Democratic rifle or saber clubs. What an early historian of state militia during Reconstruction insightfully characterized as "two distinct and dissimilar phases" in the formation of state militia charts a widening

---

1. Powell, "Correcting for Fraud"; Rable, *But There Was No Peace*. Similar features of postemancipation politics in Jamaica are noted in Heuman, *Between Black and White*, p. 118; Holt, *Problem of Freedom*, pp. 231–32.

197

breach between an emergent grass-roots movement and its formal political leadership.[2]

The authorized state militia and quasi-military associations came to reflect the growing distance between ex-slave rank-and-file Republicans and many Republican officeholders. In the minds of some members, the state militia and the Union League's local drill squad were distinct bodies.[3] Some ex-slave members of groups that had been armed as units of the state's militia unsuccessfully attempted to take up tactics of social banditry against powerful Democratic clubs in their neighborhoods.[4] On occasion, local Republican officials called on paramilitary Democratic forces rather than the ex-slave–dominated state militia to establish order.[5] In other instances, the state militia's Republican organizers of 1870 did not fully endorse groups that formed later.[6] In the end, the quasi-military society of an organizing laborers' movement could not march to the drum of the state militia. As emergent wage earners, former slaves discovered interests that collided with the terms of clientage proffered by elites of both the old order and the new.

There is perhaps no neat demarcation between visionary courage and misguided ignorance, no decisive sorting of the farsighted from the expedient, no impermeable boundary between the fragile and the resilient in the elements of this remarkable popular mobilization. Nominal opposites sometimes traveled in close company, as those who had felt the dead weight of the past long pressed against them saw their moment and shoved back.

2. Singletary, *Negro Militia,* quotation at p. 100.
3. See the account of a Fourth of July parade in Charleston in which members of the Union League and the state militia appear in separate places in the procession. Charleston *Daily Courier,* 6 July 1869, p. 1, cols. 3–4.
4. Ex-slave members of Edward Tennant's militia unit in Edgefield County seem to have made the attempt in 1875 and 1876. See Burton, *In My Father's House,* pp. 156, 255, 348n; Singletary, *Negro Militia,* pp. 43–44; Thompson, *Ousting the Carpetbagger,* pp. 75–76, 83–84; Reynolds, *Reconstruction in South Carolina,* pp. 272, 301–02.
5. Thompson, *Ousting the Carpetbagger,* pp. 70–71. In the late summer of 1876, the head of the state's constabulary force expressed relief that "Providence . . . saved us from the use of a part of" Charleston's armed Democratic clubs against striking rice workers on the Combahee. See James P. Low to Chamberlain, 8 Sept. 1876, Daniel H. Chamberlain Papers, SCDAH.
6. The unit of state militia that clashed with Democratic vigilantes in the well-known riot at Hamburg in July 1876 had recently been revived under the leadership of Doc Adams. There are indications that by the latter date, ex-slave Republican politician and Trial Justice Prince Rivers was out of sympathy with the body. The state's attorney general, William Stone, advised Governor Daniel H. Chamberlain that the company at Hamburg initially formed by Rivers in 1870 had reorganized in May 1876, when Adams was elected captain. William Stone to Daniel H. Chamberlain, 12 July 1876, Governors' Papers, SCDAH; Thompson, *Ousting the Carpetbagger,* p. 99. See also Williamson, *After Slavery,* pp. 266–71.

Bibliography

Manuscript Collections

American Missionary Association Manuscripts (AMA) (microfilm)
South Caroliniana Library:
     Aiken Family Papers
     David Wyatt Aiken Papers
     Charles P. Aimar Papers
     Allston Family Papers
     Bratton Family Papers
     Conway, Bonds Papers
     Ellis Family Papers
     Frank Goss Papers
     Hammond–Bryan–Cumming Family Papers
     Hammond Family Papers
     Edward Spann Hammond Papers
     Heyward Family Papers
     Edward Barnwell Heyward Papers
     Jennings Family Papers
     John H. King Papers
     Hugh Lide Law Papers
     Read–Lance Family Papers
South Carolina Historical Society:
     Robert F. W. Allston Papers
     Black Oak Agricultural Society, Minutes (typescript)
     Thomas B. Chaplin Journal
     Manigault Family Papers
     Middleton Family Papers
     Paul Weston Papers
     White House Plantation Correspondence [Charles P. Aimar]
Southern Historical Collection:
     David Golightly Harris Farm Journals (microfilm)
Duke University:
     James C. Beecher Papers
     Pelot Family Papers
Rutherford B. Hayes Presidential Center Library:
     Robert C. Schenck Papers (microfilm)

University of Wisconsin, Madison:
>William F. Allen Diary (microfilm)

Federal Archival Records

Record Group 105: Records of the Bureau of Refugees, Freedmen, and Abandoned Lands
>Office of the Commissioner
>Office of the Assistant Commissioner for South Carolina
>Subordinate Field Office Records for South Carolina

Record Group 393 Pt 1: Records of the United States Army Continental Commands, Departments of the South and South Carolina and 2d Military District
>>Letters Sent, vols. 1–6 2MD, ser. 4089
>>Letters Received, ser. 4111
>>Letters and Reports Received Relating to Freedmen and Civil Affairs, ser. 4112
>>Judge Advocate, Proceedings of Provost Courts, Military Tribunals, and Post Court Martial Cases, ser. 4257
>>Provost Marshal General, Letters Received, ser. 4280
>>Civil Affairs, Letters Sent, vol. 37 2MD, ser. 4357
>>Civil Affairs, Endorsements Sent Relating to Appointment of Registrars and Inspectors of Elections, vol. 43 2MD, ser. 4362
>>Civil Affairs, Miscellaneous Letters and Reports Received, ser. 4366
>>Civil Affairs, Opinions of the Chief of the Bureau of Civil Affairs Relating to the Administration of Civil Affairs, vol. 45 2MD, ser. 4368
>>Civil Affairs, Opinions of the Chief of the Bureau of Civil Affairs Relating to Registration and Qualification of Voters, vol. 50 2MD, ser. 4369

Record Group 393 Pt 4, Records of the United States Army Continental Commands, Military Installations
>>Georgetown, SC, Letters Received, Returns of Prisoners, and Reports of Arrests, ser. 482
>>Berkeley, SC, Proceedings of Provost Court, ser. 1394

National Archives Microfilm Publications M 752, Registers and Letters Received by the Commissioner of the Bureau of Refugees, Freedmen, and Abandoned Lands

National Archives Microfilm Publications M 869, Records of the Assistant Commissioner for the State of South Carolina, Bureau of Refugees, Freedmen, and Abandoned Lands

National Archives Microfilm Publications M 619, Letters Received by the Office of the Adjutant General, Main Series, 1861–1870
>>Reel 200, Testimony taken by the American Freedmen's Inquiry Commission in South Carolina

Freedmen and Southern Society Project, University of Maryland, College Park

South Carolina Department of Archives and History

Governors' Papers
    Francis Pickens
    James L. Orr
    Robert K. Scott
Legislative Papers, "Green File"

Published Federal and State Records

General Statutes of the State of South Carolina (Columbia, SC: 1883).

[Hammond, Harry]. *South Carolina: Resources and Population, Institutions and Industries* (Charleston, SC: 1883).

    Report on the Cotton Production of the State of South Carolina, in Eugene W. Hilgard, comp., *Report on Cotton Production in the United States,* 2 vols., Tenth Census (Washington, DC: GPO, 1884), vol. 2, pp. 1–70.

The Ku-Klux Conspiracy: Testimony Taken by the Joint Select Committee to Inquire Into the Condition of Affairs in the Late Insurrectionary States, Part 3 South Carolina, 3 vols. (Washington, DC: GPO, 1872).

Proceedings of the Constitutional Convention of South Carolina . . . 1868 (1868; New York: Arno, 1968).

Report of the Joint Committee on Reconstruction (Washington, DC: GPO, 1866).

Statutes of South Carolina, in *Proceedings of the General Assembly* (Columbia, SC: 1866–76).

U.S., *Statutes At-Large of the United States* (Washington, DC: GPO, 1837–).

U.S., Adjutant General's Office. *Official Army Register of the Volunteer Force of the United States Army for the Years 1861–1865, Part 8* (Washington, DC: 1867).

U.S., Navy Department. *Official Records of the Union and Confederate Navies in the War of the Rebellion,* 30 vols. (Washington, DC: 1894–1922).

U.S., Secretary of War, *Annual Reports, 1865–68.*

U.S., War Department. *War of the Rebellion: A Compilation of the Official Records of the Union and Confederate Armies,* 128 vols. (Washington, DC: 1880–1901).

Memoirs and Other Contemporary Accounts

Abbott, Richard H., ed. "A Yankee Views the Organization of the Republican Party in South Carolina, July 1867," *SCHM,* 85, no. 3 (July 1984): 244–50.

[Allston, R. F. W.]. "Rice," *De Bow's Review,* 1 (April 1854): 289–319.

    "Sea-Coast Crops of the South," *De Bow's Review,* 16 (June 1854): 589–615.

Ames, Mary. *From a New England Woman's Diary in Dixie in 1865* (Springfield, MA: Plimpton, 1906).

Andrews, Sidney. *The South Since the War* (1866; New York: Arno, 1969).

Avary, Myrta Lockett. *Dixie After the War* (Boston: Houghton Mifflin, 1937).

[Benjamin, S. G. W.]. "The Sea Islands," *Harper's New Monthly Magazine,* 57 (Nov. 1878): 839–61.

Botume, Elizabeth Hyde. *First Days Amongst the Contrabands* (Boston: Lee & Shepard, 1893).

[Capers, William Henry]. "Reply . . . On the Subjects Connected with the Culture of Black Seed or Sea-Island Cotton," *Southern Agriculturist,* 8 (Aug. 1835): 401–12.

Doar, David. *Rice and Rice Planting in the South Carolina Low Country* (Charleston, SC: Charleston Museum, 1936).

"The Education of the Freedmen," *North American Review,* 101 (Oct. 1865): 528–49.

Fields, Mamie Garven, with Karen E. Fields. *Lemon Swamp and Other Places: A Carolina Memoir* (New York: Free Press, 1983).

[Gannett, William Channing, and Edward Everett Hale]. "The Freedmen at Port Royal," *North American Review,* 101 (July 1865): 1–28.

Heard, William H[enry]. *From Slavery to the Bishopric in the A.M.E. Church* (1924; New York: Arno, 1969).

Holland, Rupert S., ed. *Letters and Diary of Laura M. Towne, 1862–1884* (1912; New York: Negro Universities PR, 1969).

Howard, Oliver Otis. *Autobiography of Oliver Otis Howard,* 2 vols. (New York: Baker & Taylor, 1907).

Jervey, Susan R., and Charlotte St. J. Ravenel. *Two Diaries from Middle St. John's Berkeley, South Carolina, February–May 1865* (Pinopolis, SC: St. John's Hunting Club, 1921).

Kemble, Frances Anne. *Journal of a Residence on a Georgian Plantation,* ed. John A. Scott (New York: Knopf, 1970).

Lawton, William M. *An Essay on Rice and Its Culture* (Charleston, SC: Walker, Evans, & Cogswell, 1871).

Leigh, Frances B[utler]. *Ten Years on a Georgia Plantation Since the War* (1883; New York: Negro Universities PR, 1969).

Leland, John A. *A Voice from South Carolina* (1879; New York: Negro Universities PR, 1971).

Manigault, Gabriel. "The Low Country of South Carolina," *The Land We Love,* 2, no. 1 (Nov. 1866): 5–11.

Moore, Frank, ed. *The Rebellion Record* (New York: Putnam, 1864).

Moore, John Hammond, ed. *The Juhl Letters to the Charleston Courier: A View of the South, 1865–1871* (Athens: Univ of GA PR, 1974).

Myers, Robert M., ed. *The Children of Pride* (New Haven, CT: Yale Univ PR, 1972).

Oliphant, Mary C. Simms, Alfred Taylor Odell, and T. C. Duncan Eaves, eds. *The Letters of William Gilmore Simms,* 5 vols, (Columbia: Univ of SC PR, 1952–56).

Pearson, Elizabeth Ware, ed. *Letters from Port Royal Written at the Time of the Civil War* (Boston: Clarke, 1906).

Reid, Whitelaw. *After the War: A Tour of the Southern States, 1865–66,* ed. C. Vann Woodward (New York: Harper & Row, 1965).

Richards, T. Addison, "The Rice Lands of the South," *Harper's New Monthly Magazine,* 19, no. 114 (Nov. 1859): 721–38.

Smith, Daniel E. Huger, et al., eds. *Mason Smith Family Letters, 1860–1868* (Columbia: Univ of SC PR, 1950).

Tremain, Henry Edwin. *Two Days of War: A Gettysburg Narrative and Other Excursions* (New York: Bonnell, Silver, & Bowers, 1905).

Turner, J[oseph] A[ddison]. *The Cotton Planter's Manual: Being a Compilation of Facts from the Best Authorities on the Culture of Cotton* (1857; New York: Negro Universities PR, 1969).

Periodicals

Beaufort *New South*
Charleston *Daily Courier*
Charleston *Daily News*
Charleston *Mercury*
Liberator
Nation
New York *Herald*
New York Times
New York *Tribune*
Rural Carolinian
Southern Agriculturist

Books and Articles

Abbott, Martin. *The Freedmen's Bureau in South Carolina, 1865–1872* (Chapel Hill: Univ of NC PR, 1967).

Abbott, Richard H. *The Republican Party and the South, 1855–1877* (Chapel Hill: Univ of NC PR, 1986).

Allen, James S. "The Struggle for Land During the Reconstruction Period," *Science and Society,* 1, no. 3 (Spring 1937): 378–401.

Armstrong, Thomas F. "From Task Labor to Free Labor: The Transition Along Georgia's Rice Coast, 1820–1880," *GaHQ,* 64 (1980): 432–47.

Basler, Roy P., ed. *The Collected Works of Abraham Lincoln,* 9 vols. (New Brunswick, NJ: Rutgers Univ PR, 1953–55).

Berlin, Ira. *Slaves Without Masters: The Free Negro in the Antebellum South* (New York: Pantheon, 1974).

"Time, Space, and the Evolution of Afro-American Society on British Mainland North America," *AHR,* 85, no. 1 (Feb. 1980): 44–78.

Berlin, Ira, Barbara Jeanne Fields, Thavolia Glymph, Joseph P. Reidy, and Leslie S. Rowland, eds. *Freedom: A Documentary History of Emancipation, 1861–1867,* ser. 1, vol. 1, *The Destruction of Slavery* (Cambridge Univ PR, 1985).

Berlin, Ira, Thavolia Glymph, Steven F. Miller, Joseph P. Reidy, Leslie S. Rowland, and Julie Saville, eds. *Freedom: A Documentary History of Emancipa-*

tion, 1861–1867, ser. 1, vol. 3, *The Wartime Genesis of Free Labor: The Lower South* (Cambridge Univ PR, 1990).

Berlin, Ira, and Philip D. Morgan, eds. *Cultivation and Culture: Labor and the Shaping of Slave Life in the Americas.* (Charlottesville: Univ PR of VA, 1993).

Berlin, Ira, Joseph P. Reidy, and Leslie S. Rowland, eds. *Freedom: A Documentary History of Emancipation, 1861–1867*, ser. 2, *The Black Military Experience* (Cambridge Univ PR, 1982).

Bethel, Elizabeth Rauh. *Promiseland: A Century of Life in a Negro Community* (Philadelphia: Temple Univ PR, 1981).

Blassingame, John W. *The Slave Community: Plantation Life in the Ante-Bellum South* (New York: Oxford Univ PR, 1972).

"Status and Social Structure in the American Slave Community: Evidence from New Sources," in Harry P. Owens, ed., *Perspectives and Ironies in American Slavery* (Jackson: Univ PR of MS, 1976), pp. 137–52.

Blassingame, John W. ed. *Slave Testimony: Two Centuries of Letters, Speeches, Interviews, and Autobiographies* (Baton Rouge: LA State Univ PR, 1977).

Bleser, Carol K. Rothrock. *The Promised Land: The History of the South Carolina Land Commission, 1869–1890* (Columbia: Univ of SC PR, 1969).

Bleser, Carol K. Rothrock, ed. *The Hammonds of Redcliffe* (New York: Oxford Univ PR, 1981).

Bloch, Marc. *Feudal Society,* 2 vols. (Univ of Chicago PR, 1961 trans.).

Burton, Orville Vernon. "Race and Reconstruction: Edgefield County, South Carolina," *JSocH,* 12, no. 1 (Fall 1978): 31–56.

In My Father's House Are Many Mansions: Family and Community in Edgefield, South Carolina (Chapel Hill: Univ of NC PR, 1985).

Carawan, Guy. *Ain't You Got a Right to the Tree of Life? The People of John's Island, South Carolina* (New York: Simon & Schuster, 1967).

Cardoso, Ciro Flamarion S. "The Peasant Breach in the Slave System," *Luso-Brazilian Review* 25, no. 1 (1988): 49–58.

Carlton, David L. *Mill and Town in South Carolina, 1880–1920.* (Baton Rouge: LA State Univ PR, 1982).

Carter, Dan T. "The Anatomy of Fear: The Christmas Day Insurrection Scare of 1865," *JSH,* 42, no. 3 (Aug. 1976): 345–64.

When the War Was Over: The Failure of Self-Reconstruction in the South, 1865–1867 (Baton Rouge: LA State Univ PR, 1985).

Clifton, James M., ed. *Life and Labor on Argyle Island: Letters and Documents of a Savannah River Rice Plantation, 1833–1867* (Savannah, GA: Beehive, 1978).

"Jehossee Island: The Antebellum South's Largest Rice Plantation," *AgH,* 59, no. 1 (Jan. 1985): 56–65.

Coclanis, Peter, A. *The Shadow of a Dream: Economic Life and Death in the South Carolina Low Country, 1670–1820* (New York: Oxford Univ PR, 1989).

Coon, David L. "Eliza Lucas Pinckney and the Reintroduction of Indigo Culture in South Carolina," *JSH,* 42, no. 1 (Feb. 1976): 61–76.

Cooper, Frederick. *From Slaves to Squatters: Plantation Labor and Agriculture in Zanzibar and Coastal Kenya, 1890–1925* (New Haven, CT: Yale Univ PR, 1980).

Cooper, William J., Jr. *The South and the Politics of Slavery, 1828–1856* (Baton Rouge: LA State Univ PR, 1978).

Coulter, E. Merton, *Negro Legislators in Georgia during the Reconstruction Period* (Athens, GA: Georgia Historical Quarterly, 1968).

Cox, LaWanda. "The American Agricultural Wage Earner, 1865–1900: The Emergence of a Modern Labor Problem," *AgH*, 22, no. 2 (April 1948): 95–114.

"The Promise of Land for the Freedmen," *Mississippi Valley Historical Review*, 45, no. 3 (Dec. 1958): 413–40.

Creel, Margaret Washington. *"A Peculiar People": Slave Religion and Community-Culture among the Gullahs* (New York Univ PR, 1988).

Daniel, Pete. *Breaking the Land: The Transformation of Cotton, Tobacco, and Rice Cultures since 1880* (Urbana: Univ of IL PR, 1985).

David, Paul A., et al., *Reckoning With Slavery: A Critical Study in the Quantitative History of American Negro Slavery* (New York: Oxford Univ PR, 1976).

Davidson, Chalmers Gaston. *The Last Foray: The South Carolina Planters of 1860, a Sociological Study* (Columbia: Univ of SC PR, 1971).

Davis, David Brion. *The Slave Power Conspiracy and the Paranoid Style* (Baton Rouge: LA State Univ PR, 1969).

The Problem of Slavery in Western Culture (Ithaca, NY: Cornell Univ PR, 1969).

The Problem of Slavery in the Age of Revolution, 1770–1823 (Ithaca, NY: Cornell Univ PR, 1975).

Slavery and Human Progress (New York: Oxford Univ PR, 1984).

Davis, Keith F. *George N. Barnard: Photographer of Sherman's Campaign* (Kansas City, MO: Hallmark, 1990).

Dawley, Alan. *Class and Community: The Industrial Revolution in Lynn* (Cambridge, MA: Harvard Univ PR, 1976).

Decanio, Stephen J. *Agriculture in the Postbellum South: The Economics of Production and Supply* (Cambridge MA: MIT PR, 1974).

Drago, Edmund L. *Black Politicians and Reconstruction in Georgia: A Splendid Failure* (Baton Rouge: LA State Univ PR, 1982).

DuBois, Ellen Carol. *Feminism and Suffrage: The Emergence of an Independent Women's Movement in America, 1848–1869* (Ithaca, NY: Cornell Univ PR, 1978).

Du Bois, W. E. B. *Black Reconstruction in America, 1860–1880.* (1935; New York: Atheneum, 1969).

Dunn, Richard S. *Sugar and Slaves: The Rise of the Planter Class in the English West Indies, 1624–1713* (Chapel Hill: Univ of NC PR, 1972).

Easterby, J. H., ed. *The South Carolina Rice Plantation as Revealed in the Papers of Robert F. W. Allston* (Univ of Chicago PR, 1945).

Edelstein, Tilden G. *Strange Enthusiasm: A Life of Thomas Wentworth Higginson* (1951; New York: Atheneum, 1970).

Engs, Robert Francis. *Freedom's First Generation: Black Hampton, Virginia, 1861–1890* (Philadelphia: Univ of PA PR, 1979).

Faust, Drew Gilpin. "Culture, Conflict, and Community: The Meaning of Power on an Ante-Bellum Plantation," *JSocH*, 14 (Fall 1980): 83–98.

James Henry Hammond and the Old South: A Design for Mastery (Baton Rouge: LA State Univ PR, 1982).

Fields, Barbara Jeanne. "Ideology and Race in American History," in J. Morgan Kousser and James M. McPherson, eds., *Region, Race, and Reconstruction: Essays in Honor of C. Vann Woodward* (New York: Oxford Univ PR, 1982), pp. 143–78.

"The Nineteenth-Century American South: History and Theory," *Plantation Society in the Americas*, 2, no. 1 (April 1983): 7–27.

Slavery and Freedom on the Middle Ground: Maryland During the Nineteenth Century (New Haven, CT: Yale Univ PR, 1985).

Fink, Leon. *Workingmen's Democracy: The Knights of Labor and American Politics* (Urbana: Univ of IL PR, 1983).

Fitzgerald, Michael W. *The Union League Movement in the Deep South: Politics and Agricultural Change during Reconstruction* (Baton Rouge: LA State Univ PR, 1989).

Fleming, Walter L. " 'Forty Acres and a Mule,' " *North American Review*, 183 (May 1906): 721–37.

Fogel, Robert William, and Stanley L. Engerman. *Time on the Cross*, vol. 1, *The Economics of American Negro Slavery*, vol. 2, *Evidence and Methods* (Boston: Little, Brown, 1974).

Foner, Eric. *Free Soil, Free Labor, Free Men: The Ideology of the Republican Party before the Civil War* (New York: Oxford Univ PR, 1970).

Politics and Ideology in the Age of the Civil War (New York: Oxford Univ PR, 1980).

Nothing But Freedom: Emancipation and Its Legacy (Baton Rouge: LA State Univ PR, 1983).

Reconstruction: America's Unfinished Revolution, 1863–1877 (New York: Harper & Row, 1988).

Foner, Philip S., and Ronald L. Lewis, eds. *The Black Worker During the Era of the National Labor Union*, vol. 2 of *The Black Workers: A Documentary History from Colonial Times to the Present* (Philadelphia: Temple Univ PR, 1978).

Ford, Lacy K., Jr. "Labor and Ideology in the South Carolina Up-Country: The Transition to Free Labor Agriculture," in Walter J. Fraser and Winifred B. Moore, Jr., eds., *The Southern Enigma: Essays on Race, Class, and Folk Culture* (Westport, CT: Greenwood, 1983), pp. 25–42.

"Rednecks and Merchants: Economic Development and Social Tensions in the South Carolina Upcountry, 1865–1900," *JAH*, 71, no. 2 (Sept. 1984): 294–318.

Origins of Southern Radicalism: The South Carolina Upcountry, 1800–1860 (New York: Oxford Univ PR, 1988).

Fox-Genovese, Elizabeth. "The Many Faces of Moral Economy: A Contribution to a Debate," *Past and Present*, no. 58 (Feb. 1973): 161–68.

"Poor Richard at Work in the Cotton Fields: A Critique of the Psychological and Ideological Presuppositions of *Time on the Cross*," *Review of Radical Political Economics.* 7 (Fall 1975): 67–80.

Within the Plantation Household: Black and White Women of the Old South (Chapel Hill: Univ of NC PR, 1988).

Freehling, William W. *Prelude to Civil War: The Nullification Controversy in South Carolina, 1816–1836* (New York: Harper & Row, 1968).

Gaspar, David Barry. *Bondmen and Rebels: A Study of Master–Slave Relations in Antigua With Implications for Colonial British America* (Baltimore, MD: Johns Hopkins Univ PR, 1985).

"Slavery, Amelioration, and Sunday Markets in Antigua, 1823–1831, *Slavery and Abolition*, 9 (May 1988): 1–28.

Gates, Paul W. *Agriculture and the Civil War* (New York: Knopf, 1967).

Geggus, David. "The Haitian Revolution," in Franklin Knight and Colin Palmer, *The Modern Caribbean* (Chapel Hill: Univ of NC PR, 1989), pp. 21–50.

Genovese, Eugene D. *The Political Economy of Slavery: Studies in the Economy and Society of the Slave South* (1965; New York: Vintage, 1967).

Roll, Jordan, Roll: The World the Slaves Made (New York: Pantheon, 1974).

From Rebellion to Revolution: Afro-American Slave Revolts in the Making of the Modern World (Baton Rouge: LA State Univ PR, 1979).

Genovese, Eugene D., and Elizabeth Fox-Genovese. *Fruits of Merchant Capital: Slavery and Bourgeois Property in the Rise and Expansion of Capitalism* (New York: Oxford Univ PR, 1983).

Gerteis, Louis S. *From Contraband to Freedman: Federal Policy Toward Southern Blacks, 1861–1865* (Westport, CT: Greenwood, 1973).

Glickstein, Jonathan. " 'Poverty is Not Slavery': American Abolitionists and the Competitive Labor Market," in Lewis Perry and Michael Fellman, eds., *Antislavery Reconsidered: New Perspectives on the Abolitionists* (Baton Rouge: LA State Univ PR, 1979), pp. 195–218.

Glymph, Thavolia, and John J. Kushma, eds. *Essays on the Postbellum Southern Economy* (College Station: Texas A & M Univ PR, 1985).

Gottlieb, Manuel. "The Land Question in Georgia During Reconstruction," *Science and Society*, 3, no. 3 (Summer 1939): 356–88.

Gray, Lewis Cecil. *History of Agriculture in the Southern United States to 1860*, 2 vols. (1933; New York: Peter Smith, 1941).

Greenberg, Kenneth S. *Masters and Statesmen: The Political Culture of American Slavery* (Baltimore: Johns Hopkins Univ PR, 1985).

Gutman, Herbert G. *The Black Family in Slavery and Freedom, 1750–1925* (New York: Pantheon, 1976).

Slavery and the Numbers Game: A Critique of Time on the Cross (Urbana: Univ of IL PR, 1975).

Hahn, Steven. "Hunting, Fishing, and Foraging: Common Rights and Class Relations in the Postbellum South," *Radical History Review*, no. 26 (Oct. 1982): 37–64.

The Roots of Southern Populism: Yeoman Farmers and the Transformation of the Georgia Upcountry, 1850–1890 (New York: Oxford Univ PR, 1983).

"Class and State in Postemancipation Societies: Southern Planters in Comparative Perspective," *AHR* 95 (Feb. 1990): 75–98.

Hall, Douglas. "The Flight from the Estates Reconsidered: The British West Indies, 1838–1842," *Journal of Caribbean History,* 10–11 (1978): 7–24.

Hall, Kermit L. "Political Power and Constitutional Legitimacy: The South Carolina Ku Klux Klan Trials, 1871–1872," *Emory Law Journal* 33 (1984): 921–51.

Hermann, Janet Sharp. *The Pursuit of a Dream* (New York: Oxford Univ PR, 1981).

Heuman, Gad. *Between Black and White: Race, Politics, and the Free Coloreds in Jamaica, 1792–1865* (Westport, CT: Greenwood, 1981).

Higginson, John. *A Working Class in the Making: Belgian Colonial Labor Policy, Private Enterprise, and the African Mineworker, 1907–1951* (Madison: Univ of WI PR, 1989).

Higgs, Robert. *Competition and Coercion: Blacks in the American Economy, 1865–1914* (Cambridge Univ PR, 1977).

Higman, Barry W. *Slave Populations of the British Caribbean* (Baltimore: Johns Hopkins Univ PR, 1984).

Hobsbawn, E. J. *Primitive Rebels: Studies in Archaic Forms of Social Movement in the 19th and 20th Centuries* (1959; New York: Norton, 1965).

The Age of Revolution, 1789–1849 (New York: New American Library, 1962).

The Age of Capital, 1848–1875 (New York: Scribner, 1975).

Workers: Worlds of Labor (New York: Pantheon, 1984).

Hoffman, Edwin D. "From Slavery to Self-Reliance: The Record of Achievement of the Freedmen of the Sea Island Region," *JNH,* 41, no. 1 (Jan. 1956): 8–42.

Holt, Thomas C. *Black Over White: Negro Political Leadership in South Carolina During Reconstruction* (Urbana: Univ of IL PR, 1977).

"Negro Legislators in South Carolina During Reconstruction," in Howard N. Rabinowitz, ed., *Southern Black Leaders of the Reconstruction Era* (Urbana: Univ of IL PR, 1982), pp. 223–46.

" 'An Empire Over the Mind': Emancipation, Race, and Ideology in the British West Indies and the American South," in J. Morgan Kousser and James McPherson, eds., *Region, Race, and Reconstruction: Essays in Honor of C. Vann Woodward* (New York: Oxford Univ PR, 1982), pp. 283–313.

The Problem of Freedom: Race, Labor, and Politics in Jamaica and Britain, 1832–1938 (Baltimore, MD: Johns Hopkins Univ PR, 1992).

Jaynes, Gerald D. *Branches Without Roots: Genesis of the Black Working Class in the American South, 1862–1882* (New York: Oxford Univ PR, 1986).

Johnson, Guion Griffis. *A Social History of the Sea Islands with Special Reference to St. Helena Island, South Carolina* (Chapel Hill: Univ of NC PR, 1930).

Johnson, Michael P., and James L. Roark. *Black Masters: A Free Family of Color in the Old South* (New York: Norton, 1984).

Jones, Gareth Stedman. "Class Expression Versus Social Control: A Critique of Recent Trends in the Social History of 'Leisure,' " *History Workshop,* no. 4 (Autumn 1977): 162–70.

Jones, P. M. *The Peasantry in the French Revolution* (Cambridge Univ PR, 1988).

Joyner, Charles. *Down By the Riverside: A South Carolina Slave Community* (Urbana: Univ of IL PR, 1984).

Klein, Rachel N. *Unification of a Slave State: The Rise of the Planter Class in the South Carolina Backcountry, 1760–1808* (Chapel Hill: Univ of NC PR, 1990).

Kolchin, Peter. *Unfree Labor: American Slavery and Russian Serfdom* (Cambridge, MA: Harvard Univ PR, 1987).

Kremm, Thomas W., and Diane Neal. "Challenges to Subordination: Organized Black Agricultural Protest in South Carolina, 1886–1895," *South Atlantic Quarterly*, 77 (Winter 1978): 98–112.

"Clandestine Black Labor Societies and White Fear: Hiram F. Hoover and the 'Cooperative Workers of America' in the South," *LH*, 19, no. 2 (Spring 1978): 226–37.

Lamson, Peggy. *The Glorious Failure: Black Congressman Robert Brown Elliott and the Reconstruction in South Carolina* (New York: Norton, 1973).

Laurie, Bruce. *Working People of Philadelphia, 1800–1850* (Philadelphia: Temple Univ PR, 1980).

Levine, Lawrence W. *Black Culture and Black Consciousness: Afro-American Folk Thought From Slavery to Freedom* (New York: Oxford Univ PR, 1977).

Littlefield, Daniel C. *Rice and Slaves: Ethnicity and the Slave Trade in Colonial South Carolina* (Baton Rouge: LA State Univ PR, 1981).

Litwack, Leon F. *Been in the Storm So Long: The Aftermath of Slavery* (New York: Knopf, 1979).

Litwack, Leon F., and August Meier, eds. *Black Leaders of the Nineteenth Century* (Urbana: Univ of IL Press, 1988).

Lofton, John. *Denmark Vesey's Revolt: The Slave Plot That Lit a Fuse to Fort Sumter* (1964; Kent, OH: Kent State Univ PR, 1983).

Logan, Rayford W., and Michael R. Winston, eds., *Dictionary of American Negro Biography* (New York: Norton, 1982.).

McFeely, Williams S. *Yankee Stepfather: General O. O. Howard and the Freedmen* (New Haven, CT: Yale Univ PR, 1968).

McMath, Robert C., Jr. "Southern White Farmers and the Organization of Black Farm Workers: A North Carolina Document," *LH*, 18 (Winter 1977): 115–19.

McPherson, James M., ed. *The Negro's Civil War: How American Negroes Felt and Acted during the War for the Union* (New York: Vintage, 1965).

Magdol, Edward. "Local Black Leaders in the South, 1867–1875: An Essay Toward the Reconstruction of Reconstruction History," *Societas* 4 (Spring 1974): 81–110.

A Right to the Land: Essays on the Freedmen's Community (Westport, CT: Greenwood, 1977).

Mintz, Sidney. "The Rural Proletariat and the Problem of Rural Proletarian Consciousness, *Journal of Peasant Studies*, 1 (April 1974): 291–323.

"Was the Plantation Slave a Proletarian?" *Review*, 2 (Summer 1978): 81–98.

"Slavery and the Rise of Peasantries," in Michael Craton, ed., *Roots and Branches: Current Directions in Slave Studies* (New York: Pergamon, 1979), pp. 213–42.

Mohr, Clarence L. "Before Sherman: Georgia Blacks and the Union War Effort, 1861–1864," *JSH*, 45, no. 3 (Aug. 1979): 331–52.

On the Threshold of Freedom: Masters and Slaves in Civil War Georgia (Athens: Univ of GA PR, 1986).

Montgomery, David. *Beyond Equality: Labor and the Radical Republicans, 1862–1872* (1967; Urbana: Univ of IL PR, 1972).

" On Goodwyn's Populists," *Marxist Perspectives*, 1 (Spring 1978): 166–73.

The American Civil War and the Meanings of Freedom (Oxford Univ PR [Clarendon PR]: 1987).

Morgan, Philip D. "Work and Culture: The Task System and the World of Low-country Blacks, 1700 TO 1880," *WMQ*, 3d ser., 39, no. 4 (Oct. 1982): 536–99.

"The Ownership of Property by Slaves in the Mid–Nineteenth-Century Low Country," *JSH*, 49, no. 3 (Aug. 1983): 399–420.

"Black Society in the Lowcountry, 1760–1810," in Ira Berlin and Ronald Hoffman, eds., *Slavery and Freedom in the Age of the American Revolution* (Charlottesville: Univ PR of VA, 1983), pp. 83–141.

Oubre, Claude F. *Forty Acres and a Mule: The Freedmen's Bureau and Black Landownership* (Baton Rouge: LA State Univ PR, 1978).

Painter, Nell Irvin. *Exodusters: Black Migration to Kansas after Reconstruction* (New York: Knopf, 1977).

Patterson, Orlando. *Slavery and Social Death: A Comparative Study* (Cambridge, MA: Harvard Univ PR, 1982).

Pease, William H. "Three Years Among the Freedmen: William C. Gannett and the Port Royal Experiment," *JNH*, 42, no. 2 (1957): 98–117.

Phillips, Ulrich Bonnell, ed. *Plantation and Frontier*, 2 vols, (Cleveland, OH: Clark, 1909).

American Negro Slavery: A Survey of the Supply, Employment and Control of Negro Labor as Determined by the Plantation Regime, ed. Eugene D. Genovese (1918; Baton Rouge: LA State Univ PR, 1966).

Life and Labor in the Old South (Boston: Little Brown, 1929).

Powell, Lawrence N. *New Masters: Northern Planters during the Civil War and Reconstruction* (New Haven, CT: Yale Univ PR, 1980).

"Southern Republicanism during Reconstruction: The Contradictions of State and Party Formation," paper, annual meeting of Organization of American Historians, 1984.

"Correcting for Fraud: A Quantitative Reassessment of the Mississippi Ratification Election of 1868," *JSH*, 55, no. 4 (Nov. 1989): 633–658

Quarles, Benjamin. *The Negro in the Civil War* (Boston: Little Brown, 1953).

Rable, George C. *But There Was No Peace: The Role of Violence in the Politics of Reconstruction* (Baton Rouge: LA State Univ PR, 1984).

Rachleff, Peter J. *Black Labor in the South: Richmond, Virginia, 1865–1890* (Philadelphia: Temple Univ PR, 1984).

Ramsdell, Charles W. *Behind the Lines in the Confederacy* (Baton Rouge: LA State Univ PR, 1944).

Ransom, Roger L., and Richard Sutch. *One Kind of Freedom: The Economic Consequences of Emancipation* (Cambridge Univ PR, 1977).

"Sharecropping: Market Response or Mechanism of Race Control?" in David G. Sansing, ed., *What Was Freedom's Price?* (Jackson: Univ PR of MS, 1978), pp. 51–70.

Reid, Joseph D., Jr. "Sharecropping as an Understandable Market Response: The Post-Bellum South," *Journal of Economic History*, 33 (March 1973): 106–30.

"Sharecropping in History and Theory," *AgH*, 49 (April 1975): 426–40.

Reidy, Joseph P. "Aaron A. Bradley: Voice of Black Labor in the Georgia Low-country," in Howard N. Rabinowitz, ed., *Southern Black Leaders of the Reconstruction Era* (Urbana: Univ of IL PR, 1982), pp. 281–308.

From Slavery to Agrarian Capitalism in the Cotton Plantation South: Central Georgia, 1800–1880 (Chapel Hill: Univ of NC PR, 1992).

Reynolds, John S. *Reconstruction in South Carolina, 1865–1877* (1905; New York: Negro Universities PR, 1969).

Ripley, C. Peter. *Slaves and Freedmen in Civil War Louisiana* (Baton Rouge: LA State Univ PR, 1976).

Ripley, C. Peter, ed. *The Black Abolitionist Papers*, 5 vols. (Chapel Hill: Univ of NC PR, 1985–92).

Roark, James L. *Masters Without Slaves: Southern Planters in the Civil War and Reconstruction* (New York: Norton, 1977).

Robinson, Armstead L. "Beyond the Realm of Social Consensus: New Meanings of Reconstruction for American History," *JAH*, 68, no. 2 (Sept. 1981): 276–97.

Bitter Fruits of Bondage (New Haven, CT: Yale Univ PR, forthcoming).

Rodney, Walter. *A History of the Guyanese Working People, 1881–1905* (Baltimore, MD: Johns Hopkins Univ PR, 1981).

"Plantation Society in Guyana," *Review*, 4, no. 4 (Spring 1981): 643–67.

Rogers, George C., Jr. *The History of Georgetown County, South Carolina* (Columbia: Univ of SC PR, 1970).

Rose, Willie Lee. *Rehearsal For Reconstruction: The Port Royal Experiment* (1964; New York: Oxford Univ PR, 1976).

Slavery and Freedom, ed. William W. Freehling (New York: Oxford Univ PR, 1982).

Rosengarten, Theodore. *Tombee: Portrait of a Cotton Planter with the Journal of Thommas B. Chaplin (1822–1890)* (New York: Morrow, 1986).

Salvatore, Nick. *Eugene V. Debs: Citizen and Socialist* (Urbana: Univ of IL Press, 1982).

Saville, Julie. "Grassroots Reconstruction: Agricultural Laborers and Collective Action in South Carolina, 1860–1868," *Slavery and Abolition*, 12, no. 3 (Dec. 1991): 173–82.

Scott, Rebecca J. "Explaining Abolition: Contradiction, Adaptation, and Challenge in Cuban Slave Society," *Comparative Studies in Society and History*, 26, no. 1 (Jan. 1984): 83–111.

Slave Emancipation in Cuba: The Transition to Free Labor, 1860–1899 (Princeton, NJ: Princeton Univ PR, 1985).

Shick, Tom W., and Don H. Doyle. "The South Carolina Phosphate Boom and the Stillbirth of the New South, 1867–1920," *SCHM,* 86, no. 1 (Jan. 1985): 1–31.

Shifflett, Crandall A. "The Household Composition of Rural Black Families: Louisa County, Virginia, 1880," *Journal of Interdisciplinary History,* 6, no. 2 (Autumn 1975): 235–60.

Shlomowitz, Ralph. "The Origins of Southern Sharecropping," *AgH,* 53 (July 1979): 557–75.

Simkins, Francis Butler, and Robert Hilliard Woody. *South Carolina During Reconstruction* (1932; Gloucester, MA: Peter Smith, 1966).

Singletary, Otis A. *Negro Militia and Reconstruction*(1957; New York: McGraw-Hill, 1963).

Smith, Alfred Glaze, Jr. *Economic Readjustment of an Old Cotton State: South Carolina, 1820–1860* (Columbia: Univ of SC PR, 1958).

Sproat, John G. *The Best Men: Liberal Reformers in the Gilded Age* (New York: Oxford Univ PR, 1968).

Stagg, J. C. A. "The Problem of Klan Violence: The South Carolina Up-Country, 1868–1871," *Journal of American Studies,* 8, no. 3 (Dec. 1974): 303–18.

Stansell, Christine. *City of Women: Sex and Class in New York, 1789–1860* (Urbana: Univ of IL Press, 1987).

Strickland, John Scott. " 'No More Mud Work': The Struggle for Control of Labor and Production in Low Country South Carolina, 1863–80," in Walter J. Fraser and Winifred B. Moore, Jr., eds., *The Southern Enigma: Essays on Race, Class, and Folk Culture* (Westport, CT: Greenwood, 1983), pp. 43–62.

Taussig, Michael T. *The Devil and Commodity Fetishism in South America* (Chapel Hill: Univ of NC PR, 1980).

Taylor, Alrutheus Ambush. *The Negro in South Carolina During the Reconstruction* (1924; New York: AMS, 1971).

Thomas, Emory M. *The Confederate Nation, 1861–1865* (New York: Harper & Row, 1979).

Thompson, E. P. *The Making of the English Working Class* (New York: Vintage, 1966).

"Time, Work-Discipline, and Industrial Capitalism," *Past and Present,* 38 (Dec. 1967): 56–97.

"The Moral Economy of the English Crowd in the Eighteenth Century," *Past and Present,* 50 (Feb. 1971): 76–136.

Thompson, Henry T. *Ousting the Carpetbagger from South Carolina* (1926; New York: Negro Universities PR, 1969).

Trelease, Allen W. *White Terror: The Ku Klux Klan Conspiracy and Southern Reconstruction* (New York: Knopf, 1971).

Uya, Okon Edet. *From Slavery to Public Service: Robert Smalls, 1839–1915* (New York: Oxford Univ PR, 1971).

Van Deberg, William L. *The Slave Drivers: Black Agricultural Labor Supervisors in the Antebellum South* (Westport, CT: Greenwood, 1979).

Wagstaff, Thomas. "Call Your Old Master – 'Master': Southern Political Leaders and Negro Labor During Presidential Reconstruction," *LH*, 10 (1969): 323–45.

Walker, Clarence E. *A Rock in a Weary Land: The African Methodist Episcopal Church during the Civil War and Reconstruction* (Baton Rouge: LA State Univ PR, 1982).

Washington, Delo E. "Education of Freedmen and the Role of Self-Help in a Sea Island Setting, 1862–1982," *AgH* 58 (July 1984): 442–55.

Wayne, Michael. *The Reshaping of Plantation Society: The Natchez District, 1860–1880* (Baton Rouge: LA State Univ PR, 1983).

Weiner, Jonathan. *Social Origins of the New South: Alabama, 1860–1885* (Baton Rouge: LA State Univ PR, 1978).

Wikramanayake, Marina. *A World in Shadow: The Free Black in Antebellum South Carolina* (Columbia: Univ of SC PR, 1973).

Wilentz, Sean. *Chants Democratic: New York City and the Rise of the American Working Class* (New York: Oxford Univ PR, 1984).

Wiley, Bell I. *Southern Negroes, 1861–1865* (New Haven, CT: Yale Univ PR, 1938).

Williamson, Harold Francis. *Edward Atkinson: The Biography of an American Liberal, 1827–1905* (Boston, Old Corner, 1934).

Williamson, Joel. *After Slavery: The Negro in South Carolina during Reconstruction, 1861–1877* (Chapel Hill: Univ of NC PR, 1965).

Wood, Peter H. *Black Majority: Negroes in Colonial South Carolina from 1670 through the Stono Rebellion* (New York: Knopf, 1974).

Woodman, Harold D. *King Cotton and His Retainers: Financing and Marketing the Cotton Crop of the South, 1800–1925* (Lexington: Univ of KY PR, 1968).

"Sequel to Slavery: The New History Views the Postbellum South," *JSH*, 53 (Nov. 1977): 523–54.

"Post–Civil War Southern Agriculture and the Law," *AgH*, 53 (Jan. 1979): 319–37.

"Postbellum Social Change and Its Effects on Marketing the South's Cotton Crop," *AgH*, 56 (Jan. 1982): 215–30.

Woodruff, Nan Elizabeth. *As Rare As Rain: Federal Relief in the Great Southern Drought of 1930–31* (Urbana: Univ of IL PR, 1985).

Woodward, C. Vann. *Origins of the New South, 1877–1913* (Baton Rouge: LA State Univ PR, 1951).

"The Price of Freedom," in David G. Sansing, ed., *What Was Freedom's Price?* (Jackson: Univ PR of MS, 1978), pp. 93–113.

Woodward, C. Vann., ed., *Mary Chesnut's Civil War* (New Haven, CT: Yale Univ PR, 1981).

Woofter, T[homas] J[ackson], Jr. *Black Yeomanry: Life on St. Helena Island* (New York: Holt, 1930).

Wright, Gavin. *Old South, New South: Revolutions in the Southern Economy since the Civil War* (New York: Basic, 1986).

Dissertations

Drumm, Marcus Austin. "The Union League in the Carolinas" (Ph.D. diss., Univ of NC, 1955).

Fitzgerald, Michael William. "The Union League Movement in Alabama and Mississippi: Politics and Agricultural Change in the Deep South during Reconstruction" (Ph.D. diss., Univ of CA, Los Angeles, 1986).

Graham, Glennon. "From Slavery to Serfdom: Rural Black Agriculturalists in South Carolina, 1865–1900" (Ph.D. diss., Northwestern Univ, 1982).

McDonald, Roderick Alexander. " 'Goods and Chattels': The Economy of Slaves on Sugar Plantations in Jamaica and Louisiana" (Ph.D. diss., Univ of KS, 1981).

Owens, Susie Lee. "The Union League of America: Political Activities in Tennessee, the Carolinas, and Virginia," abridgment (Ph.D. diss, NY Univ, 1947).

Robinson, Armstead L. "Day of Jubilo: Civil War and the Demise of Slavery in the Mississippi Valley" (Ph.D. diss., Univ of Rochester, 1976).

Saville, Julie. "A Measure of Freedom: From Slave to Wage Laborer in South Carolina, 1860–1868" (Ph.D. diss.   , Yale Univ, 1986).

Silvestro, Clement Mario. "None But Patriots: The Union Leagues in Civil War and Reconstruction" (Ph.D. diss., Univ of WI, 1959).

Stone, James Herbert. "Black Leadership in the Old South: The Slave Drivers of the Rice Kingdom" (Ph.D. diss., FL State Univ, 1976).

Tadman, Michael. "Speculators and Slaves in the Old South: A Study of the Domestic Slave Trade" (Ph.D. diss., Univ of Hull, 1977).

Index

References to local legislative units designated as district or (after 1868) as county have been combined in index entries.

Index

219